First World War
and Army of Occupation
War Diary
France, Belgium and Germany

47 DIVISION
Divisional Troops
236 Brigade Royal Field Artillery
1 March 1915 - 1 May 1919

WO95/2717/4

The Naval & Military Press Ltd
www.nmarchive.com
Published in association with The National Archives

Published by

The Naval & Military Press Ltd

Unit 10 Ridgewood Industrial Park,

Uckfield, East Sussex,

TN22 5QE England

Tel: +44 (0) 1825 749494

www.naval-military-press.com

www.nmarchive.com

This diary has been reprinted in facsimile from the original. Any imperfections are inevitably reproduced and the quality may fall short of modern type and cartographic standards.

© **Crown Copyright**
Images reproduced by permission of The National Archives, London, England, 2015.

Contents

Document type	Place/Title	Date From	Date To
Heading	WO95/2717 Mar 1915-Apr 1919 236 Brigade Royal Field Artillery		
Heading	47th Division 1-6th Brigade R.F.A. Became 236th Brigade R.F.A. Mar 1915-Apl 1919		
Heading	2nd London Division 6th London Bde. RFA Vol I 1-31.3.15		
Heading	War Diary Of The 6th London Brigade R.F.A. (T.F) From March 1st To March 31st 1915		
War Diary		01/03/1915	31/03/1915
War Diary	Lapugnoy France	01/04/1915	01/04/1915
Heading	2nd London Division 6th London Bde R.F.A. Vol II 1-30.4.15		
Heading	War Diary Of The 6th London Brigade R.F.A. From April 1st 1915 To April 30th 1915		
War Diary		01/04/1915	30/04/1915
Heading	47th Division 6th London Bde R.F.A. Vol III 1-31.5.15		
Heading	War Diary Of The 6th London Brigade R.F.A. For May 1st 1915 To May 31st 1915		
War Diary		01/05/1915	08/05/1915
War Diary	Notice Aubers Area	09/05/1915	31/05/1915
Operation(al) Order(s)	London Div. Artillery Operation Orders No.2	08/05/1915	08/05/1915
Miscellaneous	47th Lon Div. Arty Operation Order No. 3	12/05/1915	12/05/1915
Miscellaneous	47th Div. Arty Instructions	20/05/1915	20/05/1915
Miscellaneous	47th Div. Arty Proposed Howitzer Programme	28/05/1915	28/05/1915
Heading	47th Division 6th London Bde RFA Vol IV 1-30.6.15		
Heading	War Diary Of The 6th London Brigade R.F.A. 47th Lon Div From June 1st To June 30th Inclusive		
War Diary		01/06/1915	30/06/1915
Miscellaneous	Total Casualties to June 30 1915	30/06/1915	30/06/1915
Heading	47th Division 6th London Bde RFA Vol V 1-31.07.15		
Heading	War Diary Of The 6th London Brigade R.F.A. (T) From July 1st To July 31st		
War Diary		01/07/1915	31/07/1915
Miscellaneous	Reliefs Of The 47th Divisional Artillery By 15th Divisional Artillery	25/07/1915	25/07/1915
Heading	47th Division 6th London Bde RFA Vol VI From 1-31.8.15		
Heading	War Diary Of The 6th London Brigade R.F.A. From August 1st 1915 To August 31st 1915		
War Diary		01/08/1915	31/08/1915
Heading	War Diary Headquarters 236th Brigade R.F.A. (1/6 London) (47th Division September 1915		
Heading	War Diary Of The 236 Bde 6th London Brigade R.F.A. From September 1st 1915 To September 30th 1915 Vol VII		
War Diary		01/09/1915	30/09/1915
Heading	47th Division 6th London Bde R.F.A. Vol VIII Oct 15		
Heading	War Diary Of The 6th London Brigade R.F.A. From October 1st 1915 To October 31st 1915		
War Diary		01/10/1915	31/10/1915

Heading	War Diary Of The 6th London Brigade R.F.A. From Nov.1st-Nov 30th Vol IX		
War Diary		01/11/1915	02/11/1915
War Diary	Mazingarbe	02/11/1915	19/11/1915
War Diary	Auchel	18/11/1915	25/11/1915
War Diary	Noyelles	26/11/1915	30/11/1915
Heading	War Diary Of The Sixth London Brigade R.F.A. From December 1st 1915 To December 31st 1915 (Volume X)		
War Diary	Noyelles	01/12/1915	03/12/1915
War Diary	Cauchy-A-La-Tour	04/12/1915	05/12/1915
War Diary	Auchel	06/12/1915	16/12/1915
War Diary	Annequin	17/12/1915	31/12/1915
Heading	1/6 London Bde R.F.A. Jan Vol XI		
War Diary	Annequin	01/01/1916	07/01/1916
War Diary	Les Brebis	08/01/1916	31/01/1916
Heading	1/6 London Bde R.F.A. Vol XII		
War Diary	Lesbrebis Fossey Marac	01/02/1916	17/02/1916
War Diary	Anchel	18/02/1916	19/02/1916
War Diary	Bomy	20/02/1916	21/02/1916
War Diary	Anchel	18/02/1916	20/02/1916
War Diary	Bomy	21/02/1916	22/02/1916
War Diary	Courque	23/02/1916	29/02/1916
Heading	47 1/6 London Bde R.F.A. Vol XIII		
War Diary	Courques	01/03/1916	09/03/1916
War Diary	Erron Erase	10/02/1916	12/02/1916
War Diary	Dieval	13/03/1916	18/03/1916
War Diary	Carency	19/03/1916	31/03/1916
Miscellaneous	Officer i/c A.G Office Base		
War Diary	Carency	01/04/1916	30/04/1916
Heading	War Diary Of The 236th Brigade R.F.A. Late 1/6 London Bde May 1st To May 31st Vol XV		
War Diary	Carency	01/05/1916	06/05/1916
War Diary	Frevillers	07/05/1916	20/05/1916
War Diary	Carency	21/05/1916	26/05/1916
War Diary	Valhuon	27/05/1916	28/05/1916
War Diary	Barlin	29/05/1916	15/06/1916
War Diary	Aix Noulette	16/06/1916	30/06/1916
Heading	47th Divisional Artillery 236th Brigade R.F.A. July 1916		
War Diary	Aix-Noulette	01/07/1916	23/07/1916
War Diary	Hersin	24/07/1916	25/07/1916
War Diary	Sains-Les-Pernes	26/07/1915	30/07/1915
War Diary	Aubrometz	30/07/1916	31/07/1916
Heading	47th Divisional Artillery 236th Brigade Royal Field Artillery August 1916		
War Diary	Aubrometz To Beauvoir Riviere	01/08/1916	01/08/1916
War Diary	Beauvoir Riviere	02/08/1916	05/08/1916
War Diary	Vitz-Villeroy	06/08/1916	09/08/1916
War Diary	Vitz-Villeroy	10/08/1916	10/08/1916
War Diary	Lanches Havernas	11/08/1916	11/08/1916
War Diary	Havernas Behencourt	12/08/1916	12/08/1916
War Diary	Behencourt-Bottomwood	13/08/1916	13/09/1916
War Diary	Bottomwood	14/08/1916	15/09/1916
War Diary	Mametz Wood	16/09/1916	05/10/1916
War Diary	Bazentin Legrand Highwood (East) Road (S10.c.4.6)	06/10/1916	07/10/1916

War Diary	Bazentin Legrand Highwood Road	08/10/1916	08/10/1916
War Diary	Mametz	09/10/1916	13/10/1916
War Diary	Beaucourt	14/10/1916	14/10/1916
War Diary	Talmas	15/10/1916	15/10/1916
War Diary	Amplier	16/10/1916	16/10/1916
War Diary	Aubrometz	17/10/1916	17/10/1916
War Diary	Bergeneuse	18/10/1916	18/10/1916
War Diary	Crecques	19/10/1916	19/10/1916
War Diary	Belgium (S Of Watou)	20/10/1916	21/10/1916
War Diary	Zillebeke Bund	22/10/1916	25/10/1916
War Diary	Lillegate	26/10/1916	31/10/1916
War Diary	Ypres Lille Gate	01/11/1916	12/11/1916
War Diary	Ypres	13/11/1916	30/11/1916
Heading	War Diary Of The 236th Brigade Royal Field Artillery From Dec 1st 1916-Dec 31st 1916 Vol 22		
War Diary	Ypres	01/12/1916	27/12/1916
War Diary	Winnezeele	28/12/1916	31/12/1916
Heading	236 Bde RFA 1917		
Miscellaneous			
War Diary	Winnezeele	01/01/1917	21/01/1917
War Diary	Ypres	21/01/1917	31/01/1917
Heading	War Diary Of 236 Brigade RFA 1-2-17 To 28-2-17 Vol 24		
War Diary	Ypres	01/02/1917	12/04/1917
War Diary	Winnezeele & Ouderzeele	15/04/1917	15/04/1917
War Diary	Winnezeele & Oudezeele	01/05/1917	03/05/1917
War Diary	Ypres	04/05/1917	17/06/1917
War Diary	La Clytte	18/06/1917	02/07/1917
War Diary	The Bluff Ypres	04/07/1917	21/07/1917
War Diary	St Eloi	21/07/1917	20/08/1917
War Diary	La Clytte	21/08/1917	22/08/1917
War Diary	Boeschepe	22/08/1917	24/08/1917
War Diary	(Ypres) Hooge	28/08/1917	30/08/1917
War Diary	Hooge	02/09/1917	10/09/1917
War Diary	Bailleul	11/09/1917	12/09/1917
War Diary	Bluff Ypres	12/09/1917	26/09/1917
War Diary	Croix De Poperinghe	27/09/1917	27/09/1917
War Diary	(Bailleul) Strazeele	28/09/1917	30/09/1917
War Diary	Tannay	01/10/1917	01/10/1917
War Diary	Lapugnoy	02/10/1917	02/10/1917
War Diary	Acq	03/10/1917	04/10/1917
War Diary	Bailleul (Arras)	05/10/1917	21/11/1917
War Diary	Estree Cauchie	22/11/1917	22/11/1917
War Diary	Walrus	23/11/1917	23/11/1917
War Diary	Behagnies	24/11/1917	24/11/1917
War Diary	Bus (Bapaume)	25/11/1917	30/11/1917
War Diary	Gouzeaucourt	01/12/1917	12/12/1917
War Diary	Havrincourt	12/12/1917	28/02/1918
Heading	47th Divisional Artillery War Diary 236th Brigade Royal Field Artillery March 1918		
War Diary	Havrincourt	01/03/1918	03/03/1918
War Diary	Bus	04/03/1918	20/03/1918
War Diary	Bertincourt	21/03/1918	21/03/1918
War Diary	Fremicourt & Sapignies	22/03/1918	22/03/1918
War Diary	Favreuil	23/03/1918	24/03/1918
War Diary	Behucourt	24/03/1918	24/03/1918

War Diary	Achiet-Le-Petit	24/03/1918	24/03/1918
War Diary	Bucquoy	25/03/1918	27/03/1918
War Diary	Hannescamps	28/03/1918	31/03/1918
Heading	47th Div War Diary Headquarters 236th Brigade R.F.A. April 1918		
War Diary	Essarts	01/04/1918	06/04/1918
War Diary	Fonquevillers	07/04/1918	25/04/1918
War Diary	Sailly-Au-Bois	25/04/1918	06/05/1918
War Diary	Couin	06/05/1918	06/05/1918
War Diary	Gezaincourt	07/05/1918	07/05/1918
War Diary	St Ouen	08/05/1918	08/05/1918
War Diary	Liercourt	09/05/1918	21/05/1918
War Diary	Bourdon	22/05/1918	22/05/1918
War Diary	Contay	23/05/1918	28/05/1918
War Diary	Henencourt	29/05/1918	28/06/1918
War Diary	Daours	29/06/1918	29/06/1918
War Diary	Fouilloy	29/06/1918	31/07/1918
Heading	47th Divl. Artillery 236th Brigade Royal Field Artillery August 1918		
War Diary		01/08/1918	24/12/1918
Heading	236 Bde RFA 1919		
Miscellaneous			
War Diary		02/01/1919	01/05/1919

(4)

WO95/2717

Mar 1915 – Apr 1919

236 Brigade Royal Field Artillery

47TH DIVISION

1-6TH BRIGADE R.F.A.
BECAME:
236TH BRIGADE R.F.A.
MAR 1915 - APL 1919

2nd London Division

6th London Bde: R.F.A.

Vol I. 1 — 31. 3. 15.

CONFIDENTIAL

WAR DIARY

of the

6th London Brigade R.F.A. (T.F.)

from March 1st to March 31st 1915

WAR DIARY
INTELLIGENCE SUMMARY

(Erase heading not required.)

Army Form C. 2118.

Hour, Date, Place	Summary of Events and Information	Remarks and references to Appendices
Monday. March 1st	All Brigade Training stopped, so as to enable Units (F) to overhaul all their equipment, clothing etc.	
Tuesday March 2nd	The Laying & Duggery Examination arranged for today cancelled.	
Wednesday March 3rd	Captain P.J. CLIFTON promoted Major (Temporary) and Lieut. W. COOPER promoted Captain (Temporary). All horses inspected in GADEBRIDGE PARK by Assistant Director of Remounts, for casting of horses Lt-Col R.T. MACHUGH assumed temporary command of 2nd London (T.A. Divisional Artillery during absence in FRANCE of G.O.C. R.A. Medical Inspection of all ranks shoes were taken place, etc, as M.O. has not returned from leave, it was postponed.	
Thursday. March 4th	Inspection of Guns at 10 a.m. by Inspector of Ordnance Machinery. Inspection of Harness at 11.45 a.m. Inspection of Officers, N.C.O.'s + men and field Dressings. Report on inspection of horses of this Brigade very satisfactory.	
Friday. March 5th	Remounts (Chargers - Ride Horses) received to complete establishment. All officers attending courses able Billetting Area - including	

Army Form C. 2118.

Instructions regarding War Diaries and Intelligence Summaries are contained in F. S. Regs., Part II. and the Staff Manual respectively. Title pages will be prepared in manuscript.

WAR DIARY
or
INTELLIGENCE SUMMARY

(Erase heading not required.)

Hour, Date, Place	Summary of Events and Information	Remarks and references to Appendices
March 5th (continued)	Major H BAYLEY & Capt. P.A. LOVE, recalled by order. Musketry Courses arranged for this Brigade at CHALK HILL for Monday next. Boards appointed for assessing all damages.	
Saturday March 6th	Arrival of light Draught remounts to complete establishment. All indents for requirements to be submitted immediately to D.A.D.O.S. Brigade Major telegraphed Division re Monday next. An officer to sleep in Bgde Office until further orders.	
Sunday March 7th	All Horse Service taken to ST JULIEN'S FARM after preliminary inspection. Carried off Small Arm Ammunition & Ammunition Carts. Maps of FRANCE and BELGIUM received. Leave granted to take 2/Lt J.C. NOBLETT as O/C 2nd Base Details.	
Monday March 8th	Musketry Courses cancelled. Heavy Draught Remounts received. Telephone equipment, but no telephones, received. Standing Orders for Expeditionary Force, & Notes on Embarkation & Disembarkation, received. Night Operations ordered for tonight cancelled. Fairness received.	
Tuesday March 9th	All surpluses or unserviceable stores, Lists of Billets and number of	

Army Form C. 2118.

WAR DIARY
INTELLIGENCE SUMMARY
(Erase heading not required.)

(43)

Hour, Date, Place	Summary of Events and Information	Remarks and references to Appendices
Hedq'rs (continued)	men they will help, list of damage claimed settled etc, handed over to O/C. Details, 2/Lt J.C.G. POWNALL. Telephones received.	
Wednesday March 10th	Capt. W.B. COOPER left War Station for FRANCE to select billets. All impressed vehicles handed over to 2nd Line Unit.	
Thursday March 11th	Orders received for Inspection of Transport on Saturday by G.O.C. Division. 2/Lt C.E.H. ALOYD contracts measles, & his place in the D/Battery was filled by 2/Lt J.A.J. PETRE, 6th Lon Am Col. 2/Lt M.B. WELLS replaces 2/Lt J.C. WOOLLETT at O/C Base Details, who in turn goes to Amm Col.	
Friday March 12th	Lecture by GOCRA at Town Hall to all Officers & senior NCOs. Service Bicycles received. Amended "Standing Orders" received. Polydore Services to France. Today's Inspection of Transport cancelled.	
Saturday March 13th	Nil.	
Sunday March 14th		
Monday March 15th	The Brigade left HEMEL HEMPSTEAD by sections, starting with the 16th Battery at 8.45 p.m. (15-3-15), at intervals of about 2 hours, & entrained on arrival at BERKHAMPSTEAD.	
Tuesday March 16th	East section on reaching SOUTHAMPTON, entrained forthwith. The complete Brigade embarked on 2 large Troop Ships & 1 Small transport. Ships left in total darkness at 8 p.m. (16-3-15).	

Army Form C. 2118.

WAR DIARY
INTELLIGENCE SUMMARY
(Erase heading not required.)

Instructions regarding War Diaries and Intelligence Summaries are contained in F. S. Regs., Part II. and the Staff Manual respectively. Title pages will be prepared in manuscript.

Hour, Date, Place	Summary of Events and Information	Remarks and references to Appendices
Wednesday, March 17th	Disembarkation at HAVRE, after remarkably smooth crossing, at about 11 a.m. No casualties. Brigade moved off to Rest Camp on outskirts of HAVRE. Interpreter reported for duty.	
Thursday, March 18th	Entrainment by Batteries at Gare des Marchandises, HAVRE, at intervals of about 1½ hours, starting at 7.30 a.m.	
Friday, March 19th	Arrival of Units after journey of 22 hours at BERGUETTE. Information received that the Divison would form part of a different Army Corps to that originally intended. No place for Brigade forecasted. Brigade proceeded from BERGUETTE to LIERE, + billetty settled. Major Din in turn to FOUQUEREHEM, ECQUEDECQUES. At 3.30 p.m. G.O.C. who arrived to billet the Brigade at FONTES, which was reached at about 10 p.m. The work of the Billetty Officer who proceeded to FRANCE 9 days beforehand was therefore rendered entirely useless.	
Saturday, March 20th	The Brigade was attached to the 6th Infantry Brigade. The O.C. Brigade and Adjutant attended conference at NORRENT FONTES.	
Sunday, March 21st	Nil.	

Army Form C. 2118.

WAR DIARY
INTELLIGENCE SUMMARY
(Erase heading not required.)

Hour, Date, Place	Summary of Events and Information	Remarks and references to Appendices
Monday, March 22nd	The Brigade was inspected on Instructions by the Field-Marshall Commanding-in-Chief, Sir J.D.P. French, in the Park of the CHÂTEAU DE MAZYNGHEM. Field-Marshall Sir John FRENCH complimented the O.C. Brigade on the good appearance of the Brigade.	
Tuesday, March 23rd	All Officers attended lecture by Brigadier General MONTGOMERY at the G.O.C.R.A's Headquarters, MARLES.	
Wednesday, March 24th	Lt R.A CORSAN contracted measles and was taken to cleaning Hospital.	
Thursday, March 25th	Lt-Colonel R.J. MACHUGH, Capt H. BAILEY, Major A.C.GORDON, Major P.J CLIFTON, Capt W. COOPER, Lt. W.T. BARNARD, 2/Lt J.H. VAN DEN BERGH, 2/Lt V.C. LUCAS, with N.C.O's + telephonists proceeded for attachment to Regular Batteries in the firing line for 3 clear days.	
Friday, March 26th	2/Lt G. LYON-SMITH promoted Lieutenant.	
Saturday, March 27th	The Brigade moves from FONTES to LAPUGNOY	
Sunday, March 28th	Nil	
Monday, March 29th	Return to War Station of Officers who proceeded to "front" on	

Army Form C. 2118.

WAR DIARY
~~WAR DIARY~~ or
~~INTELLIGENCE SUMMARY~~

(Erase heading not required.)

Instructions regarding War Diaries and Intelligence Summaries are contained in F. S. Regs., Part II. and the Staff Manual respectively. Title pages will be prepared in manuscript.

Hour, Date, Place	Summary of Events and Information	Remarks and references to Appendices
Monday, March 29th (continued)	Thursday last. MAJOR R.R. WANSBROUGH, Lt. G. LYNSMITH, 2nd A.F. YENCKEN, Lt. R. BRUCE, Lt. A.F. BLACKWELL, 2nd Lt. T.A.O. PETRO, proceeded with 6 N.C.O.s and 6 Telephonists for attachment to Regular Batteries, in 1st & 2nd DW'ns	
Tuesday, March 30th	All officers of this Brigade on firing line recalled by wire. On arrival, one (junior) subaltern per unit was left at War Station, and all the remaining officers, including the O.C. Brigade & Adjutant, proceeded to Firing Line. Major R.R. WANSBROUGH took over command of Brigade.	
Wednesday, March 31st	Nil	

J.H. Van den Bergh 2nd Lt.
R.G.A. T.
6 London Brigade R.G.A.

Army Form C. 2118.

WAR DIARY 6 LONDON BDE. R.F.A.

INTELLIGENCE SUMMARY. For March 1915.

(Erase heading not required.)

Hour, Date, Place	Summary of Events and Information	Remarks and references to Appendices
LAPUGNOY, FRANCE April 1st 1915.	From March 1st to March 16th the Bde was occupied chiefly in completing preparations for moving over (to them) at HEMEL HEMPSTEAD to join the Expeditionary Force in FRANCE. The Bde moved on 15-16-17 March to HAVRE via SOUTHAMPTON. No casualties occurred to personnel on the journey. Four horses injured on the train journey were left behind at the port of embarkation. Two of these the A.S.C.'s charge are to be sent on to rejoin the Bde + a Farrier was left in chief of the remainder who have to prepare to bring them on when recovered. The move to FRANCE was carried out without incident: actual: bivouac the month The Bde has in billets at LA PUGNOY. Between March 25th and April 1st all officers with this exception have experience in the firing line being attached to units R.F.A.	

WAR DIARY
or
INTELLIGENCE SUMMARY

(Erase heading not required.)

Army Form C. 2118.

Hour, Date, Place	Summary of Events and Information	Remarks and references to Appendices

Relief in the 1st & 2nd Divisions much interfered in a formation was joined by none officer.

No Medical, veterinary, supply & transport service were supplied during the month with any the Lines in England or FRANCE.

R. H. MacHugh
Lt Col
6th London Bde. R.F.A.

121/5194

2nd London Divison

5th London Bde. R.F.A.
Vol II 1-30.4.15

CONFIDENTIAL

WAR DIARY

of the

6th London Brigade R.F.A.

from April 1st 1915 to April 30th 1915

Army Form C. 2118.

WAR DIARY
INTELLIGENCE SUMMARY
(Erase heading not required.)

Instructions regarding War Diaries and Intelligence Summaries are contained in F.S. Regs., Part II. and the Staff Manual respectively. Title pages will be prepared in manuscript.

Hour, Date, Place	Summary of Events and Information	Remarks and references to Appendices
April 1st 1915.	All officers who were attached to Regular Batteries at the Gunnery Line were recalled with the exception of O.C. Batteries and their senior subalterns. The O.C. Brigade & Adjutant attended a conference at the G.O.C. R.A's headquarters, CHÂTEAU DE NANTE EVENTE. Capt. C.H. WELCH, R.A.M.C., Medical Officer to the Brigade, contracted measles and was removed to Field Ambulance.	
April 3rd	Inspection, in rain, of 17th Bty by O.C. Brigade. Remainder of officers returned from Gunny Line.	
April 7th	648 fuzes (No. 65) used had been reported to the weather received.	
April 8th	Bad weather has been experienced lately. Lieut. W.R. SADLER, R.A.M.C. attached to this Brigade as Medical Officer instead of Capt CH WELCH. Adjutant & Brigade Commander orderly officer attended conference on Telephones at NARLES. 2/Lt H B WELLS (O.i/c Base Details) reported for duty with Brigade.	
April 9th	42 Gunners (1st Battery) in charge of O.C. Batteries & Senior Subaltern left LAPUGNOY in motor omnibuses for Gunny Line, with the object of preparing gunpositions. On arrival at RUE DE L'ERMETTE, they found the positions which had been assigned to them occupied by other Batteries.	
April 10th	The Advance Party were ordered to leave RUE DE L'ERMETTE at 4 a.m. & waited until 11 a.m. before receiving instructions as to their destination. Finally the 15th Battery proceeded to a position	See orders for the move, & also see Appendix I.

Army Form C. 2118.

WAR DIARY
INTELLIGENCE SUMMARY
(Erase heading not required.)

Instructions regarding War Diaries and Intelligence Summaries are contained in F. S. Regs., Part II. and the Staff Manual respectively. Title pages will be prepared in manuscript.

(48)

Hour, Date, Place	Summary of Events and Information	Remarks and references to Appendices
April 10th (continued)	South of the LA BASSÉE canal, the 16th Batty to a position north of the LA BASSÉE canal, and the 17th Battery returned to a position west of BETHUNE, in reserve. The 15th & 16th Batteries were under the tactical command of Col PARRY, R.A. (34th Brigade R.F.A).	All orders about this move were verbal.
April 11th	The guns & waggons and all the remainder of the Brigade took up their positions at dusk. Waggon lines for both Batteries are at GORRE CHATEAU.	
April 12th	15th Battery fired 24 rounds at a village in CANTLEUX to register range, fuze & line. Range 4150. 16th Battery registered enemy's howitzer from A.3.c.16. to A.9.a.68. Range 3775/4000 (Reference "BETHUNE" 1/40,000) Lt R BRUCE + 2/Lt A.F. BLACKNELL (Both of 6 London Am Col.) attached to 16th +15th Batteries respectively.	(Reference Central map)
April 13th	15th Battery registered a communication trench running from CANTIL EUX westward. Range 3725. 16th Battery registered German trench from A.9.a.60 to A.9.a.85. Range 4025.	
April 14th	Neither Batteries fired.	

1247 W 8299 200,000 (E) 8/14 J.B.C. & A. Forms/C. 2118/11.

WAR DIARY
INTELLIGENCE SUMMARY

(Erase heading not required.)

Army Form C. 2118.

(49)

Hour, Date, Place	Summary of Events and Information	Remarks and references to Appendices
April 15th	15th Battery fired on red cottage in CANTLEUX Range 3950. 16th Battery registered 3 points, including the end of a German breastwork (A.3 c.14.) Range 3775. 17th Battery were inspected by the G.O.C. 1st Army Corps, GENERAL Sir DOUGLAS HAIG, at his hour's notice. The G.O.C. expressed his satisfaction at the appearance of the men, horses, guns.	
April 16th	15th Battery did not fire. 16th Battery charged observation station, + choked 390 lines on German Trench with 11 rounds. A.3.c.1.3 Range 3800. 16th Battery also registered right extremity of "R" Breastwork. Range 3625.	
April 17th	15th Battery registered on forward German trench near Railway. Range 3350. 16th Battery opened fire – 12 rounds – on road junction about CHAPELLE ST. ROCH (A.4.c.1.4). 16th Battery, at request of O.C. 3rd COLDSTREAM GUARDS fired 12 rounds on German second trench (A.9.a 7.7.) Range 3175. Harness Inspection by O.C. Brigade & Headquarters Staff, 15th + 16th Btys. 17th Bty, which up till this date, has been in Reserve, took over the position of the 15th Bty, which proceeded to LIERE.	
April 18th	16th Bty fired 12 rounds at "S" Bend. 17th Bty fired at communication trench at CANTLEUX for registration. Range 3325/3725. 2/Lt H.B WELLS (6th London Am. Col.) attached to 17th Bty.	

Army Form C. 2118.

WAR DIARY
INTELLIGENCE SUMMARY
(Erase heading not required.)

(50)

Instructions regarding War Diaries and Intelligence Summaries are contained in F.S. Regs., Part II. and the Staff Manual respectively. Title pages will be prepared in manuscript.

Hour, Date, Place	Summary of Events and Information	Remarks and references to Appendices
April 19th	16th Bty registered "K works" (Range 3575), and fired 2 rounds in the evening, but then stopped owing to the arrival on the horizon of the relief of the INNISKILLING FUSILIERS.	
April 20th	17th Bty registered cottage at CANTLEUX. Range 4175. 16th Bty fired 12 rounds at night at "K wks" (A.3.c.29) Range 3575. 17th Bty engaged house behind CANTLEUX. Range approximately 4475.	
April 21st	16th Bty fired 12 rounds at "S Bns" (A.9.a.6.8.) at root of Infantry. Range 2525/3625. 17th Bty engaged CANTLEUX communication trench. 16th Bty moved into new position and did not fire. 16th Bty began to register in new position, but the observing officer was shelled out of the observation station. Later 16th Bty registered trenches from S.27.A.03 to A.3.A.6.5. 23 rounds fired. Range 3375 – 3575.	For reason for this move, please see Appendix II.
April 22nd	17th Bty did not fire. 15th Bty came into position again from reserve, at daybreak 22/4/15. The 15th & 16th Batteries are now under the tactical command of COLONEL HALL R.A. (36th Brigade RFA); the 17th Bty remains under the tactical command of COLONEL PARRY (34th Brigade RFA).	
April 23rd	Brigade Headquarters moves from the banks of the LA BASSÉE and to LOISNE.	

WAR DIARY or INTELLIGENCE SUMMARY

Army Form C. 2118.

(57)

Hour, Date, Place	Summary of Events and Information	Remarks and references to Appendices
April 24th	15th Bty registered K works (3600), R 2 works (3500), R 1 (3600), firing 36 rounds. Waggon-line shelled. One man wounded. 2 horses killed. 4 horses injured. 16th Bty completed registration which was interrupted yesterday. Zone registered — A3 a 02 to S 26 b 96. Ranges 3559/3550. 17th Bty fired at the end of the communication trench in CANTLEUX. A125.	
April 25th	15th Bty did not fire. 16th Bty fired 36 rounds in registing German trenches from A3 d 22 to A3 a 02. Ranges 3425—3600. 17th Bty registered four points - a Sniper's Post (3050), Canal Trench (300), German forward trench (3425), German communication trench (3700). The 16th & 17th Btys, as the result of Chateau GORRE being shelled yesterday, moved their waggon lines to LA MOTTE farm, & the banks of the LA BASSÉE canal respectively. Today the Brigade came under the tactical command of General WRAY, (RHA, Colonel HALL) instead of General ONSLOW, 2nd Division. During the night (April 25th/26th), the 15th Bty fired 6 rounds at the K works, after the 2nd army slowly war head for the enemy. Later the sound of hammering & posts war heard, and the sound ceased after the last two rounds fired.	
April 26th	16th Bty registered zone from A3 d 22 b A3 a 02. 36 rounds fired. 17th Bty registered communication trench leading along the north bank	

WAR DIARY
INTELLIGENCE SUMMARY
(Erase heading not required.)

Army Form C. 2118.

Instructions regarding War Diaries and Intelligence Summaries are contained in F. S. Regs., Part II. and the Staff Manual respectively. Title pages will be prepared in manuscript.

Hour, Date, Place	Summary of Events and Information	Remarks and references to Appendices
April 26th continued	of the LA BASSÉE canal. Range 3925–4200. H.A. BARKER & Pte P.L.G. WINTER (15th Battalion London Regiment) gazetted as 2nd Lieutenants.	
April 27th	15th & 16th Batteries reported a series of explosions in the direction of GIVENCHY, & the fact that searchlights were played on English trenches from the direction of LA BASSÉE. The 15th Bty did not fire. The 16th Bty fired 5 rounds at the gap on the south end of the J Breastwork. 17th Bty registered communication trench. Later 16th Battery switched from 17th Battery's target, firing 36 rounds. Inspection of Brigade Ammunition Column by O.C. Brigade.	
April 28th	15th Bty fired 6 rounds at working party reported near J2. 4 rounds struck the parapet. 16th Bty verified registration of K works. 17th Bty fired on Canal Trench & communication trench leading to it, to verify range (target already registered).	
April 29th	Between 12.35 & 12.45 a.m. 15th Bty fired 6 rounds at J 2. 16th Bty registered J1, J7, & J5 Bend, – 26 rounds – and sniped registration of J4. 17th Bty. fired at new extension of communication trench, and verified registration of other points.	
April 30th	15th Bty registered on K.4 & K.1 – 20 rounds, and fired 4 rounds at 11.20 p.m. at J.1. Later 15th Bty fired 5 rounds at K.1.	

Army Form C. 2118.

WAR DIARY
INTELLIGENCE SUMMARY
(Erase heading not required.)

(53)

Instructions regarding War Diaries and Intelligence Summaries are contained in F. S. Regs., Part II. and the Staff Manual respectively. Title pages will be prepared in manuscript.

Hour, Date, Place	Summary of Events and Information	Remarks and references to Appendices
April 30th continued	10th Bty 3rd 1st Fr. 17th Bty verified registration of front German trenches. J.H. Van den Bergh Lt.	VAN DEN BERGH 2/Lt

1247 W 3299 200,000 (E) 8/14 J.B.C. & A. Forms/C. 2118/11.

121/5554

47th Division

8th London Bde. R.F.A.

Potijil 1 — 31.5.15

CONFIDENTIAL

WAR DIARY

of the

6th London Brigade R.F.A.

From May 1st 1915 to May 31st 1915

WAR DIARY
INTELLIGENCE SUMMARY
(Erase heading not required.)

Army Form C. 2118.

(54)

Hour, Date, Place	Summary of Events and Information	Remarks and references to Appendices
Sat. May 1st 1915	At 6.30 a.m. Heavy bombardment heard in a northerly direction. No batteries fired, except in receipt of a message from the Infantry, the batteries could open fire. The 15th Bty took 2 minutes, & 16th Bty one minute. This appears to be quicker than the time taken by the Heavy Batteries. 13th Lon. Batty fired 2 rounds in direction of NEUVE CHAPELLE.	
Sunday May 2nd	2 rounds at T3 (A.2.d.83) 15th Lon Batty opened fire at 3.35 p.m. to verify registration of that part of zone invisible from last observing station, i.e. The ORCHARD. 14 rounds fired. At 10.37 p.m. fired 2 rounds into the ORCHARD, at request of 18th Lon. Battn. One direct hit. 17th Lon Batty did not fire.	
Mon. May 3rd	Information received from 1st Army of use by enemy of asphyxia by gas east and north of YPRES. Big conflagration (forest) G.C.W. LA BASSEE church. One of the guns of the 15th Lon Batty was placed in a forward position at 9 p.m., but was withdrawn by order at 9.30 p.m. 16th Batty fired 2 rounds at CROSS ROADS by P.8741 at request of O.C. B Company. 18th 19th Lon Regt. 2 GERMANS seen installing from M.22, wearing light blue uniforms and flat round caps. All men received masks & bicarbonate of soda, for use against gases. At the suggestion of the O.C. Brigade, a certain portion of the enemy's trenchworks were bombarded by heavy guns. 17th Lon Batty fires a few rounds to verify points on registered lines.	

CONFIDENTIAL
WAR DIARY
OF THE

6th London Brigade R.F.A

From May 1st 1915 to May 31st 1915

WAR DIARY / INTELLIGENCE SUMMARY

Army Form C. 2118.

(54)

Hour, Date, Place	Summary of Events and Information	Remarks and references to Appendices
Sat. May 1st 1915.	At 6.30 a.m. Recon. bombardment heard in a northerly direction. No batteries fired, except in a test or filler. A test was laid to see how soon after the receipt of a message from the Infantry, the batteries could open fire. The 15th Bty took 2 minutes, & 16th Bty on private 'phone their supposed to quicken than the rest by private batteries.	
Sunday May 2nd	Firing heard in direction of NEUVE CHAPELLE. 15th Lon. Batty fired 2 rounds at J3 (A.2.d.83) 16th Lon Batty opened fire at 3.30 p.m. 6 rounds registration of that part of fire invisible from last Germans station; i.e. The ORCHARD. 14 rounds fired. At 10.37 p.m. fired 2 rounds into the ORCHARD, at request of 18th Lon. Battn. One Brock Lt. 17th Lon. Batty did not fire.	
Mon. May 3rd	Information received from 1st Army of use by enemy of asphyxiating gases east and north of YPRES. Posh. trufflegraphm (trans) B.G.I. LA BASSEE Church. One of the guns of the 15th Lon Batty was placed in a forward position at 9 p.m. but was withdrawn by order at 9.30 p.m. 16th Batty fired 2 rounds at CROSS ROADS to P.944, at request of O.C. B Company, 18th 15th Lon. Regt. 2 GERMANS seen walking from M.22, wearing light blue uniforms and flat round caps. All men received masks & bicarbonate of soda, for use against gases. At the suggestion of the O.C. Brigade, a certain portion of the enemy's trenchworks were bombarded by heavy guns. 17th Lon Batty fired a few rounds to verify points on registered lines.	

Army Form C. 2118.

WAR DIARY
INTELLIGENCE SUMMARY
(Erase heading not required.)

No. 55

Hour, Date, Place	Summary of Events and Information	Remarks and references to Appendices
Tues. May 4th	15 Lon Batty fired 8 rounds at 11.15 a.m. on enemy's communication trench S.27 d.1.1, and subsequently fired 8 rounds on enemy's breastwork at 4.50 p.m. 59 rounds were fired at A2a 77 and A2 b 95. 16 Lon Batty fired 8 rounds in direction of trenches north of the S. bend. Both Batteries also fired 12 special 65= fuzes. Report received that the 1st HERTS, in front line trenches, had been unharmed by fire. This was unique.	
Wed. May 5th	Owing to misty weather, firing in the early morning was impossible. 15 Lon Batty did not fire therefore, but 16 Lon Batty fired 12 rounds at 9 a.m. to register onto in front of J1. Range 3375. Observation very difficult. 17 Lon Batty did not fire.	
Thurs. May 6th	15 Lon Batty fired on the enemy (4.15 a.m. – 6.45 a.m.) At 6.40 a.m. 16 Lon Batty fired 13 rounds between T7 and S bend. Attack by GERMANS expected. 50 rounds per gun sent to Batteries, to be dumped.	
Fri. May 7th	Note: as far as an attack by the British to so often interfered. Action expected at dawn tomorrow, but was delayed 24 hours. Clocks were misty. 15 Lon Batty fired 12 rounds at wire between T1 & T3. 16 Lon batty rectified registration on N2 & M3. Observation very difficult.	For copy of Operation Order (M.I) see Appendix D.
Sat. May 8th	15 Lon Batty fired 9 rounds on enemy's breastwork T1, + 2 rounds on T3. Range 3450 x + 3500 x. 16 Lon Batty fired 11 rounds to register wire at K3 (3425 x), later fired	

WAR DIARY
INTELLIGENCE SUMMARY

(Erase heading not required.)

Army Form C. 2118.

Hour, Date, Place	Summary of Events and Information	Remarks and references to Appendices
May 8th (contd) Sunday. May 9th Noctor Anctors area 9.5.15.	16 rounds at wire at K3 (3425') and 4 rounds at houses in the RUE D'OUVERT. The C.O. London Brigade RGA took part in the first starred attack since its arrival in the firing line. The 15 cm Batty opened fire at 4.45 a.m. and fired 50 rounds. Rocky Hill 5.30 a.m. at the enemy's wire. Several breaks 6ft were obtained, but the actual result was difficult to estimate owing to bad light and mist. Between 5.35 & 6.15 a.m. 7 rounds were fired with excellent effect at DOORWHEEL HAUS. And, the attack having been (?) up on our immediate front, fired at ease for the morning at 6.55 a.m., after 5 rounds had been fired at the enemy's earthworks. The attack was resumed, without much success, in the afternoon (3.30 p.m.) when the 15 cm Batty fired 6 rounds at the communication trench near K5, and fired again at the German objective at 4.50 with 6 rounds, at 5.25 pm, 11.45 pm. It could fired 5 rounds respectively were fired at the communication trench. The programme carried out by the 16 cm Batty was the same as the one outlined above, exactly the same targets being engaged at approximately the same times, but whereas the 15 cm Batty had only fired 82 rounds up to 6.55 am, by 6.45 am had its 16 cm Batty had accounted for 133 rounds. The 16 cm Batty fired between 7 and 10 a.m. as follows :- 6 rounds at GERMANS advancing down the open, at 8.30 am and 95 rounds at M3, M2, P14, N6, earthworks & from 6.35 & 9.9 a.m. At 4.5 pm the 16 cm Batty fired 6 rounds at the RUE D'OUVERT, and 4 rounds at 11.30 pm.	3rd Operation order (No 2)  2in Appendix E. ? ?

Army Form C. 2118.

WAR DIARY
INTELLIGENCE SUMMARY

(57)

(Erase heading not required.)

Instructions regarding War Diaries and Intelligence Summaries are contained in F. S. Regs., Part II. and the Staff Manual respectively. Title pages will be prepared in manuscript.

Hour, Date, Place	Summary of Events and Information	Remarks and references to Appendices
May 9th (continued)	The sphere of operations had not extend as far as the front of the 17th Batty, thus there took no part in the operation. Casualties as the result of today's operations – NIL. A letter was received this morning from the G.O.C. Division expressing the hope that the Division, and fifty as a complete unit for the first time, would maintain the traditions of the Territorial Force.	ast in "Aubers" area 9.5.15.
Mon. May 10th	From today, a scheme is to be adopted for "annoying" the enemy, by shelling at different spots at irregular intervals, shelling Battalion Headquarters, cross roads & which enemy are likely to pass. The FRENCH are making unhurried good progress further south. Today the 15 Ln Batty are to bombard J1, J3, and K16 Ln Batty to bombard the communication trench in the RUE D'OUVERT. 15 shown Batty fires 9 rounds between 5.45 and 6.15 am, 16 rounds at 7.10 & 24 rounds at 9.30, + 14 rounds at 3.20 pm. Six direct hits. 16 Ln Batty fired 132 rounds at irregular intervals between 12.35 a.m. + 3.15 p.m. 17 Ln Batty did not fire. Lieut N.V. BRANNETT, details for reinforcements 2nd Ln Div R.F.A.	
Tues. May 11th	Order received for the 15 Lon BATTY to bombard the points J1, J3, + the 16th Lon BATTY the entrance to the southern communication trench in the RUE D'OUVERT, at a very slow rate of fire. 15 Ln BATTY fires 9 rounds on K 5, between 5.45 am and 6.15 am, 10 rounds on K work between 7.10 + 7.30, and 24 rounds between 7.30 + 10.15 am on K 3. at 3.20 pm out of 144 rounds fires at "DOG WHISKER" being Six direct hits were obtained from this F.A. the Division (2nd London) as known as the 47th DIVISION	

Army Form C. 2118.

WAR DIARY or INTELLIGENCE SUMMARY

(Erase heading not required.)

Instructions regarding War Diaries and Intelligence Summaries are contained in F. S. Regs., Part II. and the Staff Manual respectively. Title pages will be prepared in manuscript.

58

Hour, Date, Place	Summary of Events and Information	Remarks and references to Appendices
Wed. May 12th	15 LON BATTY fired 9 rounds of working party at K work, between 6.15 + 6.45 p.m. 16 LON BATTY did not fire.	
Thur. May 13th	LT-COL R.T. MACHUGH, having reported sick, proceeded to hospital in BETHUNE, and his place was taken by LT-COL A.E. LOWE D.S.O. who also retains command the 47 Div. Am. Col. 15 LON BATTY did not fire. 16 LON BATTY fired 4 rounds at the ORCHARD, 12 rounds at N 6.	
Fri. May 14th K	15 LON BATTY fired 6 rounds at K work, and 7 rounds on communication trench nr. RUE D'OUVERT, and at 6.15 a.m. fires 23 rounds at electric work in K works, after which, at 7.30 a.m., 22 rounds were fired at the RUE DU MARAIS later, in the evening, 5.30—7.10, 45 rounds were fired at the RUE DU MARAIS and RUE D'OUVERT. Single shots at 9.50, 10.30, 11.0, + 11.55 p.m. fired 4 rounds wingfiring at the enemy second line trenches. The 16 LON BATTy fired 113 rounds nr RUE D'OUVERT.	Lt-Col A.E. LOWE was appointed Col Cr No 3 (See Apps Sit F)
Sat. May 15th ✓	day at work. 112 rounds were fired at the North end of the RUE D'OUVERT. 16 LON BATTy fired 2 rounds at southern end of RUE D'OUVERT, 39 rounds from 16 to 5 Bens, 29 rounds at north end of RUE D'OUVERT and RUE DU MARAIS. Another SS rounds were fired over the same parts. Major R.R. WAMSBROUGH noted (6th Lon. Am. Col.) appointed to command 47 Div. Am. Col. Capt. R.A. LANE (15 Lon Batty) appointed to command 6th Lon Am Col. vice Major R.R. WAMSBROUGH.	
Sun. May 16th	Today an attempt was made, on similar lines to those adopted last Sunday, to break through the enemy's lines. Considerable ground was gained, and the success achieved today gave the foundation to several more successful attacks carried out during the week	

WAR DIARY
INTELLIGENCE SUMMARY
(Erase heading not required.)

Army Form C. 2118.

(59)

Hour, Date, Place	Summary of Events and Information	Remarks and references to Appendices
Sun. May 16th (continued)	The Brigade formed part of BARTER'S FORCE.	
Mon. May 17th		
Mon. May 17th 7.30pm	Attack continued by 7.30pm, when attacks in direction of RUE D'OUVERT – CRUZE ST. ROCH – CANTICUEX. The ground captured yesterday was consolidated. The 15 Ldn Batty fired 12 rounds on the RUE DU MARAIS, and 22 rounds on G.22.c.4.5.	
Tues. May 18th	The attack continued. 15 Ldn Batty fired 140 rounds at K. works, J1, J2, J3, and RUE D'OUVERT between 3.35 + midnight. 16 Ldn Batty fired 137 rounds at S Bend.	See Instructions see Appendix G
Wed. May 19th ?	(Rations guard by BARTER'S FORCE were consolidated). 15 Ldn Batty fired 18 rounds at J.12, J.57, + D.33, 28 rounds on the RUE D'OUVERT, followed later by 4 rounds on the same objective. 16 Ldn Batty fired 60 rounds waking him at ? S Bend. At 4.15 pm 24 rounds were fired at S. Bend, + 22 rounds were fired at a GERMAN working party.	See Instructions see Appendix H
Thurs. May 20th	15 Ldn Batty fired 36 rounds on mystery gaps in K.5. 16 Ldn Batty did not fire. The attack was resumed.	
Fri. May 21st	15 Ldn Batty fired 14 rounds on gaps in K.5, 6 rounds on T3, and 2 rounds on	See instructions see Appendix I

WAR DIARY
INTELLIGENCE SUMMARY.
(Erase heading not required.)

Army Form C. 2118.

Hour, Date, Place	Summary of Events and Information	Remarks and references to Appendices
May 21st (continued)	DOGWHEEL HOUSE. 16 Siege Batty 80 rds of fire. Lieut. R. HOTT-SMITH was wounded in the arm whilst observing from the BRITISH front line trenches, and proceeded to England.	
Saturday May 22nd	15 Siege Batty fired 18 rounds on T1, T2, T3, & 18 rounds on DOGWHEEL HOUSE. 16 Siege Batty fired 2 rounds each hour at T6, T7, & S Bend: intermittently. 17 Kite Balloon Batty fired 12 rounds on enemy.	
?	180 rounds were fired at the S Bend. 6 - small bombardment in the direction of GIVENCHY. A lieutenant of the 15th Siege Batty was killed. Also one of the first men killed on the Project.	
Sunday May 23rd	15 Siege Batty fired 24 rounds on T3, and 4 rounds on T2. 16 Siege Batty fired 29 rounds on S Bend, T6, & T7.	
Monday May 24th	15 Siege Batty fired 18 rounds on RUE D'OUVERT and 99 rounds on DOGWHEEL HOUSE. 16 Siege Batty fired 83 rounds on T3, and 28 rounds later at the same objective. 17 Siege Batty fired on trenches with their guns at irregular intervals.	
Tuesday May 25th	So as to prevent the enemy from making a counterattack, the battery of the Division were ordered to form a barrage of fire. The 15 Siege Batty	

Army Form C. 2118.

WAR DIARY
or
INTELLIGENCE SUMMARY.
(Erase heading not required.)

Hour, Date, Place	Summary of Events and Information	Remarks and references to Appendices

May 25th (continued)

fired continuously on J10, and at 3.15 a.m. caught enemy infantry company of trench at J3.11 / 6 a.m. observation Mahors in RUE D'OUVERT were considered feasible. Work parties were engaged at K6 r K7 Moo Knoaris in RUE D'OUVERT were fired at, r J8 – J10 (gntrues). The 16 Lon Batty were responsible for J7 – J10, at which they fired 16 rounds. 81 rounds were fired at enemy observation stations at CHAPELLE ST. ROCHE, followed by 28 rounds at enemy observation stations in several places, fired at an enemy watergraph.

Wednesday, May 26th

? 17 Lon Batty cut wire in several places, fired at an enemy watergraph
With the same effect as yesterday, 15 Lon Batty fired 478 rounds in
J10, J12, J15, J19. The 16 Lon Batty fired 436 rounds at T5, J10, and
94 rounds at J7, J10. The 17 Lon Batty fired 7 rounds at enemy trenches
near 98, at report of infantry.

Thursday, May 27th

15 and 16 Lon Battys again formed a barrage, the final fire being 157 rounds. Br. Wk chow at Appendix K.
in J10 – J14. During the day, the observation stations of these batteries at LE RANTIN were shelled in retaliation. New observation stations had to be found. Much shelling had been issued, except to 17 Lon Batty, and is evidenced a great improvement.

Army Form C. 2118.

WAR DIARY
INTELLIGENCE SUMMARY.
(Erase heading not required.)

62

Instructions regarding War Diaries and Intelligence Summaries are contained in F. S. Regs., Part II. and the Staff Manual respectively. Title pages will be prepared in manuscript.

Hour, Date, Place	Summary of Events and Information	Remarks and references to Appendices
Friday May 28th	15 & 16 Gun Batteries did not fire. 17 Gun Batty obtained machine gun at H.8, firing in 2 minutes at request of infantry.	
Saturday May 29th	15 Gun Batty moved its position to that occupied in the first place by the 16 Gun Batty, and proceeded to register on T13, + T12, with 6 rounds. This gun was unable from that last observation. 16 Gun Batty did not fire. The 20 Gun Batty (15th) came under the command of the O.C. 1st London Brigade R.F.A.	
Sunday May 30th	Arrangements were made for the 47 Divisional Artillery to move further south, & to be replaced by the CANADIAN Divisional Artillery. Accordingly, one section of each Battery was withdrawn to the Battery Waggon Lines.	
Monday May 31st	The remaining sections in each Battery war replaced, and the Brigade (the 17 Gun Batty is not included) proceeded south, and took up positions in the neighbourhood of VERMELLES.	

J.H. Van der Bogh Lt
Captain Van Pozière R.F.A.

Secret   London Div. Artillery

OPERATION ORDERS NO. 2.   8/5/15

Reference Maps 1/40000, 1/10000

Information.(1) 1st Army will advance tomorrow with the object of breaking through the enemy's line and gaining LA BASSEE - LILLE ROAD between LA BASSEE AND FOURNES.
It sfurther advance will be directed on the line BAUVIN - DON.
(b) 1st Corps is to attack from RUE DU BOIS and advance on RUE DU MARAIS-ILLIES, maintaining its right at GIVENCHY & CUINCHY.
(c) The 1st Div. is to attack from its breastworks in front of Rue Du Bois.
Its first objectives are
Hostile trenches P. 8 - P.10 the road junction P.15 and the road thence to LA TOURELLE.
Its subsequent advance is to be directed on RUE DU MARAIS -LORGIES a defensive flank being organised from the ORCHARD (P.4) by LA QUINQUE RUE to RUE DU MARAIS.
The artillery supporting the attack of the 1st Div. is to complete such registration as may be necessary by 5 am at which hour the preliminary bombardment is to commence and continue up to the time of the Inf. assault., in accordance with the following time table:-
5am to 5-10 am Wire cutting and bombardment of hostile strong points
5-10am to 5-40 am Wire cutting and bombardment of first objective.
5-40am Infantry assault. Artillery increase their range.
(d) The 2nd Div.(less 4th (Guards) Bde.) with motor machine battery attached is to be in corps reserve in the area LOISNE-LE TOURET-LE HAMEL in readiness to continue the advance.
Intention.2. The G.O.C. intends to hold the present defensive line CUINCHY -CHOCOLAT MENIER CORNER (S.15.) opening a vigous fire attack along the entire front, untill called upon to relieve the Infantry of the 1st Div. at THE ORCHARD (P.4) LA QUINQUE RUE and RUE DU MARAIS when these points have been secured and further to make advantage of any weakening of the enemy about the RUE D'OUVERT to occupy that locality.
Detail. 3. (a) All troops are to be warned that the 1st Div. attack will cime across their front from left to right and that the right of their attack, as also any captured points will be marked by a red flag with white vertical bar in centre.
Troops of the 2nd Div. will carry a yellow flag.
Troops of Lon. Div. will be marked by a round disc with a black cross (disc 2 ft. in diameter).
Should our Inf. come under fire of our own arty. they will make their identity known by raising their caps on the points of their bayonets.
(b) Infantry. The 4th (Guards), 4th Lon. Inr. (less 8th Btn. Lon. Rgmt), 6th Lon. Inf. (less 23rd Bn. Lon. Rgmt.) Bdes will maintain their positions. The 6th Lon. Inf. Bde. however, will be prepared on the receipt of orders to relieve the troops of the 1st Div. at the points mentioned in para 2 after these points have been occupied and made good by those troops.
All the above troops will be in position by 4 am.
(c) At 5-40 am a vigorous fire attack with bursts of rifle and machine gun fire, will be opened along the whole front, the object being to prevent the enemy being withdrawn from our front to operate against the 1st Div. and to inflict losses on reinforcements may bring up to oppose the right of that Div. The heaviest possible fire will be brought to bear on any favourable target which may be offered.
(d) Arty. fire will be directed as per time table already issued. N.B. Arty. in Lon. Div. area opens fire on wire at 4-45 am.
(e) Engineers The 1st E.Anglian Fd. Co. R.E. is attached to the 4th(Guards) Bde.; 1 Sec. 3rd Lon. Fd. Co. R.E. to the 4th Lon. Inf. Bde.; 2 Sec. of the 4th Lon. Fd. Co. R.E. to the 6th Lon. Inf. Bde. emains of R.E. are placed at the C.R.Es. disposal to carry out tasks already allotted.
The 4th and 6th In.f Bdes will each be prepared to detail a company as working party when called for by the C.R.E.
(f) Wagon Line and Amm. Cols. Horses of wagon lines and Amm. Cols. not in use are to be harnessed and saddled ffrom 5 am 9th May but not hooked in.
Reserves. 4. The Div. Reserve constituted as follows, will be in position by 4-45 am 9th May.
(a) Div. Mounted Troops (Squadron Kings Edwards Horse less two troops and Lon. Cyclists less two platoons) under Maj. Hermon will be under cover at BEUVRY.
(b) 8th Bn. Lon. Rgmt. at ANNEWUIN under cover.

Secret. To 6th Lon. F.A.B.

B.M.C/453. 19th May. AAA
 Following received from BARTERS FORCE
Result of attacks by 2nd and 7th Div. yesterday was to gain the line M.5 -LA QUINQUE RUE-P.11 - P.10 -Q.7 which line has been consolidated AAA
   On the right the line continues through M.3 -L.1 - L.2 -WILLOW ROAD AAA   The Breastwork from L.2 --WILLOW ROAD was completed by the 140th Inf. Bde. last night except for 15 yards near L.2 AAA
A deliberate bombardment begins to-day the dividing line between the arty. fire of the 2nd and 7th Div. being the line Q.5- P.10-M.12 AAA
First group H.A.R. is to bombard FERME COUR D'AVOUE -Buildings P.13 - P.14-P15-P.16- Q.11 AAA
Second Div. to seize opportunity to gain ground to the line P.14, Q.12, Q.11 and the 7th Div. similarly towards L.8-L.10-L.12-M.9 AAA
Following instructions issued by 1st Army as regards reliefs of 2nd & 7th Div. by 51st(Highland) and Canadian Div. to-night AAA
The 7th Div.(less arty.) will be withdrawn to the area LILLERS-BUSNES, there to rest AAA
The 7th Div. will remain under the orders of the G.O.C. 1st Corps AAA
The 7th Div. Arty. will remain in action in its present positions and will come temporarily under the orders of the Canadian Div., when the relief of the 7th Div. is completed AAA
The 2nd Div. Arty. will remain in action in its present positions, and will come temporarily under the orders of the Highland Div., when the relief of the 2nd Div. is completed. AAA
Acknowledge AAA
          Sd. D.E.Sherlock, Bde. Maj,. 47th Div. Arty.
From 47th Div. Arty.
Time 8 am.

Secret.

To 6th Lon. F.A.B.
BM C/425 18th May AAA

First Corps is attacking at 4-30 pm to-day as follows:-
The Inf. attack will take place at 4-30 pm to-day AAA
Object is to gain and consolidate the line M. 5 LA QUINQUE RUE- P.14-
P.15.0.16-Q.12 AAA
Second Div. will attack with 4th Guards Bde. objectives P.14, P.15, P.16,
Q.12, Q.11 AAA
The 3rd Canadian Bde. is placed under orders of 7th Div. and will attack on
right of 4th Guards Bde. AA
Objective of 7th Div. -LA QUINQUE RUE Road from P.14 exclusive of M.5 inclusive AAA
The Indian Corps will attack FME DU BOIS and establish a defensive flank
in connection with left of 2nd Div. AAA
Dividing Line between Arty. of 1st & 2nd Div. Q.5, P.10, M. 12 AAA
1st Group H.A.R. will engage objectives which have been communicated to
Div. by R.G.R.A. 1st Corps AAA
The Bombardment will be-gin at 2-30 pm and continue till 4-30 pm when it
will be lifted sufficiently to allow the Inf. assault to take place. AAA
Barters Force is to remain in occupation of present lines as where before
and when co-operation can be effected with 7th Div. is to engage the
enemy actively with fire AAA
The 140th Inf. Bde. will be prepared to establish connection with the
right of the 7th Div. and will eventually connect across to the nearest
point of the British defensive line with a defensive work AAA
 This is in addition to the L.2-WILLOW ROAD work now in progress. AAA
Acknowledge. AAA

                                        Sd. D.E.Sherlock Bde. Maj.

Secret.   47th Div. Arty. Operation Order No. 3.   12/5/15
(Lon. inserted above "Div")

Ref: Map. 1/10000

1. Under instructions from 1st Corps the following is to be carried out.
(a) A deliberate bombardment of all strong points in the enemy's position in K.1 -- K.5 to V.3 -- V.5 (all inclusive) is to be systematically carried out from the earliest hour tomorrow at which accurate observation is possible, and is to continue throughout the 13th and 14th instz.
(b) 7th Div. Arty. has received instructions to bombard the sector K.3 to K.5 and P.5 to P.9; Second Div. Arty. the remainder.
(c) First Group H.A.R. has received instructions to take part in this bombardment, its objectives being selected under arrangements co-ordinated by R.G.R.A. 1st Corps, to avoid interference with observation of fire of 2nd and 7th Div. Arty.
2. The hostile breastworks both first and second lines from N.1 to P.5 and from R.1 to V.3 are to be particularly dealt with and systematically destroyed.
   This is to be effected gradually in such a manner as not to attract the enemy's attention unduly in these two sections of the front.

47th Div. Arty. Instruction.:-
3. The 5th and 6th Lon. F.A. Bdes. will open fire as early as possible tomorrow morning on points in the direction of RUE D'OUVERT and RUE DU MARAIS. They are especially to watch for the movement of troops and fire at any cross roads, observation stations, Hqrs. Etc of the Germans which can be located.
4. Due economy of ammunition is not to be lost sight of. It will therefore be advisable as soon as objectives have been accurately ranged on to deal with them with shrp bursts of fire at uncertain intervals.
                         Sd. D.E.Sherlock, Bde. Maj. 47th Div. Arty.

BM C/159

Hqrs. at Cross roads (F.29 b)
In case of sudden emergency this Bn. may be employed by G.O.C. 4th (Guards Bde. to support the defence of the right flank.
(c) 23th Bn. Lon. Rgmt. under cover at LE PREOP. Hqrs. at Canal Bridge (F.10.c)

Medical. Div. Collecting Station will be at BEUVRY (F.14.a 5.9) The existing dressing station will be maintained.

Supply. Every man to carry the current day's ration and iron ration.
(b) Supply Sections of Train to rendezvous at Refilling Point by 6 am 9th May.

Communication.7. From 3 am 9th May all wires are reserved for operations purposes. All administrative messages will be sent by despatch rider, as opportunity offers.

Reports. Reports to Div. H.Q. MARCHE AU PAULETS, BETHUNE.
              Sd. D.E.Sherlock, Bde., Maj,. Lon. Div. Arty.

Secret. 47th Div. Arty. Instructions. 20/5/15

To 6th Lon. F.A.B.
(1) The following received from 47th Div.
The offensive of the first army is to be continued towards La Bassee. Aldersons force is to secure localities L.11, L.12, M.9 and group of houses P.13, P.14, P.15, P.16.
Indien Corps is to secure localities Q.15, Q.16 R.8.
Troops of the 47th Div. holding the line will use every means by day and night to harass the enemy continually.
All avenues of approach to the enemy's forward positions are to be kept under shrapnel fire by day and night especially between dusk and 10 pm.
(2) 47th Div. Arty. will deal with communication trench K.13, J.21 CHLLE. ST. ROCHE and cross roads at CHLLE. ST. ROCHE in particular.
(3) In continuation of above, the 3rd Canadian Inf. Bde. will to-night secure localities L.12 and L.11 with two companies. The assault will take place at 7-45 pm preceeded by a heavy bombardment of 9-2" guns from 6pm to 7 pm and from guns of the Canadian Div. Arty. from 4 pm to 7-45 pm.
At the same hour a small party of the Canadian Inf. Bde. will attack points M.9 and M.12. These points will have been similarly submitted to an Arty. bombardment.
(4) All ground gained will be consolidated and joined up.
(5) The 2nd Canadian Inf. Bde. with two companies will secure K.5 at 7-45 pm
A heavy bombardment of K.5 and surrounding trenches will be carried out by 9.2" guns from 6pm to 7pm and by heavy and field guns of the Canadian Div Arty. from 4 to 7-45 pm.
After 7-45 pm the 9.2" guns will fire at L.8.
(6) As soon as K.5 is secured the trenches towards J.1 and L.8 will be secured as far as possible by bombing outwards.
All ground gained will be consolidated and joined up.
(7) 2nd Div. will keep up a slow continuous bombardment trhoughout the night on P.15 to P.16 and RUE DU MARAIS.
(8) The Heavy gun group will bombard through the night K.13 and CHLLE. ST ROCHE.
(9) All avenues of approach to enemy's forward positions are to be kept under shrapnel fire by day and night especially between dusk adn 10 pm.
(10) 47th Div. Arty. will deal with communication trench K.13, J.21, CHLLE. ST. ROCHE, and cross roads at CHLE ST ROCHE in particular.
(11) No infantry fire will be directed North of the line J.3 - L.13
(12) All troops will be in a state of constant readiness except the Div. Reserve, namely Div. Mounted Troops and 7th Lon. Rgmt.
(13) Horses will not be saddled.
BM C/509. Sd. D.E.Sherlock, Bde. Maj. 47th Div. Arty.

SECRET.   47th Div. Arty.

                Proposed Howitzer Programme   28/5/15

6-25 pm to 7-15 pm   Occasional fire by 4-5" and 6" Hows. on area 1,2,
                     H. 3. 1.15, 1.12.
7-25 pm to 7-30 pm   PAUSE. Then rates of fire slightly increased.
7-30 pm to 7-45 pm   (6" Hows fire on 1.10, 1.8, 1.9
   47 B. R.F.A.   (4.5" Hows fire 50 yards each side of 1.2, 1.7.

7-45 pm to 7-55 pm   (6" Hows fire on 1.15, 1.11, 1.12.
   47 B. R.F.A.   (4.5" Hows fire on 1.10, 1.8, 1.9,

7.55 pm to 8.8 pm   (6" Hows lift to I.15, I.11, I.12
   47 B.R.F.A.   (4.5" Hows. lift to I.10, I.8, I.9.

8-10 pm   I N F A N T R Y A S S A U L T

From 7pm to 8-40pm   Shrapnel as follows:-

CURTAIN.   15th & 16th Lon. Batteries J.10, J.13, J.14.

RIGHT BARRAGE 50th Bty. R.F.A. I. 15, to CHAPPELLE ST. ROCHE.
               56th   Ditto (How) H.3 to I. 15

Left Barrage 12th & 13th Lon. Batteries J.9 to J.12

Also 70th Battery R.F.A. on points J.14, J.17, J.18.

BM C/848
                    SD   D.E.Sherlock
                            Bde. Maj, 47th Div. Arty.

47th Division

8th London Bde: R.F.A.

Vol IV 1 — 30. 6. 15

CONFIDENTIAL
WAR DIARY

of the

6th London Brigade R.F.A. T.F.

47 Lon Div.

From June 1st to June 30th inclusive.

WAR DIARY

INTELLIGENCE SUMMARY

Army Form C. 2118.

Instructions regarding War Diaries and Intelligence Summaries are contained in F.S. Regs., Part II. and the Staff Manual respectively. Title pages will be prepared in manuscript.

(Erase heading not required.)

Hour, Date, Place	Summary of Events and Information	Remarks and references to Appendices
Tuesday June 1st	Last night the 15th & 16th Lden Batterys occupied their new positions at VERMELLES, as did one section only of the 17 Lden Batty. Registration was commenced at once. The 15 Lden Batty fired 13 rounds on A.29.c.10.7., 9 rounds on A.29.C.9.4., 7 rounds on A.28.D.2.8., and 9 rounds on G.11.b.6.8. The 16 Lden Batty registered cardinal points in its zone. The 17 Lden Batty, being incomplete, did not register. Their position however was shelled, and one wagon belonging to 117 Bty RFA was hit, but no one hurt.	Reference to the map refer throughout to the "Combined Sheet. BETHUNE 1/40000 (Trench 6th.ones sheet). unless otherwise stated).
Wednesday June 2nd	Registration continued. 15 Lden Batty fired 4 rounds on A.29.c.10.7., 10 rounds on G.4.b.4.4., and 18 rounds on G.8.a.9.0. 16 Lden Batty fired 20 rounds in registering the right section of principal points in its zone. The 17 Lden Batty did not fire.	
Thursday June 3rd	Registration continued. 12 rounds were fired at A.30 & A.18, and later 2 rounds at the same objective. The 16 Lden Batty fired 24 rounds in completing its registration. During the afternoon the enemy shelled the BRITISH front line trenches with, according to others, their Brigade replied with 2 shell for every one GERMAN shell. In this way the 16 Lden Batty fired 54 rounds at the BOIS CARRÉ, a small clump of trees, about 100 yards in front of the GERMAN front line trenches, forming what is an observation station. The 17 Lden Batty registered further points in its zone, G.11.d.6.7., G.17.b.2.4., and G.17.d.0.1. Tonight the BRITISH attacked FIVENCHY, when, in spite of successful artillery fire, they were repulsed from the positions gained by Minenwerfer. Owing to the dispersed nature of the country, exercise for horses may only take place in batches of 16 or 17.	

WAR DIARY
INTELLIGENCE SUMMARY.
(Erase heading not required.)

Army Form C. 2118.

Hour, Date, Place	Summary of Events and Information	Remarks and references to Appendices
Friday. June 4th.	15 Sieg Batty fired 11 rounds on A.30.6.4.8. and later fired 2 rounds on the same target. 16 Sieg Batty fired 10 rounds in registering southern limit of extension of zone. 17 Sieg Batty registered extension of same zone as 16 Sieg Batty.	
Saturday. June 5th.	15 Sieg Batty fired 25 rounds in A.30.6.4.8., and later fired 21 rounds on same target. 16 Sieg Batty, at request of G.O.C. 140 Inf. Bde fired 3 rounds on working party in G.11.d. 17 Sieg Batty, in consequence of reconnaissance report of infantry, that extensive wire entanglement existed between G.23.6.5-7. and G.23.6.6-7, fired on both these points.	
Sunday. June 6th.	15 Sieg Batty fired 4 rounds at 4.30 p.m., 4 rounds at 5.35 p.m. at 4 rounds at 6.10 p.m. on A.30.6.4.8. 16 Sieg Batty did not fire. 17 Sieg Batty, in reply to 2 rounds from the enemy, fired 4 rounds on LES BOIS CARRE. At 5.30 p.m. 17 Sieg Batty fired 12 rounds on BOIS CARRE and GERMAN front trenches, at G.23.a. At 8 p.m. fired 2 rounds on HULLUCH ROAD. a few officers attended a demonstration of the working and effect of gas.	
Monday. June 7th.	O.C. Batteries and Officer Commanding of the 36th Bde R.F.A. examined positions and observation stations of my batteries, with a view to "taking over." 15 + 17 Sieg Batties did not fire. 16 Sieg Batty fired 5 rounds at working party.	
Tuesday. June 8th.	15 Sieg Batty fired 12 rounds on G.4.6.53., 5 rounds on G.4.6.9.9., 11 rounds on A.30.6.4.8. and 11 rounds on G.4.6.5.3. 16 Sieg Batty did not fire.	

Army Form C. 2118.

WAR DIARY
INTELLIGENCE SUMMARY.
(Erase heading not required.)

Hour, Date, Place	Summary of Events and Information	Remarks and references to Appendices
June 8th (continued)	7 Ln Batty, in reply to 2 rounds on our front trenches, 2 rounds H.E. on our communication trenches, and 3 rounds on LE RUTOIRE from the enemy, fired 4 rounds, 4 rounds and 6 rounds on the BOIS CARRÉ. At 8.30 p.m. one section of each battery of this Brigade withdrew from its position at VERMELLES and proceeded to LAPUGNOY to rest.	
Wednesday June 9th	The remaining sections of each battery were relieved by sections of batteries of the 35 Brigade R.F.A. and, together with the Brigade Headquarter Staff, proceeded to LAPUGNOY, which was reached in the early hours of Thursday morning. The whole of the Small Arms Ammunition section of the Brigade Ammunition Column, and one section of Gun Ammunition, went detached from the Brigade, and were stationed at DROUVIN, under 2Lt. H.B. WELLS, to supply the 140 Infantry Brigade and the 19 Ln Batty (who remained in action) with ammunition. Nil.	
Thursday June 10th Friday June 11th	36 men, under Lt. N.V. BRASNETT, arrived at LAPUGNOY from Base Details, to fill up deficiencies caused by death, sickness, and increased establishment of the Brigade Ammunition Column. Lt. BRASNETT returned to Base Details.	
Saturday June 12th	The G.O.C. 47 (Ln) Division, Major-General C. St.L. BARTER came to LAPUGNOY and addressed each battery in turn. He expressed his	

WAR DIARY

INTELLIGENCE SUMMARY.

(Erase heading not required.)

Army Form C. 2118.

Instructions regarding War Diaries and Intelligence Summaries are contained in F. S. Regs., Part II. and the Staff Manual respectively. Title pages will be prepared in manuscript.

(66)

Hour, Date, Place	Summary of Events and Information	Remarks and references to Appendices
June 12th (continued)	gratitude to the Brigade for the splendid work it has done in this Sector, and his pleasure at the excellent work carried at by each Officer & man, especially the Telephonists. He impressed on all ranks the need for keeping themselves in a clean and sanitary condition.	
Sunday, June 13th.	Lt. R.A. CORSAN & Lt. C.E.H. LLOYD, both of whom had suffered from measles, arrived at LAVENTIE from ENGLAND.	
Monday, June 14th.	The Horses of the 15 & 16 Ln. Batteries and Brigade Headquarters Staff were inspected, by the O.C. Brigade.	
Tuesday, June 15th.	The Horses of the 17 Ln. Batty were inspected by the O.C. Brigade.	
Wednesday, June 16th.	A detailed inspection of the Headquarters Staff & 15 Ln Batty was held by the O.C. Brigade, after which the Horses of the Am. Col. were inspected. This afternoon Regimental Sports took place in excellent weather. At 11.45 p.m. a message was received warning the Brigade to get ready to move off at half an hour's notice.	
Thursday, June 17th.	At 3 a.m. a message was received that no move would take place for the present. A visit was received from the G.O.C. 1st Corps, Lieut-General Sir CHARLES MUNRO, who described the work of the Brigade as "magnificent." A detailed inspection was held of the 16 Ln Batty. The Brigade was warned to be ready to move at one hour's notice.	
Friday, June 18th.	A detailed inspection of the 17 Ln Batty took place.	

Army Form C. 2118.

WAR DIARY
INTELLIGENCE SUMMARY
(Erase heading not required.)

(67)

Hour, Date, Place	Summary of Events and Information	Remarks and references to Appendices
Saturday. June 19th.	The 6 Lon. Amm. Col. was inspected in detail by the O.C. Brigade. 2nd Lt. H.B. WELLS went into hospital, suffering from severe neuralgia.	
Sunday. June 20th.	This evening the 15 Pdr Lon Batteries proceeded into action, the former being attached to the 36 Brigade RFA, and occupying its former position at VERMELLES, and the latter to the 41 Brigade RFA near CAMBRIN. The 6 Lon Amm. Col. was divided, part going to each battery. Brigade Headquarters and the 17 Lon Battery unit remained at rest at LAPUGNOY.	
Monday. June 21st.	⎫ Nil	
Tuesday. June 22nd.	⎬ All blankets were withdrawn and returned to Railhead.	
Wednesday. June 23rd.	⎭ Capt. M.J.K. O'MALLEY proceeded on 7 days to ENGLAND on 7 days leave.	
Thursday. June 24th.	⎫ Nil	
Friday. June 25th.	⎬	
Saturday. June 26th.	Under authority of His Majesty the King, the Field Marshal Commanding-in-Chief awarded the DISTINGUISHED CONDUCT MEDAL to the following man of the 6th London Brigade RFA :- No. 1699 Gunner A.W. NORTH. 16 County of London Battery RFA For coolness and gallantry whilst acting as telephonist in the Observation Station at FESTUBERT, during the heavy bombardments to which it was subjected.	

Army Form C. 2118.

WAR DIARY
or
INTELLIGENCE SUMMARY.

(68)

(Erase heading not required.)

Instructions regarding War Diaries and Intelligence Summaries are contained in F.S. Regs., Part II. and the Staff Manual respectively. Title pages will be prepared in manuscript.

Hour, Date, Place	Summary of Events and Information	Remarks and references to Appendices
Sunday, June 27th.	Lieut. W.R. SADLER (RAMC) proceeded to ENGLAND on 5 days' leave.	
Monday, June 28th.	Capt. P.A. LIVE proceeded to ENGLAND on 7 days' leave.	
Tuesday, June 29th.	Up to this date, the 47th (London) Division, of which this Brigade is included, formed part of the 1st Army Corps, commanded by Lieut. Gen. Sir CHARLES MUNRO. From this date, the 47th (London) Division, the 1st Division, and the 48th (South Midland) Division, form the 4th Army Corps, commanded by Lieut. General RAWLINSON. The 4th Corps is still part of the First Army, commanded by General Sir DOUGLAS HAIG. Major P.T. CLIFTON proceeded to ENGLAND on 5 days' leave. The 15 & 16 Lon Batties are attached to the 1st Division.	
Wednesday, June 30th	The HESDIGNEUL Rra Cross Rds has been allotted to this Brigade on 3 days for work for Battery manœuvre. A telegram was received stating that the 16 Lon Batty, being no longer required by the 1st Division, would proceed tonight to LABUGNOY. At 11.45 p.m. a further message was received saying that, in the services of this Battery were still required, they would remain in action and occupy the position F.30 & 40. Since going into action on June 21st, the 15 Lon Batty has been occupied principally in registering and retaliating. No work of great importance was carried out. During this period, Machine Gun Hostile	

Army Form C. 2118.

WAR DIARY
INTELLIGENCE SUMMARY.
(Erase heading not required.)

Hour, Date, Place	Summary of Events and Information	Remarks and references to Appendices
	was destroyed by the 15 cm Batty and 8 direct hits were obtained. This was one at rear of Infantry. Other targets engaged were FORT HOHENZOLLERN (A.29.), the HAISNES Cross roads, FOSSE N° 8, — at the latter target 37 rounds were fired on June 23rd, and 8 rounds on June 25: on this occasion 2 GERMAN observers disappeared. — On June 27, 95 rounds were expended (43 rounds on B.25. & 6.7.) & 52 rounds on A.30. & 3.8. From Monday June 21st to Saturday June 26th, the 16 cm Batty occupied the time in registering the gun A.28. c.2.2. — A.21. d.4.1. For every one round fired by the GERMANS, 6 rounds were fired by the 16 cm Batty. From June 26th to the morning of June 29th, not a round was fired. During this period (on the night of June 28th) the left section was withdrawn preparatory to the change of line. The remaining section fired 40 rounds in 10 minutes in the evening of June 29th, in support of a demonstration & the reply of 3 mines. On June 30th, the Battery was ordered back to LAVENTIE. This order was cancelled at the eleventh hour, and the night section came into its new position (F. 30. C. 4.0) at 10 p.m. J.H. Vanden Bergh Lt.	

Army Form C. 2118.

WAR DIARY
or
INTELLIGENCE SUMMARY.
(Erase heading not required.)

Instructions regarding War Diaries and Intelligence Summaries are contained in F.S. Regs., Part II and the Staff Manual respectively. Title pages will be prepared in manuscript.

Hour, Date, Place	Summary of Events and Information	Remarks and references to Appendices
	TOTAL CASUALTIES to June 30 1915	
	OFFICER:—	
	WOUNDED:— Lieut. G. LYON SMITH	15 Lin Batty.
	OTHER RANKS:—	
	KILLED:— Gr. WHITING	15 Lin Batty
	DIED OF WOUNDS:— Bdr. FARROW	15 Lin Batty
	Gr. DEVERELL	15 Lin Batty
	Gr. MILES	15 Lin Batty
	Gr. DARBYSHIRE	15 Lin Batty
	Dr. RUSSALL	16 Lin Batty
	WOUNDED:—	
	DIED OF SICKNESS:—	
	INJURED, as result of Shell Fire:— Bdr. MACLAREN	16 Lin Batty
	Bdr. IRONS	17 Lin Batty
	J.H. Van den Berg Lt.	

12/673

47th Division

8th London Bde RFA.

Vol V

1 - 31 July - 15

CONFIDENTIAL.

WAR DIARY
of the
6th London Brigade R.F.A. (T)

from July 1st to July 31st

Army Form C. 2118.

WAR DIARY
INTELLIGENCE SUMMARY.
(Erase heading not required.)

Instructions regarding War Diaries and Intelligence Summaries are contained in F. S. Regs., Part II. and the Staff Manual respectively. Title pages will be prepared in manuscript.

Hour, Date, Place	Summary of Events and Information	Remarks and references to Appendices
Thursday, July 1st 1915	The 15 Ln Batty (now attached to the 26 Bde RFA, and lent to 2nd Division) fired 18 rounds on GERMAN front line trenches, and 5 rounds on the cross roads at HAISNES. The 16 Ln Batty (now attached to the 39 Bde RFA, and lent to 2nd Division) fired on GERMAN front line trenches between LES BRIQUES and AUCHY. During this period the 15 & 16 Ln BATTIES were the only batteries of the Division in action.	References throughout are made to the AUCHY-LENS trench map, unless otherwise stated.
Friday, July 2nd	Lt-Col. A.C. LOWE, D.S.O., + 2/Lt. J.H. VAN DEN BERGH proceeded to ENGLAND on 7 days' leave. Capt. MACVEAGH (2/18th Ln. Bde. RFA) attached to 15 Ln Batty.	
Saturday, July 3rd Sunday, July 4th Monday, July 5th Tuesday, July 6th	NIL	
Wednesday, July 7th	Capt. W. COOPER proceeded to ENGLAND on 7 days' leave. Arrangements have now been made whereby one Officer and 2 "other ranks" proceed to ENGLAND on seven days' leave each Tuesday. Up to this date, the 15 & 16 Ln Batties have, since July 1st, daily fired, in retaliation only, at the same targets — the 15 Ln Batty at the crossroads at HAISNES and at "HOHENZOLLERN" fort and the 16 Ln Batty at the GERMAN front line trenches between AUCHY & LES BRIQUES. Lieut. N.V. BRASNETT reported for duty from Base Details and posted to 6 Ln group. Lt. R.A. CORSAN promoted Captain (Temporary), dated April 1st	

Army Form C. 2118.

WAR DIARY
INTELLIGENCE SUMMARY.
(Erase heading not required.)

(71)

Instructions regarding War Diaries and Intelligence Summaries are contained in F. S. Regs., Part II. and the Staff Manual respectively. Title pages will be prepared in manuscript.

Hour, Date, Place	Summary of Events and Information	Remarks and references to Appendices
Thursday. July 8th.	One section of the 15 Lon Batty left its position at VERMELLES, and one section of the 16 Lon Batty left its position at ANNEQUIN and proceeded to a new position at MAZINGARBE, as did one section of the 17 Lon Batty from LAPUGNOY, where the 17 Lon Batty and Brigade Headquarters has remained. All the above took place after dusk today.	
Friday. July 9th.	Each battery registered its zone in its new position, with its one available section. The 16 Lon Batty registered G.28.B.c.1; G.28.c. Q.5; and G.34. The remaining section of each battery came into action at MAZINGARBE, and Brigade Headquarters proceed thither from LAPUGNOY.	
Saturday. July 10th.	15 Lon Batty fired 16 rounds on enemy's first line trench G.28.6.5. 15 Lon Batty also fired at a working party of 6 GERMAN gunners cutting clear at G.23.c.8, whereupon they retired. 16 Lon Batty fired 22 rounds, from G.28.6.9.5 — G.28.6.5.0, in registration and retaliation. 17 Lon Batty registered G.34.a – G.34.c. Arrangements were concluded whereby the 17 Lon Batty will fire with the new "80-fuze" Before the whole Brigade before is now firing with ammunition.	
Sunday. July 11th.	The new-line of each battery, write up-to-date, has been very this ammunition.	

WAR DIARY
INTELLIGENCE SUMMARY

Army Form C. 2118.

Hour, Date, Place	Summary of Events and Information	Remarks and references to Appendices
Sunday July 11th (continued)	close to the Battery positions, were moved to DROUVIN, about 4 miles further back. The 15 cm Batty this afternoon fired 33 rounds in retaliation on a GERMAN forward trench. The 16 cm Batty fired 8 rounds in retaliation. The 17 cm Batty fired several rounds in retaliation on G.34.c.7.9. and subsequently registered a Rable gun emplacement in 29.B.	
Monday July 12th	Orders were received early this morning that the 47 Div Arty would be relieved tonight by the 48 (South Midland) Div Arty. The Batteries of this Brigade therefore did not fire today. At 10.45 p.m. the move was cancelled.	
Tuesday July 13th	Between 11 p.m. & midnight. Lt R. BRUCE proceeded to ENGLAND on 7 days' leave. With a view to a Roble attack, the O.C. Brigade together with the G.O.C.R.A. reconnoitred suitable artillery positions on two lines of defence — one passing through GRENAY, the other passing through SAILLY LABOURSE. 15 cm Batty fired 6 rounds at working party in forward GERMAN trench, and subsequently 47 rounds in retaliation. 16 cm Batty fired 56 rounds on front line trenches & 13 rounds in retaliation. 17 cm Batty fired a few rounds at transport on crossroads at 4.25.d. in the evening: fire during the day was impossible owing to the presence & fire of enemy observation balloons in the direction of ELEU ANION and LENS.	
Wednesday July 14th	15 cm Batty fired a total of 14 rounds at forward GERMAN trenches in	

WAR DIARY
INTELLIGENCE SUMMARY.

(Erase heading not required.)

Army Form C. 2118.

No. 73

Instructions regarding War Diaries and Intelligence Summaries are contained in F.S. Regs., Part II. and the Staff Manual respectively. Title pages will be prepared in manuscript.

Hour, Date, Place	Summary of Events and Information	Remarks and references to Appendices
July 14th (continued)	retaliation. Subsequently 15 cm Batty registered crossroads at LOOS (10 rounds) and then fired 11 rounds at same. 16 cm Batty did not fire. 17 cm Batty fired on billets at LOOS, as a reprisal for GERMAN shrapnel which fell in front of NOEUX and near GRENAY Chemel.	
Thursday, July 15th	15 cm Batty fired a total of 25 rounds in retaliation on enemy's front trenches, and the 16 cm Batty fired a total of 48 rounds on the same objective, in retaliation. The 17 cm Batty fired on sentries observed at traffic passing crossroads at H.25.d., and on two occasions at working parties.	
Friday, July 16th	15 cm Batty fired 10 rounds in retaliation on forward GERMAN trenches. 16 cm Batty also fired in retaliation, on registered positions G.34.b.7.7, G.35.a.1.6, G.29.c.9.1, G.35.c.7.3. 17 cm Batty again fired on several occasions at transport at H.25.d. Sous Officier T. LEGRIX [underlined] proceeded to ELBEUF on 8 days' leave.	
Saturday, July 17th	The O.C. Brigade reconnoitred positions for Batteries, so as to enable them to carry-out wire-cutting operations. Brigade Head quarters moved to MAZINGARBE CHATEAU. 15 cm Batty fired a total of 38 rounds on GERMAN front line trenches in retaliation, and 3 rounds on crossroads at LOOS. 16 cm Batty fired 19 rounds in registering to same points as yesterday, and 16 rounds in retaliation. 17 cm	

WAR DIARY
INTELLIGENCE SUMMARY

Army Form C. 2118.

Hour, Date, Place	Summary of Events and Information	Remarks and references to Appendices
July 17th (continued) Sunday. July 18th	Batty fired in retaliation on G.34.a.8.0-2. Capt. P.A. LOVE – O.C. 6th Lon Amm. Col. went sick and was removed to field Ambulance, his place as O.C. Am. Col. being taken by Capt. C.P. BERNE, 16 Lon Batty. 15 Lon Batty fired a total of 28 rounds in retaliation on forward GERMAN trenches, and 16 Ln Batty fires 10 rounds. 17 Ln Batty fired 23 rounds in reply to hostile fire, which ceased. A working party of 30 men were dispersed. At 11.45 p.m. 17 Ln Batty fired 4 rounds on enemy's trenches at request of infantry. A Corporal, Bombardier & Gunner of K. 15 Ln Batty were accidentally wounded whilst examining an unexploded GERMAN shell.	
Monday. July 19th	15 Ln Batty fired 5 rounds in retaliation on GERMAN trenches, + 16 Ln Batty 24 rounds. 17 Ln Batty also fired at this objective. 30 men of the 5th London Bde RFA + 40 men of the 7th London Bde RFA were attached to the Batteries of this Brigade, to assist in railway cutting.	
Tuesday. July 20th	Lieut. W.J. BARNARD proceeded to ENGLAND on 7 days' leave, thereby leaving the 16 Ln Batty with 2 officers only. 2nd Lieut. J.A.W. PETERS attached to 16 Ln Batty from 6 Ln Amm. Col.	
Wednesday. July 21st	Capt. & Adjt. M.J.K. O'MALLEY, sick, was evacuated to 6th Field Ambulance. 15 Ln Batty	

WAR DIARY
INTELLIGENCE SUMMARY.
(Erase heading not required.)

Army Form C. 2118.

Hour, Date, Place	Summary of Events and Information	Remarks and references to Appendices
July 20th (continued)	fired 15 rounds in retaliation on forward GERMAN trenches, & 16 LON Batty fired a total of 8 rounds, also in retaliation, on the same target. 17 Lon Batty likewise retaliated.	
Wednesday. July 21st	Captain & Adjutant M.J.K. O'MALLEY, sick, was evacuated to 6th Fld ambulance. 15 Lon Batty fired a total of 36 rounds on billets at LOOS, & 7 rounds on GERMAN forward trenches, all in retaliation. 16 Lon Batty fired 23 rounds in retaliation; of these, 8 rounds were fired at LOOS, and remainder distributed along the GERMAN front line trenches. Later, 32 rounds were fired at the latter target. At 3 periods during the day the 17 Ln Batty retaliated on G. 34. c. 6.8. Three N.C.O's and one man of the 15 Ln Batty were wounded, as the result of examining a GERMAN "blind" shell. One man of 17 Ln Batty was wounded, during bombardment of 17 Ln Batty upper line at NOYELLES.	
Thursday. July 22nd	Retaliating, 15 Ln Batty fired 12 rounds on LOOS billets, and a total of 17 rounds on GERMAN front line trenches. 16 Ln Batty fired 91 rounds on LOOS billets & GERMAN front line trenches, & 17 Ln Batty fired on LOOS billets. The Trench bombardment was particularly severe — Rifle explosive — on PHILOSOPHE, LES BREBIS, and neighbourhood this afternoon. One man at 17 Ln Batty Wagon line at NOYELLES wounded. 16 rifles per battery, and rifles of Brigade Head Quarter Staff & Bde Amm. Col. were withdrawn: these units are to be re armed with Carbines.	

Army Form C. 2118.

WAR DIARY
INTELLIGENCE SUMMARY.
(Erase heading not required.)

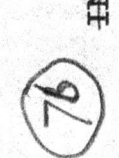

Hour, Date, Place	Summary of Events and Information	Remarks and references to Appendices
Friday, July 23rd.	15 Hr Batty fired a total of 80 rounds on GERMAN front line trenches in retaliation for fire on ours. This Battery also fired 11 rounds registering a new point — G. 28. B. 3.7. The 16 Hr Batty fired 13 rounds in retaliation, for the same reason as the 15 Hr Batty. 17 Hr Batty fired 3 rounds on G. 34. c. 6. 9.	
Saturday, July 24th.	15 Hr Batty fired a total of 48 rounds on GERMAN front line trenches in retaliation. 16 Hr Batty retaliated similarly with 24 rounds. 17 Hr Batty fired at G. 34. c. 6.8., and dispersed a working party. Tonight, one gun from each of the 15, 16, 17 Hr Batteries, and one gun of the 13 Hr Batty (un manned by Major A. C. SCAMMEL) took up new forward positions (prepared by working parties from 5th + 7th Hr Brigades RFA, for wirecutting.	
Sunday, July 25th.	15 Hr Batty, with 3 guns only, fired 13 rounds on G. 28. c. 8.3., 6 rounds on a GERMAN working party, and 8 rounds on LOOS cemetery and billets in retaliation for GERMAN bombardment of PHILOSOPHE. 16 Hr Batty fired 2 rounds on LOOS, and 17 Hr Batty replied to hostile bombardment of MAROC. Wire cutting took place tonight. Observation was for range rather than effect. The 15 Hr Batty fired 6 rounds, 16 Hr Batty 5 rounds, 17 Hr Batty 7 rounds, + 13 Hr Batty 12 rounds. The result were	

Army Form C. 2118.

WAR DIARY
or
INTELLIGENCE SUMMARY.

(74)

(Erase heading not required.)

Instructions regarding War Diaries and Intelligence Summaries are contained in F.S. Regs., Part II. and the Staff Manual respectively. Title pages will be prepared in manuscript.

Hour, Date, Place	Summary of Events and Information	Remarks and references to Appendices

July 25th (continued) — satisfactory. The best result was obtained by the 17 Lwr Batty. Range 1750. In all other cases, the gun positions were over 3000 yards away. The working parties from the 5th & 7th London Brigades returned to their units.

Monday. July 26th. 15 Lwr Batty retaliated with 22 rounds on GERMAN forward trenches. By order of 47 Division HQ, 16 Lwr Batty fired on chimney seen in GERMAN trenches, & after firing 16 rounds satisfied themselves that chimney was not in first or second line of GERMAN trenches. 17 Lwr Batty fired 2 rounds at transport on crossroads at H.25.d., thereby stopping traffic. Last night, guns were brought back from the "intercutting position".
2 Lt J.C. WODLLETT proceeded to ENGLAND on 7 days' leave. 15 Lwr Batty fired 28 rounds in retaliation on GERMAN first and second line trenches; on this objective 16 Lwr Batty retaliated with 10 rounds, and also fired 3 rounds at Loos Pylons. 17 Lwr Batty did not fire.

Tuesday. July 27th. Major H.D. SPRAGUE (2/6th London Brigade RFA) and Capt E.J. NATCHAM (2/3rd East Anglian Brig.II RFA) attached to 16 + 17 Lwr Batties respectively.
On section of the 15 Lwr Batty was last night relieved by a section of "A" Battery (71st Brigade RFA) — Kitchener's Army. This section of the 15 Lwr Batty proceeded forthwith to GOSNAY. 16 Lwr Batty fired 4 rounds on GERMAN first line trenches, + 20 rounds on LOOS — all in retaliation. A draft of four men received from Base Details.

Wednesday. July 28th. The remaining section of the 15 Lwr Batty, and one section of the 16 Lwr Batty were relieved by sections of Batteries of the 71st Bde RFA, last night. "D" Battery of the 70th Bde RFA relieved

Thursday. July 29th.

WAR DIARY
INTELLIGENCE SUMMARY.
(Erase heading not required.)

Army Form C. 2118.

Instructions regarding War Diaries and Intelligence Summaries are contained in F.S. Regs., Part II. and the Staff Manual respectively. Title pages will be prepared in manuscript.

(78)

Hour, Date, Place	Summary of Events and Information	Remarks and references to Appendices
July 29th (continued)	was in position at VERMELLES, should have relieved the 17 Ln Batty, but having lost its way, failed to put in an appearance till 4 a.m. As it was then daylight, the relief had to be postponed.	
Friday, July 30th	The remaining section of the 16 ln Batty & the first section of the 17 Ln Batty were relieved last night, & proceeded to GOSNAY. At midday today, Lt.Colonel A.C.LOWE D.S.O. landed over his command to Colonel HEATH, O.C. 71st Brigade RFA. The 6 Ln Amm. Col. proceeded to GOSNAY.	
Saturday, July 31st	The remaining section of the 17 Ln Batty and the Brigade Headquarter Staff proceeded last night to GOSNAY.	

T.H. Van den Bergh

47th.Div.
5th.Lon.F.A.B.
6th.Lon.F.A.B.
7th.Lon.F.A.B.
8th.Lon.F.A.B.
~~4th.Bde.~~
3rd.Bde.R.G.A.

Reliefs of the 47th.Divisional Artillery by 15th.Divisional Artillery will be carried out as follows:-

Night of 27th/28th. July, 1915.

One Section 72nd.Bde.R.F.A. relieves one section 18th.Lon.Bty.
" " 70th.Bde.R.F.A. " " " 13th. " "
" " 71st.Bde.R.F.A. " " " 15th. " "
" " 73rd.Bde.R.F.A. " " " 22nd. " "

Night of 28th/29th.July,1915.

Remaining sections of these Batteries carry our reliefs and the following additional reliefs take place.

One Section 72nd.Bde.R.F.A. relieves one section 20th.Lon.Bty.
" " 70th.Bde.R.F.A. " " " 14th. " "
" " 71/73th.Bde.R.F.A. " " " 17th. " "
" " 70/73st.Bde.R.F.A. " " " 16th. " "

Night of 29th./30th.July, 1915.

Remaining sections of these Batteries carry out reliefs. One Officer from each battery will remain with the relieving battery for 24 hours after relief is completed.

The section of the 21st.Lon.Battery and the single gun of the 12th.Lon.Battery will be relieved in accordance with orders to be issued later.

Orders as to billets of units on relief will be issued later.

Captain, R.F.A. for
Brigade Major,
47th.Div.Arty.

B.M. c/948.
25/7/15.

121/6598

47th Division

1st London Bde R.F.A.

Vol VI

From. 1 - 31. 8. 15

CONFIDENTIAL

WAR DIARY

OF THE

5th LONDON BRIGADE. R.F.A.

FROM August 1st 1915. to August 31st 1915.

Army Form C. 2118.

WAR DIARY
INTELLIGENCE SUMMARY.
(Erase heading not required.)

Instructions regarding War Diaries and Intelligence Summaries are contained in F.S. Regs., Part II. and the Staff Manual respectively. Title pages will be prepared in manuscript.

Hour, Date, Place	Summary of Events and Information	Remarks and references to Appendices
Sunday. August 1st	The 6th London Brigade RFA is now complete at GOSNAY (Chateau de Danas) A series of inspections is about to be embarked on - Horses, Kits, harness stores are all being inspected by O.C. Units (F). The guns of the Brigade were inspected by the I.O.M, IV Corps, who made a satisfactory report.	
Monday. August 2nd	Captain and Adjt. M.J.K. O'MALLEY rejoined the Brigade from the Base. Orders Cadre received.	
Tuesday. August 3rd Wednesday. August 4th	Major A. BAYLEY proceeded to ENGLAND on 7 days leave. Examination took place of class of 20 recruit signallers, under a three months course of instruction. This is the first of monthly examinations.	
Thursday. August 5th	The 1st Kent Comm: Col is now carrying out Battery Gun Drill with the guns of batteries. Brigade Headquarters moved to the Mill House, GOSNAY.	
Friday. August 6th	Major P.J. CLIFTON, sick, proceeded to Hospital. The race course, on HESDIGNEUL Common, is at the disposal of the Batteries of this Brigade for two days per week. (proposed)	
Saturday. August 7th	The A.D.V.S. 47 Div. lectured to the class of A Shoeing Smiths, undergoing a six weeks course of instruction. The Brigade Rifle on Illuminated concert in the evening; the band of the 6th London Field Ambulance gave Selections: the following amongst others, were present:- G.O.C RA 47 Div. Arty + Staff, Major DOYLE IV Corps, Staff of 142 Inf. Bde., Staff of 47 Div, etc	

Army Form C. 2118.

WAR DIARY
INTELLIGENCE SUMMARY.
(Erase heading not required.)

Instructions regarding War Diaries and Intelligence Summaries are contained in F. S. Regs., Part II and the Staff Manual respectively. Title pages will be prepared in manuscript.

(80)

Hour, Date, Place	Summary of Events and Information	Remarks and references to Appendices

Sunday, August 8th — The Preliminary rounds of a Brigade Boxing Competition took place this afternoon. Battery Sergeant Major W.G. RUSSELL 15 km Battery — gazetted Second Lieutenant, dated July 18th.

Monday, August 9th — All signallers are being re-drilled. The 16 km Battery moved its present waggon lines and gun park to a position higher in the woods of the BOIS DES DAMES. A working party of 100 men of this Brigade proceeded to LES BREBIS to construct gun pits on the second line of defence, under supervision of 2/Lt C.E.H. LLOYD. All billets are being systematically searched, so that all ordnance & supply stores can be handed to the Salvage Company. Capt. M.J.K. O'MALLEY won 2nd prize in open Jumping Competition at 7th London Brigade RFA Sports. Lt-Col A.C. LOWE, D.S.O, and Major A.C. GORDON proceeded to ENGLAND on 4 + 7 days leave respectively. A draft of 5 men arrived from BASE. 2/Lt T.A.W. PETRE attached from 6 Lon: Amm: Col. to 17 km Battery during absence on duty of 2/Lt C.E.H. LLOYD.

Wednesday, August 11th — The Brigade Boxing Competition was concluded. It was proposed the Bonfire at MARLES, but, as no suitable accommodation could be found, it was decided to let the Brigade remain where it is, in consequence 2/Lt W.G. RUSSELL proceeded to BASE. The A.D.V.S. (47 Div.) inspected (?)

Thursday, August 12th — horses, for purposes of casting. Vacancies in non-commissioned ranks, caused by death or sickness, are being filled by promotion to temporary acting rank.

(73989) W.4141—463. 400,000. 9/14. H.&J.Ltd. Forms/C. 2118/10.

WAR DIARY
INTELLIGENCE SUMMARY.
(Erase heading not required.)

Army Form C. 2118

(81)

Place	Date	Hour	Summary of Events and Information	Remarks and references to Appendices
	Friday, August 13th Saturday 14th		Nil	
	Sunday, August 15th		Major P.T. CLIFTON, 17 Ldn Batty, rejoined the Brigade from the Base. 2nd Lt H.B.WELLS was struck off the strength of the Brigade from today's date. Men who have been inoculated with one dose only are to be re-inoculated. 100% of the Brigade have been inoculated.	
	Monday, August 16th		Major R.R. WANSBROUGH, having relinquished the command of the 47 (LON) DIVISIONAL AMMUNITION COLUMN, re-assumed command of the 6th Ldn Amm. Col. will effect from today's date. Brigade Sports were held in HESDIGNEUL Common, the Band of the 6th Ldn Field Ambulance was in attendance.	
	Tuesday, August 17th		Capt. C.P. BEATTIE proceeded to ENGLAND on 7 days leave. A Broom was appointed to examine the Class of Sharp Smiths who have undergone a six week course of instruction.	
	Wednesday, August 18th		2nd Lt J.A.W. PETRO proceeded to LES BREBIS, to assist 2nd Lt C.E.H. LLOYD in digging gun pits on the defensive lines. Two 18-pr guns fetched from 15th Div. Arty. for batteries of this Brigade to practice with.	
	Thursday, August 19th		HESDIGNEUL COMMON is no longer at the disposal of Artillery Brigades of the 47 DN for any purpose.	
	Friday, August 20th		17 Ldn Batty moved its present Waggon Line to a place in the BOIS DES DAMES.	
	Saturday, August 21st		Lieut. G. LLOYD-SMITH, R.F.A., rejoined the Brigade from the 3/6th London Brigade R.F.A.	

Army Form C. 2118

WAR DIARY
or
INTELLIGENCE SUMMARY.
(Erase heading not required.)

(82)

Place	Date	Hour	Summary of Events and Information	Remarks and references to Appendices
	August 21st (continued)		was posted to the 15 Ldn Batty. Major R.R. WANSBROUGH promoted Lieutenant-Colonel.	
	Sunday. August 22nd		2/Lieut C.E.H. LLOYD appointed temporary Aide-de-camp to Brigadier-General T.C. WRAY, M.V.O., C.R.A. 47 Div. Each unit inspected by O.C. Brigade after Church Parade. Passenger Boats + mail steamer service between ENGLAND and FRANCE stopped.	
	Monday. August 23rd		The 6th London Brigade R.F.A Tug o' War team, captained by R.S-M J.T. HOOD, and coached by B.S-M. A.V. DAVIS, having beaten the 8th London (Howitzer) Brigade R.F.A in the preliminary heats, and the 7th London Brigade R.F.A. in the final heat, qualified to represent the 47 Divisional Artillery in the Divisional Sports on Wednesday next. Lt. R. BRUCE ..... 6th Ldn. Am. Col... transferred to 16 Ldn Batty. Lt. W.T. BARNARD.. 16 Ldn Batty .... transferred to 6th Ldn. Am. Col. Lt. J.E. WOOLLETT... 15 Ldn Batty .... transferred to 6th Ldn Am. Col. 2/Lt. T.A.W. PETRO... 6 Ldn. Am. Col ..... attached to 17 Ldn Batty. ⎤ with effect from tomorrow's date. Service between ENGLAND and FRANCE resumed. Officers and Men of this Brigade will in future proceed on leave each WEDNESDAY instead of TUESDAY.	
	Tuesday. August 24th		Inspection of Transport (Cook's Waggon, Cook's Cart, Medical Cart, + Water Carts) by Col BLYTHE.	
	Wednesday. August 25th		2/Lt. V.C. LUCAS proceeded to ENGLAND on 7 days' leave. A whole holiday granted by G.O.C. R.A. so that all ranks could attend Divisional Sports at LOZINGHEM. Chief Judge was Lt-Col. A.C. LOWE, D.S.O. (6th London Brigade R.F.A.); Chief Marshal – Capt. M.J.K. O'MALLEY (6th London Brigade R.F.A	

WAR DIARY
INTELLIGENCE SUMMARY.
(Erase heading not required.)

Army Form C. 2118

(83)

Place	Date	Hour	Summary of Events and Information	Remarks and references to Appendices
	August 25th (continued)		The following events were won by teams or individuals of the 6th London Brigade R.F.A:— (1) Team Driving. (2) Relay Race. (3) Quarter Mile Open. and (4) Light Draught Horse........ 3rd Prize. (5) Officers Jumping (Open)........ 3rd Prize.	
	Thursday. August 26th		The O.C. Brigade and Adjutant attended Divisional Artillery conference at LOZINGHEM. The Veterinary Officer, Lt. W.P.S. EDWARDS was attached to 1st Division; his duties will be performed by the A.D.V.S., 47 Div. Capt. J. ABSON. Inspection of Technical Stores Wagon of the Ammunition Column.	
	Friday. August 27th		The 15 Pdr Battery moved its present gun wagon line to a new position in the BUS DES DAMES	
	Saturday. August 28th		Lt. G. LYON-SMITH appointed Orderly Officer & H.Q.C. Brigade. Lt. J.C. WOOLLETT transferred from 6th Ln. Amm. Col. to 15 Pdr Batty. Lt. T.H. VAN DEN BERGH transferred from Brigade Headquarters Staff to 6th Ln. Amm. Col. T.H. Van den Bergh Lt.	
	Sunday August 29th		Nil	
	Monday August 30th		Capt O'Nally left GOSNAY for LES BREBIS with telephonists. A party of 40 men under Lt. BRUCE, left GOSNAY & proceeded to NOYELLES. Lt BRUCE returned to GOSNAY after conducting the party.	
	Tuesday August 31st		An additional party of 20 men, under Lt. BLACKWELL, left GOSNAY & proceeded to NOYELLES. Lecture by Capt. M.Combrie, chemical Adviser, 1st Army, "On Smoke Helmets & Touch in at NOYELLES. Lt. BRUCE + 2 N.C.O.s attended. J.M.Smith Lt.	

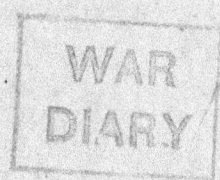

Headquarters.

236th BRIGADE, R.F.A.
(1/6 London)

(47th Division)

S E P T E M B E R

1 9 1 5

47th Division

D/7493

CONFIDENTIAL

WAR DIARY
OF THE
236 Bde.
6th LONDON BRIGADE. R.F.A.

from SEPTEMBER 1st 1915 to SEPTEMBER 30th 1915

— Vol VII

Army Form C. 2118.

WAR DIARY
or
INTELLIGENCE SUMMARY.
(Erase heading not required.)

(84)

Instructions regarding War Diaries and Intelligence Summaries are contained in F. S. Regs., Part II. and the Staff Manual respectively. Title pages will be prepared in manuscript.

Place	Date	Hour	Summary of Events and Information	Remarks and references to Appendices
	Wednesday September 1st		Bde. headqr Brigade RFA moved from BOSNAY. 15th 16th 17th how batteries at PLACE à BRUAY Bde. how ammunition column at HANLICOURT	
	Thursday September 2nd		Lt. W.P.S. EDWARDS A.V.S. returned from 1st Division	
	Friday September 3rd		18 pdr guns returned to 7th Brigade. Lt. BRUCE took charge of the guns. One 15 pdr gun lent to dy 17th Battery & dy 5th London FA.B.	
	Saturday September 4th		Lt-Col A.C. LOWE left BRUAY to understudy G.O.C. R.A. 47th Division conal Artillery at LESBREBIS. 2/Lt V.C. LUCAS left BRUAY for woumended Capt. O'MALLEY at LES BREBIS	
	Sunday September 5th		Church Parade at 4th Corps H.Q. LABUSSIÈRE. 2/Lt J.A.W. PETRO assisted by 2/Lt A.F. YEMCKEN, took a section Recruit 17 K.O.H Batty to attend the 15th Division Army	
	Monday September 6th		Capt. R.A. CORSAN left BRUAY to assist Major H. BAYLEY at MAZINGARBE. Working parties returned.	

Army Form C. 2118

WAR DIARY
or
INTELLIGENCE SUMMARY.
(Erase heading not required.)

Instructions regarding War Diaries and Intelligence Summaries are contained in F. S. Regs., Part II. and the Staff Manual respectively. Title pages will be prepared in manuscript.

Place	Date	Hour	Summary of Events and Information	Remarks and references to Appendices
	Tuesday September 7th		CAPT R.A. CORSAN came down from MAZINGARBE and took back 26 men from the 15th Lon Batty for a working party.	
			25 men from the 15th Lon Batty went up to LES BREBIS as a working party for 47th Div. Aug. H.Q.	
			6 men from 15th Lon Batty went up to detached section of 17th Batty with 15th Division to assist 7/L PETRO.	
	Wednesday September 8th		Issue of BLANKETS - one per man	
			COURT MARTIAL at HAILLICOURT. President = MAJOR P.J. CLIFTON	
	Thursday September 9th		Nil	
	Friday September 10th		COURT MARTIAL (held again) President - MAJOR P.J. CLIFTON.	
	Saturday September 11th		Nil	
	Sunday September 12th		Church Parade at 4th Corps H.Q. at LABUSSIÈRE	
	Monday September 13th		Lt. BRASNETT was struck off the strength of the Brigade & posted to Training School at ST. VENANT for trench mortar battery. 31.8.15	
			15th Battery sent out section to the firing line under CAPT CORSAN & 2/Lt NOBLETT. Teams returned here.	

1577 Wt. W10791/1773 500,000 1/15 D. D. & L. A.D.S.S./Forms/C. 2118.

Army Form C. 2118.

WAR DIARY
or
INTELLIGENCE SUMMARY.

(Erase heading not required.)

(8b)

Place	Date	Hour	Summary of Events and Information	Remarks and references to Appendices
Tuesday September 14th		Nil	2/Lt VAN DEN BERGH proceeded to join "MASSY GROUP" at LES BRÉBIS	
	Wednesday Sept. 15th		BRUAY - out of bounds for British troops.	
			CAPT. COOPER reported at 47th Div. Arty. at 7 P.M. for the purpose of bringing up 2 guns from 18th How. Batty. Shrader was cancelled and Capt. COOPER returned to Place à BRUAY.	
			2/Lt J. C. WOOLLETT returned from MAROC & became O.C. 18th How. Batty.	
			Capt. COOPER returned to 17th Battery.	
Thursday Sept 16th			Interpreter CANDOUX joined the brigade to replace Interpreter LEARY. Medical A.D.M.S. A.D.V.S. and D.A.D.O.S.	
Friday September 17th			2/Lt BLACKWELL returned to de Couvienes and 15th Battery. 2/Lt WOOLLETT & Lt BRUAY are proceeded to MAROC. Capt. COOPER & Lt BRUAY transfer to 47th Div. Arty.	
Saturday September 18th			Working party returned to 15th Battery. Lt W.R. SADLER R.A.M.C. to Captain.	
Sunday September 19th			CHURCH PARADE at Lt Colo A. Q. L'ADUISIERE	
Monday September 20th			MAJOR GORDON left BRUAY proceeded to 141st Infantry Bde as Liaison Officer. 1 Section (under Lt BRUCE) proceeded to the firing line. Lt BRUCE returned	

1577 Wt. W10791/1773 500,000 1/15 D. D. & L. A.D.S.S./Forms/C. 2118.

WAR DIARY or INTELLIGENCE SUMMARY

Army Form C. 2118.

(Erase heading not required.)

Place	Date	Hour	Summary of Events and Information	Remarks and references to Appendices
	Tuesday September 21st		Lt. Brook R.G.A. left Place A Bray and bivouacked at Hallucourt near the 6th Lon. B.A.C. The 6 remaining guns of this Brigade and 18 guns of the 7th Lon. F.A.B. formed the 47th Reserve Div. Arty. (Chambers Group) under the command of Col. Chambers, O.C. 7th Lon. F.A.B. Lt. Bruce proceeded to 141st Infantry Brigade as Liaison Officer. 1st day of Bombardment.	
	Wednesday September 22nd		The day was spent in cleaning up camp & putting up bivouacs. 2nd day of Bombardment.	
	Thursday September 23rd		Our fire returned effective from 5th Lon F.A.B. - one from 17th Lon Batty. knocked up 4 of the dummy guns. 3rd day of Bombardment. Spare Stores were stored at 47th R.A. Storage at Hallucourt.	
	Friday September 24th		4th day of Bombardment	
	Saturday September 25th		6th Lon F.A.B. moved from Hallucourt to Les Brebis and bivouacked at Les A. Infantry attacked at 5.50 a.m. Capt. Corsan was ordered up to act as Mullet Wireless Observer in Maroc attached to 15th Battery. Lt. Bruce was wounded during the initial attack just by O.K. Batt. London Regiment just as he reached the German front line trenches. Fired on Dublin Grazier during the infantry attack. 15th (attached) Section (under Capt Corsan) fired during the attack.	Detached Section (under 7th R.G.A.)

Army Form C. 2118.

WAR DIARY
or
INTELLIGENCE SUMMARY.
(Erase heading not required.)

Place	Date	Hour	Summary of Events and Information	Remarks and references to Appendices
	Sunday September 26th		Remaining section of the 16th Battery went up to N. MAROC to join the section already in the firing line. The 16th battery is under the command of Major GORDON. Still with Infantry Brigade. Capt. COOPER Major GORDON returned to LES BREBIS. 149th Infantry Bde. Detached section 17th Battery returned to the wagon line. 2/Lt LLOYD returned to duty to the 17th Battery from H.Q. 5th Divn Arty.	
	Monday September 27th		One gun from 17th Battery was sent up to 13th Lon Batty to observe a gun badly damaged by an explosion in the breech. 16th Battery fired 3 rounds registering.	
	Tuesday Sept. 28th		Lt. R. BRUCE officially reported killed. Wounded by Capt. R. WOOD, Chaplains 14th Infantry Bde. 2/Lt LLOYD for 5 captured German field Guns & AND ONE captured machine gun to VAUDRICOURT, where they were inspected by FIELD MARSHAL SIR JOHN FRENCH.	
	Wednesday Sept. 29th		At 8.30 A.M. enemy shelled the aeroplane at LES BREBIS - horses were immediately withdrawn for 2 hours. 2/Lt J.A.N. PETRO took a party of 30 men to get in captured field guns 8 in LOOS 16th Battery fired on enemy's trenches north of LOOS	

Army Form C. 2118

WAR DIARY
or
INTELLIGENCE SUMMARY.
(Erase heading not required.)

Instructions regarding War Diaries and Intelligence Summaries are contained in F. S. Regs., Part II. and the Staff Manual respectively. Title pages will be prepared in manuscript.

Place	Date	Hour	Summary of Events and Information	Remarks and references to Appendices
Thursday	Sept 30th		6th London Brigade, R.F.A. moved from LES BREBIS to L21c (between LES BREBIS and NOEUX-LES-MINES) less 16th Lon Batty guns + wagons in action + 2 guns of the 15th Battery. Major Mark ?	

121/7384

7th Division

8 In London Bde RFA

Vol XIII

Oct 15

CONFIDENTIAL

WAR DIARY
of the
6th London Brigade R.F.A.

from October 1st 1915 to October 31st 1915

Army Form C. 2118.

WAR DIARY
or
INTELLIGENCE SUMMARY.
(Erase heading not required.)

Instructions regarding War Diaries and Intelligence Summaries are contained in F. S. Regs., Part II. and the Staff Manual respectively. Title pages will be prepared in manuscript.

Place	Date	Hour	Summary of Events and Information	Remarks and references to Appendices

1577 Wt.W10791/1773 500,000 1/15 D. D. & L. A.D.S.S./Forms/C. 2118.

Army Form C. 2118

WAR DIARY
or
INTELLIGENCE SUMMARY.
(Erase heading not required.)

Instructions regarding War Diaries and Intelligence Summaries are contained in F. S. Regs., Part II. and the Staff Manual respectively. Title pages will be prepared in manuscript.

Place	Date	Hour	Summary of Events and Information	Remarks and references to Appendices
	October 1st Friday		6th London Bde RFA moved from NOEUX-LES-MINES to HESDIGNEUL race course. Major GORDON rejoined the Brigade from the 141st Infantry Bde H.Q. Capt. COOPER - Bowill to 16th Battery out of action + joined 1st Brigade. Lt VAN DEN BERGH rejoined the Brigade from 5th London Bde RCA. Lt WOOLLETT joined 2 guns 1/16 15th battery out of action. Lt. Col. A.C.C.L	
	October 2nd Saturday		Lt. Col. A.C. LOWE D.S.O. rejoined the Brigade from 47th Div. Arty	
	October 3rd Sunday		Church Parade for 5th, 6th + 7th F.A. Brigades. 6th Brigade completed establishment with New (fuze 80) ammunition. 6th Brigade moved from HESDIGNEUL race course into billets at LABEUVRIÈRE	
	October 4th Monday		Lt. Col. MASSEY (comdg 5th How. F.A.B.) in Command of the 5th, 6th + 7th London F.A. Brigades.	
	October 5th Tuesday		6th London Bde R.F.A. moved from LABEUVRIÈRE to MARLES-LES-MINES, into billets	
	October 6th Wednesday		Capt. M.J.K. O'malley returned to the Brigade from 47th Div. Arty. & took up again the duties of adjutant. Major Lt. Bayley returned to the Brigade from 47th Div. Arty	

1577 Wt. W10791/1773 500,000 1/15 D. D. & L. A.D.S.S./Forms/C. 2118.

WAR DIARY
INTELLIGENCE SUMMARY
(Erase heading not required.)

(9)

Place	Date	Hour	Summary of Events and Information	Remarks and references to Appendices
	October 7th Thursday		The Brigade started through nightering places & equipment.	
	October 8th Friday		The Brigade was held in readiness to move at 2 hours notice.	
	October 9th Saturday		General Rawlinson spoke to the Division representatives (Col. Adj. & their 21 sub alt, a 30 Pdr. powered battery par to take sentry this Infantry Brigade) at DROUVIN. *	
	October 10th Sunday		Church Parade at 10.45 AM for whole brigade. *Order to move at 2 hours notice cancelled.*	
	October 11th Monday		Nil	
	October 12 Tuesday		2/Lt L.W.R. MOORE & 2/Lt W. O'MALLEY joined the Brigade from the 2/6th on F.A.3.	
	October 13th Wednesday		Col & Adjutant went to MAZINGARBE & reconnoitred 16 sap positions for the Brigade. Battery commanders went up to reconnoitre positions. 26 men per battery & 30 from the Am. Col. & Lt MARLES in 5 squadrons to dig gunpits near PHILOSOPHE. Lt MOORE took charge of the party.	

Army Form C. 2118

WAR DIARY
or
INTELLIGENCE SUMMARY

(Erase heading not required.)

(2)

Place	Date	Hour	Summary of Events and Information	Remarks and references to Appendices
~~Friday Oct~~ October 15th	Fri	Mng.	Brigade Headquarters left MARLES & proceeded to MAZINGARBE ar L 23 d/37 b 75. On section formed battery came into action at h/r near Quality Street. 15th Batty position at G 21 C 31. 16th Batty - at G 27 A 55. 17th " " " G 21 C 02. Reference map = Trench map Sht 36.n.w.3. 13th How Batty attached 16th A Col LOWE DSO - batty position = G 16 C 10 4, near LE RUTOIRE. 15 Lon Batty registered H 31.b.1.4., H.31.4.1.6½, H.25.B.1.2½. + PITS 14. 15 Lon Batty } registered approximately, but owing to the very &c. mist left accurate registration 16 Lon Batty } to a later date. 17 Lon Batty 6th Lon B.A.C. proceeded to NOEUX-LES-MINES. (L.19.C) from MARLES.	Street
October 16th	Sat.			
October 17th	Sun.		Though still misty, the batteries of LOWE Group were able, partially, to complete their registration. 2/Lt. JAN PETRO, 6th Lon Amm. Col., transferred to 17 Lon. Batty.	

WAR DIARY
INTELLIGENCE SUMMARY

Army Form C. 2118

Place	Date	Hour	Summary of Events and Information	Remarks and references to Appendices
October	18th Mon.		Concentration of fire at 1 p.m. on Woods No 5 + 4. (H.25.d.1.8.- H.25.d.5.8, + H.25.d.5.8 - H.26.c.3.9) Six rounds per gun fired at 1 p.m., followed by 4 rounds per gun at 1.10 p.m., fired quickly. Bombardier A.T. FARQUHARSON (17th Bty) wounded. 2nd Lt T.H. VAN DEN BERGH, 16th Bty, appointed Orderly officer to O.C. Brigade, & transferred to Brigade Headquarters staff. "Under authority granted by His Majesty the King, the Field Marshal Commanding in Chief appoints the undermentioned officer to be a 'Companion of the Distinguished Service Order':- Major Hadrian Bayley, 15th County of London Battery, R.F.A, 6th London Brigade R.F.A, in recognition of services rendered at LE PLANTIN, May 12th - 26th 1915.	
October	19th Tues		2nd Lt. G.I R.R. WANSBROUGH proceeded to ENGLAND (6th Lon Amm Col) Lt. W.J. BARNARD appointed to command 6th Lon Amm Col, vice Lt. CLERMAN PEVROUGH Capt. M.J.K. O'MALLEY (Adjutant, 6th London Brigade R.F.A) transferred to 17th Division Lt G. LYON SMITH appointed Adjutant of the Brigade, vice Capt M.J.K. O'MALLEY 13th Lon Baty moved its position to G.33.c.5.9. Batteries retaliated rapidly for every one GERMAN shell, one 18 pdr + one 15 pdr shell is being fired in retaliation	

WAR DIARY
or
INTELLIGENCE SUMMARY.
(Erase heading not required.)

Army Form C. 2118

Instructions regarding War Diaries and Intelligence Summaries are contained in F. S. Regs, Part II. and the Staff Manual respectively. Title pages will be prepared in manuscript.

Place	Date	Hour	Summary of Events and Information	Remarks and references to Appendices
	Oct. 20th Wed.	Morn	All batteries fired 10 rounds of shrapnel on H.19.d.4.0 — H.25.b.10.3. as far as possible in retaliation of fire on PUITS 14 bis, + on WORDS, 3,4, 5, + 6. Retaliation as before.	
		4 pm	Leave for the Division was re-opened. Capt. R.A. CORSAN, wounded, reported to 15 kn Batty from the Base.	
	Oct. 21st Thurs	2 p.m.	Concentration of fire (5 rounds per gun) on trench H.19.a.8.0 — H.19.a.7.8. Above was repeated. Retaliation as usual.	
		2.20 p.m.	Horses of Brigade inspected by Deputy Director of Remounts; to horses cast as being unsuitable, though fit, size, or other qualifications.	
	Oct. 22nd Fri.	—	Retaliation only. There was much shelling by the GERMANS: LOOS, the CHALK PIT was much shelled accidentally (rumoured), + the DOUBLE GRASSIER were all shelled; we retaliated. (Three smoke shells were retaliated).	
			Bdr RUTSON + Gr WOOTTEN (16 kn Batty) wounded.	
	Oct. 23rd Sat.		This afternoon there was intermittent shelling by the GERMANS; we retaliated. Concentration fire, to take place at 4.30 pm postponed.	
	Oct. 24th Sun.		This morning this afternoon there was gas shell desultory shelling by the GERMANS, to front line trenches, CHALK PIT WOOD + LOOS being their principle target. We retaliated, with no round (18 pdr) or no round (15 pdr) for every one of their rounds. Concentration of fire — 13 + 15 kn Batts on trench H.19.d. 4.3.0 — H.25. b.97.; 16 + 17 kn Batts on trench H.19.d. 4.3.0 — H.25. b. 4.7.	
		4 pm	District Artok. 18 pr Wagon (only + limber saluted. Batteries reported on large number of misfires due to the fact that "T tubes" are not now received in sealed tins.	

Army Form C. 2118

WAR DIARY
or
INTELLIGENCE SUMMARY
(Erase heading not required.)

(95)

Place	Date	Hour	Summary of Events and Information	Remarks and references to Appendices
	Oct. 25th Mon.	11.0 a.m.	Concentration of fire; target:- Trench H.15.a.9.4. – H.15.6.1.2. At 11 a.m. 2 rounds per gun were fired; 11.10 a.m. 2 rounds per gun; 11.25 4 rounds per gun; the last to be fired in salvoes. Owing to the extremely bad weather, Battery Commanders were unable to give certain information about the enemy's position required by the O.C. Brigade able to inspect targets of H. 15, 16, 17 Km Battys, as arranged. Instructions accorded to construct large "dug-outs", 15 feet below ground level; each dug-out is to be in communication with the one next to it by means of an underground passage. Lt. R. BRUCE. R.F.A (T) 6th London Brigade, officially announced "Died of Wounds."	
	Oct. 26th Tues.		2/Lt A.F. YENCKEN proceeded to ENGLAND on 7 days' leave. The O.C. Brigade inspected the trenches of the 6th Lon. Amm. Col. Retaliation – In future Pocket guns are to fire 5 times as many rounds as the GERMANS have fired. There was no concentration of fire today. 13 Km Batty registered H.19.6.8.1., H.25.6.8.5, & H.25.6.6.2. In return for intermittent shelling of our front line trenches all day by the GERMANS, our batteries retaliated on the GERMAN front line. 15&16 Km Battys spotted flashes of GERMAN battery at H.10.6.8.7.	
	Oct. 27th Wed.	3 a.m.	Concentration of fire on Wood 6, & Strasser H.25, 26, & 31. 6 rounds per gun were fired as quickly as possible.	
		5 a.m.	The above was repeated. There was no reply by the enemy.	
		12.5 p.m.	GERMANS obtained direct hit on gun emplacement of 13 Km Batty. One man seriously wounded; three others slightly wounded. Enemy shelled trenches in front of POITS Ht Ens, CHALK PIT, CHALK PIT WOOD, & LOOS. We retaliated.	
	Oct. 28th Thurs.	11.0 a.m.	Representatives of all units of IV Corps inspected by His Majesty the King between LABUISSIÈRE &	

1577 Wt. W10791/1773 500,000 1/15 D. D. & L. A.D.S.S./Forms/C. 2118.

WAR DIARY
INTELLIGENCE SUMMARY

Army Form C. 2118

Place	Date	Hour	Summary of Events and Information	Remarks and references to Appendices
Oct. 28th (continued)			HESDIGNEUL. 30 picked men, in charge of Lt. W.J. BARNARD represented the Brigade. His Majesty was known from his tent but was uninjured. Weather very unfavourable. Intermittent shelling of trenches, CHALK PIT, &c. as yesterday. He retaliated. The Ammunition Column received 77 Light Draught horses, in accordance with its new establishment. Heavy Draught horses are being returned.	
Oct. 29th	Friday		Capt. W.R. SADLER (R.A.M.C. – M.O. i/c 6th Howitzer Brigade R.F.A.) proceeded to ENGLAND on 10 days' leave. Shelling and retaliation as before. 13 hr. Battery had two men wounded in Waggon Line which was also shelled. 13 hr. Battery moved gun position to G. 33. a. o. q. All units of LOWE GROUP are supplying men for working parties in the trenches; men are also being supplied for the building of huts in Waggon Lines. Lt-Col. R.W.A. CHRISTIE having proceeded on leave, Lt-Col A.C. LOWE, DSO, assumed command of CHRISTIE GROUP in addition to LOWE GROUP.	
Oct. 30th	Sat.	3 p.m.	Concentration of fire on enemy trenches in H.19.b. This quietened enemy's fire which had been heavy all day, their targets being as before. 8 Cell-trench were issued to each battery, for the use (temporarily, until the huts are ready) of men in Waggon Lines. 15 hr. Battery moved their Waggon Line owing to bad state of ground caused by continued wet weather.	
Oct. 31st	Sun.	2.35 p.m.	LOOS, CHALK PIT, + our first line trenches again shelled; we retaliated. Shells still fell near gun positions of 15+17 hr. Batteries. Capt. R.A. CORSAN led to be dug out, but was uninjured. Officers' dugout of 15 hr. Battery knocked in. 17 hr. Battery moved their Waggon Line. Fire increased – 6 men per Brigade + 5.15 a.m. tomorrow morning. There will be a concentration of fire at 2.30 a.m.	

J.H. Van den Bergh Lt.

47th Division

D/7694

CONFIDENTIAL

WAR DIARY

OF THE

6TH LONDON BRIGADE R.F.A.

from Nov. 1st — Nov. 30th

Vol. IX

Army Form C. 2118.

WAR DIARY
INTELLIGENCE SUMMARY

(Erase heading not required.)

(97)

Instructions regarding War Diaries and Intelligence Summaries are contained in F. S. Regs., Part II and the Staff Manual respectively. Title pages will be prepared in manuscript.

Place	Date	Hour	Summary of Events and Information	Remarks and references to Appendices
Nov 1st	Monday	2:30 a.m. 5:15 a.m.	All batteries fired 8 rounds per gun, beginning with a salvo, on hostile trenches.	
		6 p.m. 6.55 p.m.	All batteries concentrated fire on trenches H.25.d.1.0. – H.31.6.2.4. There was very heavy shelling of our front line and communication trenches, all day, especially the corner Pt. 70 on two occasions, when hostile French Artillery retaliated, GERMAN fire ceased, but on another occasion they continued.	
			"Under authority granted by His Majesty the King, the Field Marshal Commanding in Chief, appointed the undermentioned Officer to be a "Companion of the Distinguished Service Order:–
			Major Adrian Charles Gordon, 16th Country of London Battery R.F.A., 6th London Brigade R.F.A.,
			in recognition of services rendered at LOOS, Sept 25th – 26th 1915.
Nov 2nd	Tuesday	4:30 p.m. 6.45 p.m.	Concentration of fire on trenches H.25.6.6.5. – H.25.6.7½; H.13.d.2.0 – H.13.d.2.4.
			During day GERMANS shelled communication trenches in section A.2, French in G.30.d. It seems that our howitzers do not retaliate sufficiently, in return for their 5.9 shell. GERMAN field guns invariably cease fire, when our field guns retaliate.
			2/Lt J.A.W. PETRO & 2/Lt A.E. BLACKWELL proceeded to ENGLAND on 9 days' leave. As the journey has now to be undertaken via HAVRE instead of BOULOGNE, 2 extra days are allowed.

1577 J.A.W. PETRO & 2/Lt A.E. BLACKWELL Wt. W10791/1773 500,000 1/15 D. D. & L. A.D.S.S./Forms/C. 2118.

Army Form C. 2118.

WAR DIARY

INTELLIGENCE SUMMARY.

(Erase heading not required.)

Instructions regarding War Diaries and Intelligence Summaries are contained in F.S. Regs., Part II. and the Staff Manual respectively. Title pages will be prepared in manuscript.

Place	Date	Hour	Summary of Events and Information	Remarks and references to Appendices
MAZINGARBE	Nov. 2nd (continued)		2/Lt HAMILTON-DAVIS transferred from 47th Divisional Ammunition Column to 6th London Brigade R.F.A.	
	Nov. 3rd Wednesday.		Throughout the day there was considerable shelling on our front line, particularly in Section A.1.; by light field guns and howitzers. At yesterday, hostile field gun fire was effectively stopped by our fire gun fire, but rifle fire from trenches continued. 2/Lt. W.T. O'MALLEY, 6th Ln. Amm. Col., attached to 15th Ln. Batty, during absence, on leave, of 2/Lt A.F. BLACKWELL.	
	Nov. 4th Thursday.	8 p.m. 9.30 p.m. midnight 4 a.m. 5 a.m.	Light was bad for observation until 11 a.m. In future, our Artillery will only retaliate by request of our infantry. A.1. was again shelled during the day, but no request was received by 15 Ln. Batty. to fire, nor by 17 Ln Batty. 16 Ln Batty retaliated at request of infantry. Less shelling than previous days. Bombardment of trenches in H.26.c., by all batteries of LOWE GROUP.	
	Nov. 5th Friday.		Shelling today was not heavy. CHALK PIT was shelled with light incendiary shell; 16 Ln Batty retaliated at request of Infantry. 2/Lt HAMILTON DAVIS, having arrived from 47th D.A.C. was posted to 16 Ln Batty. 150 cartridges accidentally ignited by a spark from a brazier in gun-pit of 15 Ln Batty. 2 men badly burned. One man of 15 Ln Batty hit in face by a cartridge accidentally placed in rifle trap. 13 Ln Batty 9, having been ordered to rejoin 5th London Brigade R.F.A., left LOWE GROUP.	
	Nov. 6th Saturday.		Dense mist throughout the day. Observation impossible. Enemy shelled CHALK PIT at about 3 p.m. The 47th (London) Division was inspected by the LORD MAYOR OF LONDON. 10 men were sent to represent the Brigade, and were inspected near MAZINGARBE Church. Eighteen 18-pounder guns, eighteen firing battery, first line, and ammunition column wagons were received by the Divisional Artillery at NOEUX-LES-MINES Station. The	

1577 Wt.W10791/1773 500,000 1/15 D. D. & L. A.D.S.S./Forms/C. 2118.

WAR DIARY
INTELLIGENCE SUMMARY

Army Form C. 2118.

Place	Date	Hour	Summary of Events and Information	Remarks and references to Appendices
MAZINGARBE	Nov. 6th (continued)		5th London Brigade RFA, being out of action, received their full complement of guns missing first. The remaining 6 18-pdr guns, 6 gunlimbers, 6 firing battery wagons, 6 first-line wagons, and 6 Ammunition Column wagons, together with 2 cases of stores, were handed over to the 6th London Brigade RFA. They were fetched by the 6th Lon. Am. Col., and are being retained and prepared by this unit at NOEUX-LES-MINES, until the arrival of the remainder of the guns etc.	
		8.30 p.m. 10. p.m. 11. p.m.	15th Battery fired at H.25.d.2½.1. – H.25.d.0.3. – H.25.d.0.7. – H.25.d.5.9.	
		1 a.m.	16th Lon. Batty " H.26.c.0.7. – H.26.c.3.9.	2 salvoes at each hour.
		3 a.m. 4 a.m.	17th Lon. Batty " H.25.c.6.4. – H.25.c.9.6. – H.25.c.5.10 – H.19.d.1.7.	
	Nov 7th Sunday		The following message was received from 47 Div. Arty: "The intermittent bombardment which has taken place during the last few days is to cease, & short bombardments will take place instead." Weather was again foggy & observation difficult.	
Aras.		4 p.m.	Bombardment of trench H.13.d.2.5 – H.13.d.5.5, by all batteries of the 5th London Brigade RFA. Lt. Col R.W. CHRISTIE RFA, having returned from leave, reassumed command of CHRISTIE GROUP. Gun Orders issued to batteries for war of telephones and wireless.	
	Nov 8th Monday.		Lt-Col A.E. LOWE DSO proceeded to ENGLAND on 10 days leave.	
		6.30 a.m. 6.40 " 7.15 "	Short bombardment of cross-roads in H.26.c. and about 100 yards along each road.	
		2.30 p.m. 9.10 p.m. 10.0 p.m.	Short bombardment of trench H.13.d.2.5 – H.13.d.8.5.	
			There was heavy shelling of the battery position and observation stations & the ground between them. 16th Lon. Batty sustained one casualty, and the 17 Lon. Batty sustained two – all slightly wounded. 16th Lon. Batty spotted the flashes of 2 Rifle Batteries. Atmosphere was very clear and observation was very good. Lt W.J. O'MALLEY, attached 15 Lon. Batty, returned to 5th Lon. Col.	

Army Form C. 2118.

WAR DIARY
or
INTELLIGENCE SUMMARY.

(Erase heading not required.)

Instructions regarding War Diaries and Intelligence Summaries are contained in F. S. Regs., Part II. and the Staff Manual respectively. Title pages will be prepared in manuscript.

Place	Date	Hour	Summary of Events and Information	Remarks and references to Appendices
MAZINGARBE	Nov. 9th Tuesday	1 p.m.	2Lt C.E.H. LLOYD proceeded to ENGLAND on 9 days' leave. Short bombardment of trench H.25.c.9.7. to H.25.c.10.3. and communication trench from H.25.c.9.6. to H.26.a.4.6.	
		7 p.m. 7.20 p.m. 7.50 p.m.	Short bombardment of tracks from H.20.c.4.9. to H.20. Central, & from H.20.a.51. to H.20 central. In all cases, unless otherwise stated, 2 Jalousies per battery employed. Railway Alley wire again shelled, also CHALK PIT WOOD, and QUALITY STREET. 15th, 16th, 17th Kor Batteries each observed flashes of 2 hostile batteries.	
	Nov. 10th Wednesday	2.0 p.m. 9.0 p.m.	Short bombardment of trenches round Wood VI (H.25.d.). Short bombardment of tracks running from H.20.a.51.? to H.20 central H.20.c.4.8 } In retaliation for the latter bombardment, GERMANS shelled CHALK PIT: slightly far. 16th, 17th Kor Batteries each observed flashes of hostile batteries.	
	Nov. 11th Thursday	5.55 a.m. 4.30 p.m.	Short bombardment by all field Guns on their night-lines Short bombardment of H.20.c.6.5 - H.26.a.9.9. (Suspected light H.V. Velocity gun). RAILWAY ALLEY was again shelled at intervals during the day. 17 Kor Batty observed flashes of hostile guns, and observed a mound, strongly fortified, evidently made of reinforced concrete. The report made about this mound by the O.C. 17 Kor. Batty was republished in its entirety in IV Corps Intelligence Summary.	
	Nov. 12th Friday	8.0 a.m. 8.20 a.m. }	Short bombardment of PUITS 13 Bis.	
		5.30 p.m. 5.45 p.m. 6.20 p.m. }	Short bombardment of HULLUCH, and roads about it.	

Army Form C. 2118.

WAR DIARY
or
INTELLIGENCE SUMMARY.

(Erase heading not required.)

Instructions regarding War Diaries and Intelligence Summaries are contained in F. S. Regs., Part II. and the Staff Manual respectively. Title pages will be prepared in manuscript.

(101)

Place	Date	Hour	Summary of Events and Information	Remarks and references to Appendices
MAZINGARBE	Nov. 12th (continued)		A very quiet day, but RAILWAY ALLEY was again intermittently shelled. There were occasional bursts of fire on our front line and communication trenches. 17 km Batty again shelled the flashes of 2 Batteries	
	Nov. 13th Sat.	9 a.m.	2Lt. H.L. BURGIS 3/6th London Brigade RFA, reports for duty, from ENGLAND, and was attached to the 140th ly Bty as Liaison officer	
		2.50pm 3.0pm	Slow Bombardment looking for Rear, in conjunction with No 1 Group Hv.F. of front-line trenches & communication trench in H.26.a. H.25.6.9.5 — H.25.d.0.5. (Weds 3 rd. bombed)	
	Nov. 14th Sun.	5.45am 6.5am	Bombardment of trenches H.19.6.5.4. — PUITS 13, and H.19.6.8.4. — H.20.c.4.8.	
		3.45 pm	Bombardment of trench south west of HULLUCH, H.13.d.2.10 — H.13.d.2.5. Remainder of 18-pounder equipment — 6 guns, & 12 wagons for batteries, complete, together with 6 wagons for Brigade Ammunition Column, which were sent to arrive at 2 p.m. at NOEUX-LES-MINES Station, arrived at 9 p.m., having been detrained, were parked in an adjacent field for the night. The first allotment of 18(pdrs) and equipment which has arrived 10 days ago, were taken today by road to AUCHEL to await the arrival of the Brigade on coming out of action. The 2nd instalment of 18 pdr guns, which arrived today, were allotted by batteries, repeating for duty from ENGLAND, and were attached to 15 km Batty. 2/Lt M.V. EDDIS, 3/6th London Bn Scott RFA, repeating for duty from ENGLAND	
	Nov. 15th Mon.	5.15am 6.0am	Bombardment of trench south-west of HULLUCH from H.13.d. This evening, at 4:30 p.m. Rest of the 15th, 16th, +17th km Batteries were relieved by sections of the 14th km, 116th + 12th London Batteries. The section of the 15th, 16th + 17th km Batteries thus relieved, proceeded	

1577 Wt.W10791/1773 500,000 1/15 D. D. & L. A.D.S.S./Forms/C. 2118.

Army Form C. 2118.

WAR DIARY
INTELLIGENCE SUMMARY.
(Erase heading not required.)

Instructions regarding War Diaries and Intelligence Summaries are contained in F. S. Regs., Part II. and the Staff Manual respectively. Title pages will be prepared in manuscript.

(102)

Place	Date	Hour	Summary of Events and Information	Remarks and references to Appendices
MAZINGARBE	Nov. 16th Tues.		to NOEUX-LES-MINES, where they remained for the night. The sections which arrived at NOEUX-LES-MINES last night, parked their 15 pdr near the Station, dumped their 15 pdr ammunition in a selected spot, and, having taken on their 18 pdrs, which arrived on Sunday last, proceeded to AUCHEL, to rest. The remaining sections of the 15th, 16th, 17th Lm. Batties were relieved at 4:30pm, and proceeded to NOEUX-LES-MINES, where they remained for the night.	
	Nov. 17th Wed.		Having parked their 15 pdr guns and ammunition at NOEUX-LES-MINES Station, the sections relieved last night proceeded to AUCHEL to rest. Brigade Headquarters moved to AUCHEL. A small leading party was left at NOEUX-LES-MINES.	
AUCHEL	Nov. 18th Thurs.		Major H. BAYLEY DSO. proceeded to ENGLAND on 12 days' leave. Steps were immediately taken to check all 18-pdr equipment. The 18 pdr guns which had been parked at AUCHEL under guard, since Sunday last, were fetched from the Gunpark. Thus the whole Brigade is not complete with 18-pdr guns and equipment. The addition of an attached Officer per Battery has been sanctioned. 2/Lt M.G. WHITTEN, + 2/Lt H.P. BARROW, 2/6th London Brigade RFA, having arrived from ENGLAND were taken on the strength of the Brigade. 2/Lt M.G. WHITTEN was posted to the 16th Lm. Batty and 2/Lt H.P. BARROW attached to the 16th Lm. Batty. 2/Lt M.U. EDDIS attached to the 15th Lm. Batty, and 2/Lt H.L. BURGIS posted to 6th Ln. Am. Col. Capt. W. COOPER, attached to 16th Lm. Batty, rejoined 17th Lm. Batty. Capt. R.A. CORGAN returned from the Base, to duty with 15th Lm. Batty.	
	Nov. 19th Fri.		2/Lt J.C. WOOLLETT 15th Lm. Batty and 4 telephonists per unit proceeded to MARLES LES MINES, on	

1577 Wt. W10791/1773 500,000 1/15 D. D. & L. A.D.S§./Forms/C. 2118

Army Form C. 2118.

WAR DIARY
or
INTELLIGENCE SUMMARY.
(Erase heading not required.)

Instructions regarding War Diaries and Intelligence Summaries are contained in F.S. Regs., Part II. and the Staff Manual respectively. Title pages will be prepared in manuscript.

Place	Date	Hour	Summary of Events and Information	Remarks and references to Appendices
AUCHEL	Nov. 19th (continued)		Course of instruction in telephony. Inspections of 18 pdr equipment, clothing etc, were held by O.C. Units. One man per unit sent to Headquarters IV Corps for course of advanced telephony.	
	Nov. 20th Sat		A Course of Instruction in gunnery was held at the Headquarters of the 47th Divl. Am. Col, under superintendence of Capt. F.J. CLARKE R.F.A.; the following officers were attended :- 2nd M.J. EDDIS, 15th Bn Battery, 2nd Lt H. DAVIS 16th Bn Battery, 2nd Lt H.L. BURGIS 5th Bn Am. Col, 4 NCO's per unit also attended the course. A section of guns were loaned for the course by the end of the 15th, 16th Bn Batteries. An Inspection of Clothing was held by the O.C. Brigade before the Brigade moved off to Divine Service. Inter Battery Competition instituted.	
	Nov. 21st Sun			
	Nov. 22nd Mon.		A Course of Instruction in Military Correspondence, Indents, etc. was instituted, Lectures being given by S.M. J.T. HOOD. All Subaltern officers are attending. Men are also having instruction in the following:- Shoeing, chiropody, cooking. Men who have been inoculated one only, are being reinoculated. The 15th & 16th Bn Batteries went on a route march, at the end of which their teams were inspected by the O.C. Brigade. In the evening these units were invited to a Cinematograph Performance by the O.C. Brigade. The following promotions were gazetted:- Second Lieutenants to be Temporary Lieutenants, dated July 28th:- C.F.H. LLOYD, J.A.W. PETRO, A.F. YENCKEN, & J.H. VAN DEN BERGH; dated August 20th:- V.C. LUCAS, J.C. WOOLLETT, & A.F. BLACKWELL.	
	Nov. 23rd Tues.			
	Nov. 24th Wed.		The Brigade Headquarters Staff, 17th Bn Battery, & 6th Bn. Am. Col. went on a route march, at the end of which the O.C. Brigade inspected their harness. In the evening, by invitation of the O.C. Brigade, a cinematograph performance in the AUCHEL Cinematograph Theatre. These units attended	

WAR DIARY

INTELLIGENCE SUMMARY.

Army Form C. 2118.

Place	Date	Hour	Summary of Events and Information	Remarks and references to Appendices
AUCHEL				
	Nov. 24th Wed.		Major P.T. CLIFTON, 17th Batty, proceeded to ENGLAND on 12 days' leave. Capt. W. COOPER, 17th Batty, proceeded to ENGLAND on 7 days' leave. Capt. W. COOPER is in command of the 47th Divisional Artillery Reserve Party.	
	Nov. 25th Thur.		One officer from Brigade Headquarters + 6th Am. Col., and 2 officers per Battery left AUCHEL, with a view to "taking over" from the 5th London Brigade RFA, in action near LOOS. Officers of the 5th London Brigade RFA billeted at AUCHEL to take over guns & of the 6th London Brigade RFA. Arrangements have been made for this Brigade to man the guns of the 5th London Brigade RFA, whilst the latter are refitting at AUCHEL.	
NOYELLES.	Nov. 26th Fri.		The Brigade moved from AUCHEL at 6.30 a.m. Gunners of the 6th London Brigade RFA took over the guns and positions of the 5th London Brigade RFA at 1 p.m. The Brigade forms part of POOLE GROUP, and is engaged in counter battery work, i.e. it is employed solely for engaging hostile batteries. Arrangements are being made for aeroplane observation, & a wireless apparatus has been erected at Brigade Headquarters, which are at NOYELLES-LES-VERMELLES. The 15 + 17th Lon Batteries occupy the positions they formerly occupied, before relieved by the 14th + 12th Lon Batteries respectively, viz, G.27.c.o.b., + G.27.a.&.g. The 15th Lon Batty is in a position due north of VERMELLES. G.2.c., 6½.B. Wagon lines, + Am. Col. are at NOEUX-LES-MINES.	
	Nov. 27th Sat.		A few rounds were spent in registration, and during the day five hostile batteries were engaged. In all cases, except one, the enemy ceased fire. CITÉS ST. PIERRE and ST. LEONARD were also fired on, by order of POOLE GROUP.	
	Nov. 28th Sun.		Fifteen hostile batteries were engaged. In three cases fire was returned, and in three cases the enemy opened fire with 5.9, it was too misty to form definite observations. The Wagon lines at NOEUX-LES-MINES were shelled. No casualties.	

Army Form C. 2118.

WAR DIARY
or
INTELLIGENCE SUMMARY.
(Erase heading not required.)

Instructions regarding War Diaries and Intelligence Summaries are contained in F. S. Regs., Part II. and the Staff Manual respectively. Title pages will be prepared in manuscript.

(105)

Place	Date	Hour	Summary of Events and Information	Remarks and references to Appendices
NOVELLES				
November	29th	Noon	Thirty two hostile batteries were engaged. Direct hits were obtained on one case. Enemy reared fire in seventeen cases. Batteries are firing an average of 200 rounds each daily. In the absence of Major H. BAYLEY DSO (on leave), Capt. R. A CORBAN is commanding the 15th How Batty; 2/Lt. C.E.H. LLOYD is in command of the 7th How Batty during the absence on leave of MAJOR P.J. CLIFTON, and Capt W. COOPER. The 15th & 17th How Batty positions were heavily shelled today. No casualties occurred in the 17th How Batty. In the 15th How Batty, one gunner was wounded, and one gun temporarily put out of action, a piece of shell hitting and damaging the cradle. In 2 hours the gun concerned was in action again.	
Nov.	30th	Tues.	Twenty seven hostile batteries engaged, of which thirteen reared fire. An average of 140 rounds per battery were fired today. Capt. P.A. LOVE, having reported from Base Details, was posted to the 6th How Ammunition Column, to assume command.	

CONFIDENTIAL

WAR DIARY
of the
SIXTH LONDON BRIGADE R.F.A.

from December 1st 1915 to December 31st 1915

(Volume XII)

Army Form C. 2118.

WAR DIARY

INTELLIGENCE SUMMARY

(Erase heading not required.)

Instructions regarding War Diaries and Intelligence Summaries are contained in F. S. Regs., Part II. and the Staff Manual respectively. Title pages will be prepared in manuscript.

Place	Date	Hour	Summary of Events and Information	Remarks and references to Appendices
NOYELLES Wednesday	Dec 1st	-	Thirty hostile batteries were engaged, and in fifteen cases the enemy ceased fire. A very successful shoot with an aeroplane observer was undertaken today. Corrections were sent by the observer by wireless to Brigade Headquarters, and were telephoned thence to the Battery which was firing. Three targets were engaged by the 16th How Batty — a hostile battery, and 2 crossroads. In each case the target was hit, after only very few corrections. The 15th How Batty also engaged a target, but owing to the failing light, the senior had to be discontinued, and went the 17th How Batty able to fire by aeroplane, for the same reason. Leave postponed until Saturday. Major Lives at NOEUX. Lieut. L.W.B. MOORE left this station for ENGLAND.	
Thursday	Dec 2nd	-	The Brigade was relieved by the 7th Brigade R.H.A.; the 15th La Batty took over the position and guns of the 16th Lon Batty. The 16th Lon Batty (with the guns of the 16th La Batty, which had been used by the 15th Lon Batty), & 17th Lon Batty (with guns of 12th Lon Batty), together with Brigade Headquarters, proceeded to NOEUX-LES-MINES, where they stayed for the night.	
Friday	Dec 3rd	-	The Brigade, less 15th Lon Batty and one section of the Brigade Ammunition Column (commanded by Lieut. W.T. BARNARD), proceeded from NOEUX-LES-MINES to CAUCHY-A-LA-TOUR, a village occupied by the 7th Lon dn Brigade R.F.A. The billets were unsatisfactory and the billetts, consisting mainly of barns, were bad.	
CAUCHY-A-LA-TOUR. Saturday.	Dec 4th	-	Major A.C. GORDON D.S.O. and Lieut. G. LYON SMITH proceeded to ENGLAND, each on 10 days' leave. Permission was obtained from 47 DIV ARTY to move the Brigade to AUCHEL, owing to the unsatisfactory billetts and horselines at this station. Brigade billetting party proceeded to AUCHEL this afternoon.	
Sunday.	Dec 5th		The Brigade less 15 Lon Batty and one section of BAC, moved from this station to AUCHEL units	

Army Form C. 2118.

WAR DIARY
or
INTELLIGENCE SUMMARY.
(Erase heading not required.)

Place	Date	Hour	Summary of Events and Information	Remarks and references to Appendices
CAUCHY ALATOUR Dec 5th (continued)			were inspected on the march by the O.C. Brigade.	
AUCHEL	Dec 6th Monday.		2/Lieut. A.G. WHITTEN attached to 47th Div. Signal Company, and 2 telephonists per unit, for a course of telephones. 2/Lt. H. DAVIES, 2/Lt. M.U. EDDIS, + 2/Lt. H.L. BURGIS attached to 47th D.A.C., + 2 NCO's per Unit, for a course of gunnery. All Signallers in Units redrilled.	
	Dec 7th Tuesday.		2/Lt. W.J. O'MALLEY, 6th Bn B.A.C., transferred to 47th D.A.C. 15th Bn Batty were today relieved by the 20th Bn Batty, for whom they left their guns. 15th Bn Batty proceeded to NOEUX-LES-MINES where they remained for the night. 15th Bn Batty proceeded from NOEUX-LES-MINES to AUCHEL; the section of the 6th Bn Am. Col. is remaining in action until further orders. Lecture given at RAIMBERT on the "Buffer" by member of staff of I.O.M. IV Corps. At many officers as possible attended. O.C. Brigade attended a conference at 47 Div. Arty H.Q. at LILLERS. Capt. W. COOPER, 17 Bn Batty, and R.S.M. J.T. HOOD are attending the 47th D.A.C. Gunnery Course, as Instructors. Lt-Col. R.R. WANSBROUGH proceeded to ENGLAND. Lecture given at 47th DAC Officers Mess by Captain CARTHEW R.F.C. on "Cooperation Between Artillery & Aircraft". Course for Artificers instituted at RAIMBERT. The lectures by RSM HOOD on "Military Correspondence, Indents" etc were continued.	
	Dec 8th Wednesday			
	Dec 9th Thursday.		Inspection of all horses of the Brigade by ADVS postponed. Lecture by member of HQ'rs Staff at H.Q. 5th Bn BoR RFA. Billets of the Brigade inspected by Senior Medical Officers, and is satisfactory. report was made. 42 men arrived as a draft from 47th D.A.C.; all units are now supernumerary. Capt. W. COOPER temporarily attached to 16th Bn Batty with effect from this date.	

1577 Wt. W10791/1773 500,000 1/15 D.D. & L. A.D.S.S./Forms/C. 2118.

Army Form C. 2118

WAR DIARY
INTELLIGENCE SUMMARY
(Erase heading not required.)

Place	Date	Hour	Summary of Events and Information	Remarks and references to Appendices
AUCHEL Friday.	Dec. 10th	—	Lieut. V.C. LUCAS, 16th Hun. Battery, proceeded to LIETTRES, to attend at the Gunnery School, First Army. The detached section of the Brigade Amm. Col., having been relieved by a section of the Seventh London Brigade A.C., proceeded to AUCHEL, from NOEUX-LES-MINES. Lecture given to Subaltern Officers by R.S.M. HOOD on "The duties of NCO's in Wagon Lines."	
Saturday.	Dec 11th		Capt. R.A. CORSAN and Lieut. W.J. BARNARD proceeded to ENGLAND on 7 days' leave. The O.C. Brigade proceeded by motor car to the firing line to see proposed gun positions for this Brigade. All horses of the Brigade inspected by the A.D.V.S. 47th Div.	
Sunday.	Dec 12th		The Brigade attended Church Parade, after which clothing and equipment was inspected by the O.C. Brigade. The Young Officers Gunnery Course.	
Monday.	Dec 13th		Battery Commanders proceeded by motor to the firing line, to see their new gun positions and wagon lines. The 18 pounder guns originally allotted to this Brigade, and which had been handed over to the 5th London Brigade RFA at AUCHEL on the occasion when this Brigade took over the guns of the 5th London Brigade RFA in action at NOYELLES, were received back by this Brigade in exchange for the guns originally allotted to the 5th London Brigade RFA. The allotment for leave has been decreased: 10 men per Brigade, instead of 16, must proceed on leave each week. A Brigade Concert was held in the Cinema Theatre, AUCHEL.	
Tuesday.	Dec 14th			
Wednesday.	Dec 15th		The night sections of the 15th, 16th, 17th, & 19th London Batteries left AUCHEL, proceeded to ANNEQUIN, to occupy their respective positions as follows:— A.25.6.1.8., A.25.6.1.7., A.25.6.1.7., A.25.6.1.5., A.25.6.13. of A, B, C & D Batteries, 71st Brigade, on being relieved by the	Map References Hereunder are to:— Sheet 36c N.W. 1/40,000 (Provisional Edition No 2)

Army Form C. 2118

WAR DIARY

INTELLIGENCE SUMMARY

(Erase heading not required.)

Instructions regarding War Diaries and Intelligence Summaries are contained in F.S. Regs., Part II. and the Staff Manual respectively. Title Pages will be prepared in manuscript.

(109)

Place	Date	Hour	Summary of Events and Information	Remarks and references to Appendices
AUCHEL	Dec 15th (continued) Thursday.		right sections of "LOWE GROUP", proceeded to VERQUIGNEUL. The right sections of batteries which came into action last night, registered. The left sections of "LOWE GROUP", together with Brigade Headquarters & 6th Lon. Amm. Col., left AUCHEL, proceeded into action at ANNEQUIN. Group Headquarters are at F.29.c.8.4. A section of the 7th Lon. Amm. Col. will be attached to the 6th Lon. Amm. Col. for purposes of supplying the 19th London Battery with ammunition. The 19th London Battery is attached to this Brigade for tactics only, not administration. Wagon lines are as follows :- 15th & 19th Lon. Batteries at LABOURSE, 16th & 17th Lon. Batteries at VERQUIGNEUL. B.A.C. at VERQUIN. Left sections registered. 17th Lon. Batty. set on fire a bomb store at foot of FOSSE 8.	
ANNEQUIN.	Dec. 17th Friday.		All batteries continued registering the German front line. An establishment of 50% Shrapnel & 50% H.E. Explosive is to be maintained. Log Books, + Registration Books are daily kept by O.C. Batteries. Arrangements for cooperation in case of attack have been concluded between O.C. "LOWE GROUP" + O.C. 41st Brigade R.F.A. on our left (i.e. north).	
	Saturday. Dec 18th		Observation very bad. German front line trenches shelled by LOWE GROUP Batteries, in retaliation for Rifle fire and bombing on our trenches. 17th Lon Batty fired several times by request of Infantry, who reported that our shelling last night stopped the German bombing. All horses of the Brigade inspected in Wagon lines by D.D.R. Lieut. J.C. WOOLLETT and 2nd Lieut. H. DAVIS proceeded to ENGLAND on 7 days' leave.	
	Sunday. Dec. 19th		Major H. BAYLEY D.S.O. proceeded to AIRE to attend a conference, leaving 10 days in Germany.	

Army Form C. 2118

WAR DIARY
INTELLIGENCE SUMMARY
(Erase heading not required.)

Place	Date	Hour	Summary of Events and Information	Remarks and references to Appendices
ANNEQUIN (continued)	December 19th Sunday		Enemy shelled our trenches intermittently all day - we retaliated each time which caused the enemy to cease firing. 17th Battery obtained several direct hits on the parapet of the CHORD and LITTLE WILLIE. At 11.15, 11.25 pm and 11.30 pm a big bombardment took place on the light lines. Each Battery fired about 200 rounds. Bavarian regiment was relieving another. 23rd + 24th LONDON regiments were in front lines.	
	December 20th Monday		At 1.5 pm, 1.52 pm + 2.40 pm 15th Battery fired on trench at A.28.c.10.5; they silenced a trench mortar shelling our front line at A.28.c.2.3. 17th Battery report that from 7 to 7.30 am digging went on in several places in the LITTLE WILLIE, and Germans were seen passing various points where the parapet had been knocked in on the previous day. At the loop hole at G.4.c.2.10 through which men could be seen passing." The 17th Battery fired 30 rds at a machine gun reported at G.5.b.2.7. 19th Battery fired 12 rds on G.4.c.97 in reply to enemy shelling G.4.a several rounds.	
	December 21st Tuesday		Shelling took place on both sides steadily all day. From 2 Am to 8 Am 15th Battery fired 150 Shrapnel + 136 HE on the CROSS TRENCH. At 8.55 pm the 17th Battery fired 62 HE on G.4.c.39 at reputed front Infantry who were being shelled heavily in STICKY and NORTHAMPTON trenches. The 19th Battery fired at intervals during the afternoon on G.4.b.97 + G.5.a.13 in reply to enemy shelling G.4.a.	

1875 Wt. W593/826 1,000,000 4/15 J.B.C. & A. A.D.S.S./Forms/C. 2118.

WAR DIARY or INTELLIGENCE SUMMARY

Army Form C. 2118

Place	Date	Hour	Summary of Events and Information	Remarks and references to Appendices
ANNEQUIN	Dec 22nd Wednesday		From 8 am to 2 pm 16th Battery fired 83 Shrapnel & 249 H.E. on CROSS TRENCH. 12.5 pm & 1.30 pm 15th How Battery fired on trench A28c95 & G4b25 in reply to enemy shelling STICKY trench & point line in A28c. From 2 pm to 8 pm 19th How Batty fired 272 Shrapnel & 94 H.E. on CROSS Trench & Communication trench in the vicinity. At 2.50 pm 15th How Battn fired 15 rds at enemy emplacement at O.P. on the Dump at G5a57 — Several direct hits to parapets received but emplacement undamaged. At 9.15 pm 17th How Batty fired 61 H.E. on LITTLE WILLIE and CROSS TRENCH requested by Infantry. At 9.50 pm 16th How Batty fired 18 Shrapnel within own lines – HINDENBURG trench, requested by Infantry. At 10 pm 15th Batty fired on rifle lines – HIT northern part. LITTLE WILLIE – at request from Infantry. 19th How Batty fired on CROSS TRENCH reported by Infantry. 18th How Battalion (LONDON IRISH) in front eps. 2nd Division on our left – 1st Division on our right.	
	Dec. 23rd Thursday		6.30 am to 1 am 16th Battery fired 43 Shrapnel & 71 H.E. on CROSS TRENCH. Caused registrations during the day. At 9.40 am 15th Battery fired 28 rds on G4 & 26 & stopped enemy firing on A28.c52 at 11.45 am. 15th Battery fired 30 rds on A28 c67, aux. 11.45 am. 16th Battery fired 10 Shrapnel & 24 H.E. on A28a21 in reply to enemy shelling front line trenches. 8 am to 2 pm 19th How Batty fired 257 Shrap. & 42 H.E. on CROSS Trench. 2 pm & 8 pm 19th How Batty fired 100 Shrap. & 95 H.E. on CROSS trench & machinegun positions. At 11 am K enemy shelled Battalion in Quarry Alley with 5.9. 2.30 pm 17th Batty fired 30 H.E. on field telescope & dugout with loophole at G28a24.	

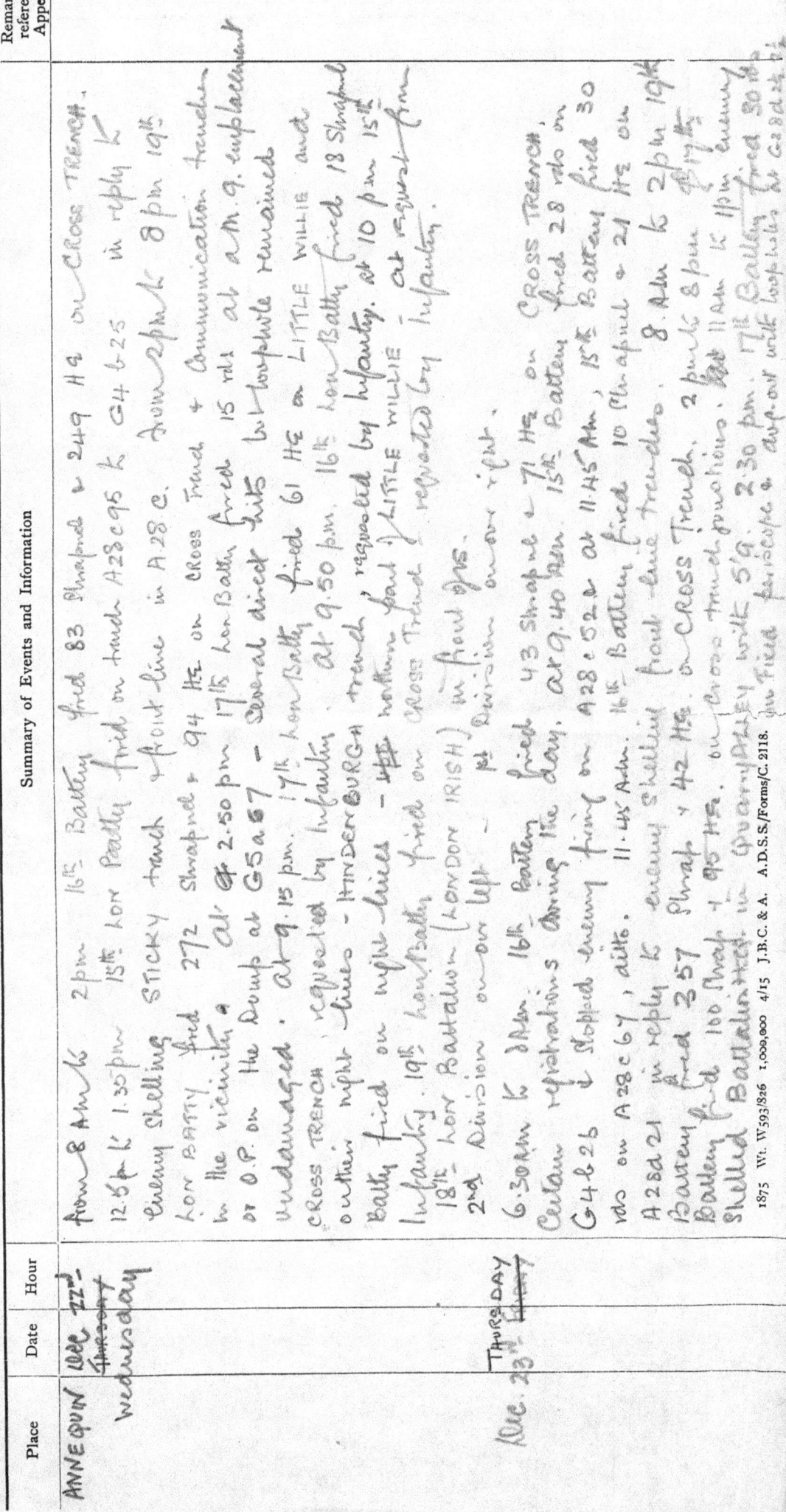

WAR DIARY or INTELLIGENCE SUMMARY

(Erase heading not required.)

Army Form C. 2118

Place	Date	Hour	Summary of Events and Information	Remarks and references to Appendices
ANNEQUIN	Dec 24 Friday	7 Am to 8.30 Am	All batteries on G4b in support Infantry, approximately 45 rds HE and 60 rds Shrapnel pr Battery expended – mine exploded by us.	
		9.30 Am	14th Battery fired 9 rds H.E. on working party in PEKIN ALLEY.	
		12.10 p.m.	15th Battery fired 28 Shrapnel & 20 HE. on A 28 c 85 in reply to enemy shelling A 28 c. – enemy ceased firing.	
		1.15 pm to 3 pm	15th Battery fired 127 Shrapnel & 80 HE. on G 4 b 2.10 in reply to enemy shelling G4a. Enemy ceased firing with great difficulty.	
		1.15 pm	19th Battery fired 15 Shrapnel on G4 b 97. Enemy shelling G4a.	
		6.30 pm	All batteries fired on C 4 b on account S.O.S. signal (sine green no shells). At VAN DEN BURGH & R.S.M. HOOD proceeded onboard.	
	Dec 25 Saturday		XMAS DAY. Steady bombardment all day. 15th how Battery fired 10 rds pr hour on A 28 a 86 to A 28 a 21 from 8 Am to 1 pm, after that time 3 and 2 rounds pr hour alternately on the same target.	
		16th	how Battery fired the same on B 4 b	
		17th	how Battery fired the same on cross track	
		19th	how Battery fired the same on A 97 & G5 d 43.	

WAR DIARY or INTELLIGENCE SUMMARY

Place	Date	Hour	Summary of Events and Information	Remarks and references to Appendices
ANNEQUIN	Dec 26th Sunday		17th Battery at 10 A.M. fired 16 Hrs. on Suspected O.P. on Dorais dump in reply to enemy shelling railway cut in G8 — our first shot hit enemy ceased firing. 10.30 A.M. 16th Battery fired 11 Shrapnel + 5 Hrs. on Cross trench in retaliation and again at 12.30 p.m. fired 11 Shrapnel, 1.52 p.m. [4B Shrapnel 12 HE], 2 p.m. single gun from 15th Battery at A.26.b.77 repeated 4 rnds 15. D.C. 17th How Battery observed "25 men working along railway from A.28.b.1.8.k "AUCHY ALLEY". Movement on roof Slate Square red house about A.29.a.0.5. Then an 3 artificial observation mounds in the roof wire also have men running mainly between front & 2 Ford Both Yards. A tape stretched on stakes behind German front line probably marking a new trench from junction "Cross Trench" + Little Willie (k to the W by the Mound produced by the explosion Mu Crater 46 HinderBurg Trench." O.C. 19th Battery reports that there is a look out post 19th London Battalion relieved the 18th.	
	Dec 27 Monday		8.25 A.M. 10.32 A.M. 12.30 p.m. 15th Battery fired on A.28.b.4.4. & A.28 d.1.4 - enemy shelling our trenches – battery ceased firing. 4th afternoon Dep-NH 10.15 A.M. mounted men going along road from A.30.c.8, & A.30.c.10. 10.20 A.M. 17th Battery fires on dispersed working party at A.29.b.2.0. 11.10 A.M. 16th Battery reported (wire across) A.5.b.77 & C.6.a.42 & C.6.c.38. 1 p.m. Shells from German field guns were falling in the region of A.25 b.16 from AUCHY 1.30 p.m. 19th Battery registered PEKIN Alley. 3.13 p.m. 16th Battery fired on Cross trench in retaliation. 3.30 p.m. 17th Battery fired on Cross trench at request of Infantry.	

WAR DIARY or INTELLIGENCE SUMMARY

Army Form C. 2118

(1/4)

Place	Date	Hour	Summary of Events and Information	Remarks and references to Appendices
ANNEQUIN	Dec 28th Tuesday		Battery fired a few rounds in Calibration. Checking wires and registration during the early part of the morning. At 11.20 17th Battery fired 16 Shrapnel ~ 20 Hz. at 400' O.P. at A.29.a.4.4½. in reply to enemy shelling railway at A.27.d.6.6. Vicinity of Battery O.P. from 8.20 to 9.11 Am 19th Battery fired 12 rounds on communication trench in C4.a. At 11.43 Am. 19th Battery fired on German support Batty. at PERIN Alley Trench. At 12.56 pm. 1.50 pm. 3.55 pm. 15th Battery fired 44 rds. in all on A.23 a 13 in reply to enemy firing on trenches A.23 c.22.— enemy ceased firing. At 2.40 pm 17th Battery fired 8 Shrapnel + 10 Hz at home in front of DOUVRIN Clocktower (archected officers men) remainder into trees obtained. At 2 pm to 2.45 pm 19th Battery fired 14 Hz. at C4 b.97 b. stop enemy machine gun rifle fire on British aeroplane. At 3.15 pm 19th Battery fired 4 Shrapnel on A 30 a 7t (Reconnaissance/report in PERIN Alley). 15th Battery fired 99 Hz. during the night on now A 30 d 9.9½. is A.29.a.2.6. At 4 pm. 10 pm. 1 am. 16 am. 16th Battery fired 43 Shrapnel 35 Hz. on Cross trench d trenches running behind Dose B. During the night 17th Battery fired 12 Shrapnel 4.12 Hz. on suspected trench position in C.4.b.	
	Dec 29th Wednesday	8.45 Am 8.58 Am	17th Battery fired 5 Shrapnel & bHz on trains arrived in PRINS. at B.3.35 & 19th Battery fired 6 HE on enemy trench mortar. 9 Am to 9.15 Am 15th Batty fired 25 Shrapnel 13 HE. on A 28.c.9.15 enemy trench mortar firing 9.45 Am 19th Battery fired 15 Shrapnel + 4 HE on A 28 c 95.	

WAR DIARY

Army Form C. 2118

 115

Place	Date	Hour	Summary of Events and Information	Remarks and references to Appendices
ANNEQUIN	Dec 29th Wednesday (continued)	10.50 a.m.	17th Battery fired 10 rds H.E. on trains biell. 10.55 a.m. 17th Battery fired 10 rds on suspected O.P. at A.20.b.3.5. 11.25 a.m. 11.50 a.m. 15th Battery fired 31 H.E. G.4.97 - enemy shelling D.2 Plaine. 11.3 K 1.27pm 19th Battery fired 6 shrapnel + 12 H.E. at G.4.97. 1.5pm 16th Battery fired 17th how Battery fired 6 rds on Cross Trench at request of infantry. 1.25 pm 17th how Battery fired 6 rds on CROSS TRENCH reported by infantry in reply to enemy shelling railway with H.V. fuzo. 1.30 K 1.35 pm. 15th Battery fired 6 H.E. on G.4.b.29 - enemy shelling Quarry in C.4.a - enemy ceased firing 1.29 pm k 10 pm. 19th Batty fired 24 Shrapnel + 35 H.E. on G.4 b.97 3pm k 3.30pm 17th Battery fired 32 H.E. on Bill's Bluff. 3 k 3.30 15th Battery fired 32 H.E. on Bills Bluff as ordered. 4pm. 16th fired 12 Shrapnel. 4 H.E. on Cross trench and again at 9.20pm, 3.16am & 6.10am. 7.10 pm 17th Batty fired 12 Shrapnel & 12 H.E. on Cross trench at request of infantry. 8.25pm k 6 .16 a.m. 19th Batty fired 25 Shrapnel & 7 H.E. on New trench portion at G.4. b.38 - minimum M.V.	
	Dec 30/15 Thursday	9.20 a.m.	16th battery fired 10 Shrapnel + 1 H.E. on a disposed working party at A.29.b.35. 9.55 a.m.k 11 a.m. 17th Battery fired 6 Shrapnel + 11 H.E. on working party. All batteries retaliated whenever trenches + O.P.s during the day. About 4.30 pm the Germans exploded a mine opposite the Quarries below in Stone GROUP found a beveret fire built with.	

WAR DIARY or INTELLIGENCE SUMMARY

Army Form C. 2118

Place	Date	Hour	Summary of Events and Information	Remarks and references to Appendices
ANNEQUIN	Dec. 31st Friday.		At 8.20, 9.10, & 10.20 16th How Batty fired at suspected O.P. (A.30.a.8.½.) where a single German has been observed, and at a second suspected O.P. (A.29.a.4.4.) was engaged with 24 rounds of Shrapnel + 3 rounds of H.E. at 10.45 a.m. The 14th How Batty also observed the Germans at A.30.a.8.½., + engaged the house with 6 rounds. The 17th How Batty at 11.30 a.m. fired 12 rounds of H.E. at the suspected O.P. at A.29.a.4.4. During the day the enemy shelled our trenches in A.27.8. (15th Lon Batty retaliated) and enemy ceased firing) & G.4.a. (19 Lon Batty retaliated with a total of 74 rounds on trenches in G.4.b.). 16th How Batty at 11.30 a.m. engaged a periscope and suspected machine gun emplacement with 20 rounds of H.E. (G.4.B.2.8.) At request of Infantry 17 Lon Batty fired 20 rounds H.E. on Cross Trench. During the afternoon the Germans shelled our billetts in CAMBRIN in reply to which the 15th + 17th Lon Batties fired on billetts in HAISNES with 8 rounds and 20 rounds respectively.	

B.J. Low
Lt-Col. R.F.A.
Commanding SIXTH LONDON BRIGADE R.F.A.

Army Form C. 2118

WAR DIARY
or
INTELLIGENCE SUMMARY
(Erase heading not required.)

(116)

Place	Date	Hour	Summary of Events and Information	Remarks and references to Appendices
ANNEQUIN	Dec. 31st	8.20, 9.10, & 10.20	At 8.20, 9.10, & 10.20 16th How Batty fired at suspected O.P. (A.30.a.8.4) where a single German has been observed, and at a second suspected O.P. (A.29.a.4.4) was engaged with 24 rounds of Shrapnel & 3 rounds of H.E. at 10.45 a.m. The 14th How Batty also observed the Germans at A.30.a.8.2, & engaged the house with 6 rounds. The 17th How Batty at 11.30 a.m. fired 12 rounds of H.E. at the suspected O.P. at A.29.a.4.4. During the day the enemy shelled our trenches in A.27.&. (15th How Batty retaliated, and enemy ceased firing) at G.4.a (19 How Batty retaliated with a total of 74 rounds on trenches in G.4.&.) 16th How Batty at 11.30 a.m. engaged a periscope and suspected machine gun emplacement with 20 rounds of H.E. (G.4.&.2.8.) At recent of infantry 17 How Batty fired 20 rounds H.E. on Corps Trench. During the afternoon the Germans shelled our billetts in CAMBRIN in reply to which the 15th & 17th How Batties fired on billetts in HAISNES with 8 rounds and 20 rounds respectively.	

R. J. Low
Lt-Col. R.F.A.
Commanding SIXTH LONDON BRIGADE R.F.A.

WAR DIARY or INTELLIGENCE SUMMARY

Army Form C. 2118

Place	Date	Hour	Summary of Events and Information	Remarks and references to Appendices
ANNEQUIN	Dec 29th Wednesday (continued)		10.50 A.m. 17th Battery fired 10 rds HE on trenches B.11.b. 10.55 A.m. 17th Battery fired 10 rds on suspected OP at A.30.b.3.5. 11.25 A.m. K.7.50.a.m. 15th Battery fired 31 H.E. on G.4.b.9.7. — enemy shelling D.2 Plaine. 11.3 K.1.27pm 19th Battery fired 6 shrapnel & 12 H.E. at G.4.b.9.7. 1.5 pm 16th Batty fired 12 rounds and 9.Ste. on Cross Trench at request Infantry. 1.25 pm 17th Hon: Batty fired 6 rds on CROSS TRENCH requested by Infantry. 1.30 K.7.36 pm. 15th Batty in reply to enemy shelling railway with H.V. Fuse. 1.30 K.7.36 pm. 15th Batty fired 6 H.E. in reply to enemy shelling. Wary in G.4.a — enemy ceased firing. 1.29 pm-K 10 pm. 19th Batty fired 24 shrapnel & 35 H.E. on G.4. Bay. 3pm-K 3.30pm 17th Battery fired 32 H.E. on Bills Bluff. 3 K 3.30 15th Battery fired 32 H.E. on Bills Bluff as ordered. 4pm. 16th fired 12 shrapnel 4.12.H.E. on Cross Trench — Shrapnel & 12.H.E. on Cross Trench at 9.20 pm, 3.16 a.m. & 6.10 A.m. 7.10 pm 17th Batty fired 12. 16 Pm. 19th Batty fired 25 Shrapnel & 4 H.E. on Infantry. 8.25 pm 16 at G.4.b.3.8 — minut N.E. of New Trench position.	
	Dec 30th Thursday		9.20 A.m. 16th Battery fired 10 Shrapnel + 1 HE on & disposed working party at A.29.6.3.5. 9.55 A.m. & 11 A.m. 17th Battery fired 6 Shrapnel + 1 H.E. on working party. All batteries retaliated on enemy trenches & O.P.s during the day. About 30 pm the Germans exploded a mine during the quarrie battered stone group and a bear as fire rifle fire in line opposite the quarries —	

1/16 London B.M. R.I.a
Jan
Vol XI

Army Form C. 2118

Volume III

WAR DIARY
or
INTELLIGENCE SUMMARY
(Erase heading not required.)

Place	Date	Hour	Summary of Events and Information	Remarks and references to Appendices
ANNEQUIN	Jan. 1st 1/16 Friday Saturday	12.10am	One minute after the incoming of the New Year, all batteries of LOWE GROUP fired 5 rounds on their night lines. There was constant shelling during the day, to which we retaliated. The 15 How Batty caused the enemy to cease fire in each case. 16 How Batty set on fire a small R.E. store at A.30.c.1.2. and dispersed a working party. 15, 16, 17 How Battys fired by request of Infantry during the night. Capt. P.A. LOVE, 6th Lon. A.C. proceeded to ENGLAND on seven days' leave. The following Officers were promoted to Temp. Lieutenants:— 2nd Lt. M.G. WHITTEN. 2nd Lt. H.P. BARROW. The following were mentioned in the General Officer's Commanding-in-Chief the British Army in the Field's Despatch, published today:— Major H. BAYLEY D.S.O. 15th London Battery Major A.C. GORDON D.S.O. 16th London Battery Gunner J.A. WHITING. 15 London Battery (since killed in action)	
Sunday	Jan. 2nd		There was again considerable shelling on the part of the enemy. LOWE GROUP retaliated.	

WAR DIARY
or
INTELLIGENCE SUMMARY

Army Form C. 2118

Place	Date	Hour	Summary of Events and Information	Remarks and references to Appendices
	Jan 25th		Shell holes about G.27.a.1.8. it would appear that the Germans have been using Lachrymatory shells. The Colonel, Orderly Officer, & Battery commanders of the 3rd London Brigade R.F.A. came up preparatory to taking over from the 1st London Brigade R.F.A. The B attery commanders went round the night. From 11.30 to about 4 p.m. enemy shelled the Loos Sector and at times the bombardment was intense, especially on Loos Pylons and houses south of Crassier. Enemy aircraft very active all day. Much work has been done on the saps in front of the German lines. Main Loos - Maroc communication trench was shelled with many howitzers at 3 p.m — 40 to 50 shells. 16th Battery caused a thick cloud of black smoke to rise from German trenches by an H.E. shell. 17th London Battery reports a gun firing from old St Laurent Church on Notre Dame and Fosse 5. — That 17th London Battery report picking up fuze of this gun marked as follows:— H.Z.14 Vorst o Hamlitz hundertz saplt for fugs inferior (velocity manufactured by S.W.N (unlentette Platz) unknown maker) in 1915. 329 is 329 is the Factory series number.	

1875 W¹. W 593/826 1,000,000 4/15 J.B.C. & A. A.D.S.S./Forms/C. 2118.

Army Form C. 2118

WAR DIARY
or
INTELLIGENCE SUMMARY
(Erase heading not required.)

Instructions regarding War Diaries and Intelligence Summaries are contained in F.S. Regs., Part II. and the Staff Manual respectively. Title Pages will be prepared in manuscript.

Place	Date	Hour	Summary of Events and Information	Remarks and references to Appendices
	Jan 23rd		Hulluch direction. This S[un] m[or]n[in]g v[er]y near German front line trench as the arrival of the shell synchronises with the sound of the discharge. The 16th B Battery report a misfire from a 2 H.V. behind Fosse 8 registering on trenches in enfilade. G.34.d. 17th Battery report that the sig[na]ller is no longer for[war]d as an OP. In MSt 9.1. we put up a mine to frustrate Germans putting up a mine in the same sect[or]. We consolidated our position on our side of the crater travelling support being very effective. 15th Battery hit on front line trench crossing Lens & Bethune road. Enemy retaliated on ours with 5.9 from 10 miles. The hour fronts suffered 7 casualties today. 1 killed and 6 wounded. 2 men in the 15th wounded, 1 killed & 2 wounded in 3rd, and 1 wounded in the 15th Battery.	
			Very quiet day. A little hostile shelling on MS a and b; otherwise no shelling in loos sector or battery positions near Fosse 7 and in Maroc. German aircraft active in the morning. Flares observed in trenches 1202° from Q34 a 46 – also gun flashes & loose road.	
	Jan 24th		Enemy artillery inoperative during the day. Intermittent firing on front lines and communication trenches. 16th Battery reports that from the small of mount	

Army Form C. 2118

WAR DIARY
or
INTELLIGENCE SUMMARY
(Erase heading not required.)

Instructions regarding War Diaries and Intelligence Summaries are contained in F.S. Regs., Part II. and the Staff Manual respectively. Title Pages will be prepared in manuscript.

Place	Date	Hour	Summary of Events and Information	Remarks and references to Appendices
	Jan 20th		Enemy fire on our trenches in Loos sector with 3" + L.E shells and 4.2 were fairly active throughout the day. In enemy rear retaliation followed and were successful. The 15th Battery reported a number of vivid H.E. shell bursts obtaining very visible bursts on this whilst their allotted zones with a view to possible concentration of fire.	
	Jan 21st		There was a certain amount of shelling during the day in the Loos sector, more especially in the centre sub-sector. Batteries retaliated and were successful. Hostile enemy conditions ceased for each time. Quality started Fosse 7, and huns B. Batteries were heavily shelled yesterday morning. 17th Battery reported that at 12 noon yesterday a staff Officer + two Other their further head and shoulders above the trench in front of Artillery Mansions. The Germans immediately opened fire on O.P.s near them. Lieut A.F. Yencken 17th Battery proceeded on 7 days leave of absence to England.	
	Jan 22nd		During the day there was only slight intermittent firing in front and support trenches in Loos sector more especially in MS a and b. The B Battery positions near Fosse 7 were heavily shelled all day. Guns shelling battery positions were :— 4.2 from Cité St Pierre; S.9 from Donnhain, a 4.2 (very high velocity) more	

WAR DIARY
or
INTELLIGENCE SUMMARY

Army Form C. 2118

Place	Date	Hour	Summary of Events and Information	Remarks and references to Appendices
	Jan 17th		frontline trenches just north of Chalk Pit & halfway down the C.P.R. 1st & Btn joined frontline & communication trenches opposite. 4 inlieners up opposite last section during day. There appeared to be tunnel	
	Jan 18th		Quietest day in Loos sector yet. The enemy hardly shelled at all, except a little on our frontline trenches. Many aeroplanes up which may have accounted for this. German artillery very active probably owing to the absence of our aeroplanes. 3rd & 15th Batteries firing on frontline trench M 5 d 7½ 9½ to M 5 d 1½ 6 which was effective in causing the enemy to cease firing. During the day up to about 2.45 p.m. each Battery retaliated on the enemy's support & communication trenches.	
	Jan 19th		Enemy shelled our trenches in Loos sector at frequent intervals during the day. Our retaliation was successful in causing hostile fire to cease each time. There was a but concentration in the trenches in front of 12 noon in practice against the mine going up. This was successful & the batteries set off their rounds very quickly.	

WAR DIARY or INTELLIGENCE SUMMARY

Army Form C. 2118

Place	Date	Hour	Summary of Events and Information	Remarks and references to Appendices
	Jan 15th		Battery firing on front line and 17th Howr. Battery exploding supports communication trenches. Appeared unsuccessful in causing enemy to cease fire. 3rd Howitzer Battery were hit a disputed Maxim gun emplacement at G.36.d.9.2. Apparently there was a German relief taking place from 10.45 pm to 12.30 a.m. and a regiment of infantry battalions came into their night-line. Quite a lot of retaliation during the day for enemy shelling our front and 2nd line trenches. Germans shelled Lens-Bethune road intermittently. Fired the main road at N.7 a 3.0 caused the enemy to cease firing. Concentration of fire from 2 pm to 3 pm appeared successful and the fire of the 140th infantry Brigade was heavily shelled from 10 a.m. to 11 a.m. The 140 B infantry Brigade fire over from the 141 infantry Brigade only a slightly different front retaliating the right Bttr #2 becoming the center the left, & u near right. This caused some trouble with wire but the communication was satisfactorily maintained.	
	Jan 16th		2nd & 3rd Howitzer Batteries registered their new zones. 2nd Battery new OP at G.33 c.10.9. Apparent intense shelling all day enemy shelling our front line trenches from M.5 d 8.2 to M.5 a 4.4. 15th Battery retaliated on front line trenches & caused enemy to cease firing, from 8 am to 10.30 am enemy shelled	

WAR DIARY
INTELLIGENCE SUMMARY
(Erase heading not required.)

Army Form C. 2118

Place	Date	Hour	Summary of Events and Information	Remarks and references to Appendices
LES BŒUFS	Jan. 10th (continued)		Lieut. W.T. BARNARD, 6th Lon. A.C., attached to 15th Lon. Batty. Lieut. J.H. VAN DEN BERGH, Orderly Officer to O.C. Brigade, transferred to 6th Lon. A.C. 2/Lt. M.U. EDDIS, 15th Lon. Batty, transferred to H.Q. Staff, & appointed Orderly Officer to O.C. Brigade. 2/Lt. H.L. BURGIS, 6th Lon. A.C., attached to 15th Lon. Batty.	
	Jan 11th		Enemy shelled our trenches all day. We retaliated and in the majority of cases enemy ceased firing. Enemy shelled Loos from 2 p.m. to 4.30 p.m. at irregular intervals. O.C. 2nd Battn. reports that Generally speaking retaliation did not stop their shelling him.	
	Jan 12th		Practically no firing from either side during the morning owing to the amount of balloons up. In the afternoon the light was bad. Firing in trenches Ms & M6d cannot to stop the enemy shelling Loos Sector. Water in D and C crassier was shelled from 1 pm to 2 pm.	
	Jan 13th		During the day there was a certain amount of firing to the machine trenches & right Subsection of Loos Sector. In every case firing ceased on retaliation. B attn. continued to register various points. At 3.30 p.m. enemy concentrated their fire in Railway so Orchard. At intervals during the night B Battery fired on their night lines. 15th London Battery fired 20 into Hulluch on the Lens road.	
	Jan 14th		From 8 am to 10.30 am shelled right & left trenches of machine trenches. 15th London	

Army Form C. 2118

WAR DIARY
or
INTELLIGENCE SUMMARY
(Erase heading not required.)

(3)

Instructions regarding War Diaries and Intelligence Summaries are contained in F.S. Regs., Part II. and the Staff Manual respectively. Title Pages will be prepared in manuscript.

Place	Date	Hour	Summary of Events and Information	Remarks and references to Appendices
ANNEQUIN	Jan. 7th Friday		The 1st London Brigade R.F.A. is being attached to this Brigade (Lowe Group) in its new position, + sections of the 1st, 2nd, 3rd City of London Batteries are on the south side of FOSSE 7.	
			One portion of the GERMAN Trenches (the Chord + Pays Willie) were bombarded today by the combined RHA + LoWE Group sections at ANNEQUIN. Section of LoWE Group at FOSSE 7 registered.	
			The remainder of the 3rd BTR RHA came into action at ANNEQUIN tonight, thereby relieving the remainder of LoWE Group sections. These, (together with the remaining sections of the 1st Lon. BDE R.F.A. relieved the remainder of the French.	
			Brigade Headquarters moves to LES BREBIS.	
LES BREBIS	Saturday Jan. 8th		LoWE GROUP (6th + 1st London Brigades RFA) is now in position. The 15th + 16th Lon. Batteries are on the Northern side of FOSSE 7, + batteries of the 1st London Brigade are on the south side of FOSSE 7. The 17th Lon. Batty. is in MAROC. The 16 + 17 Lon. Batteries seek to have an gun detailed (but near the battery position) in such a position so as to be able to enfilade hostile trenches. LoWE Group cover the front of the 141st Inf. Bde. The 17th Lon. Batty. position was shelled, but no damage done.	
Sunday Jan. 9th			The day was chiefly spent in registering. A little registration, + principally retaliation. A bombardment by our 5 inch howitzers took place. The 3rd London Battery also took part in + find communication trenches continuously, + un retaliated at request of Infantry.	
Monday Jan. 10th			During the day the enemy shelled our front line, 2nd line, + communication trenches continuously, + we retaliated at request of Infantry.	

1875 Wt. W593/826 1,000,000 4/15 J.B.C. & A. A.D.S.S./Forms/C. 2118.

Army Form C. 2118

WAR DIARY
INTELLIGENCE SUMMARY
(Erase heading not required.)

Place	Date	Hour	Summary of Events and Information	Remarks and references to Appendices
ANNEQUIN	Jan. 2nd (continued)		Although in the majority of cases the enemy ceased fire, when LOWE group retaliated, in many cases they opened fire again shortly afterwards. All Batteries fired during night by report of Infantry. Major H. BAYLEY DSO was appointed Commandant of 47th Div. Gunnery School, & proceeded to GOSNAY where the classes will be held. Lieut. H.P. BARROW & 2nd Lieut H. DAVIS proceeded to the School for instruction.	
Monday Jan. 3rd			Enemy shelling was very small today, until 3 p.m., when light field guns & howitzers opened fire on our trenches in A.21. & A.25.	
Tuesday Jan. 4th			The day was quiet. Light was very clear & many observation balloons & aeroplanes were up. 17" Hm Batty observed flashes of Kohler guns at A.24.B.2.5. This gun position was shelled by our heavy artillery. By report of Infantry, 17 Hm Batty fired at Trench Mortar (J.4.b.2½.5½),+ caused it to cease fire. Our Infantry were relieved tonight by the "Dismounted" Division. R.S.M. HOOD proceeded to GOSNAY, to assist in instructing at the Gunnery School.	
Wednesday Jan. 5th			Another quiet day. Very little firing by either side owing to number of aeroplanes (both British & hostile) It has been observed that the GERMANS are beginning to adopt our system of concentrating their fire on small localities. Today, for instance, they fired in concentration 3 times, each concentration lasting six minutes. A.28.c. was their target.	
Thursday Jan. 6th			Except for the usual retaliation, no fire was undertaken today. This evening sections of the 15, 16, + 19th Hm Batteries were relieved by sections of Batteries belonging to the 3rd Brigade R.H.A, + proceeded to relieve FRENCH Batteries of the 18th French Division near FOSSE 7, (QUALITY STREET).	

Army Form C. 2118

WAR DIARY
or
INTELLIGENCE SUMMARY
(Erase heading not required.)

Instructions regarding War Diaries and Intelligence Summaries are contained in F. S. Regs., Part II. and the Staff Manual respectively. Title Pages will be prepared in manuscript.

Place	Date	Hour	Summary of Events and Information	Remarks and references to Appendices
	Jan 26th		One section of each battery of the 3rd London Bgde RFA (ie. 7th 8th & 9th London Bttries (1st London Bgde)) took over respectively from the 1st, 2nd, & 3rd London Batteries 1st London Bgde RFA. Hostile artillery again active during the day. From 1.45 pm to 2.30pm enemy bombarded the Copse and the Chalk Pit; communication trenches with light H.V. guns, 4.2, & 5.9 from lines very heavily. The gunners were driven alongside their new trenches. Observation Balloon went down as soon as the shelling ceased. During the night new trench and saps were kept under fire. The remaining sections of the 3rd London Bgde RFA took over from the remaining sections of the 1st London Bgde RFA.	
	Jan 27th		Extraordinarily heavy bombardment on our trenches during the morning. Some front Batteries shot much ammunition in retaliation. At 1 p.m. hostile bombardment suddenly ceased and the afternoon was fairly quiet. Mauvre church Tower was knocked down by S.G. Own lynx batteries fired on their night lines during the night. The Germans made a small attack on a Battalion frontage near Pütz 14 but they achieved nothing. The day passed off without any further trouble.	

WAR DIARY
or
INTELLIGENCE SUMMARY

(Erase heading not required.)

Army Form C. 2118

Instructions regarding War Diaries and Intelligence Summaries are contained in F. S. Regs., Part II. and the Staff Manual respectively. Title Pages will be prepared in manuscript.

Place	Date	Hour	Summary of Events and Information	Remarks and references to Appendices
	Jan 28th		Enemy infantry bombarded our trenches between Intinnin Lines-Blethern road but did not attempt to extent them. Yesterday, [Fire?] and Mauser were heavy. 17th Battery report that very little work was done on new German front line probably owing to our guns firing at intervals during the night. Guns fired on their night lines during the night at intervals.	Cranier and visited Fox 7 and positions 5.9 gun
	Jan 29th		Quiet day. Very little hostile artillery activity. When enemy shelled trenches nr L. H.V guns at various pts. But very little evident. During night enemy fired on or near Intinnin Pts. Lt. G. of Blackwell & Lt. G. W. Peters Intinnin 7 day's relieved to England.	between 1.30 & 2.30 pm. at such times of our inspection
	Jan 30th		Very quiet day owing to Fog. Enemy shelled Kanal Junc.-Blethern road in Mevern Church with tracks of fire during the day. 9th & 17th Battalion left new trenches during the day. Dummy the night 8th & 17th Battalion take over trenches on Intinnin ... junctions.	

1875 Wt. W593/826 1,000,000 4/15 J.B.C. & A. A.D.S.S./Forms/C. 2118.

WAR DIARY
or
INTELLIGENCE SUMMARY

Army Form C. 2118

Place	Date	Hour	Summary of Events and Information	Remarks and references to Appendices
	Jan 31st		Quiet morning. Enemy concentrated fire on the trenches which the 16th hrs Revel & Hooghen at 3pm probably in retaliation for our shelling the barricade. Enemy shells which our communication trench took with 3 '4.2 at intervals from St Pierre. Liaison Officer (Center Battalion) reports that no direct hits were obtained on Sniper House during Northly Park's Group fire. Lt J.H. Van den Bergh & Lt S.C. Woollett proceeded to 47 ½ tc. Divisional Gunnery school at Guzney. At 7.30 pm own Group & any units with other artillery violently bombarded German trenches then their communication trenches & their right look along their line. This strafe lasted about half an hour.	

H.T. Gore?
Lt Col
Cmdg 6th Div Bde R.F.A.

47

1/6 London Bde
R.F.A

Vol XII

WAR DIARY or INTELLIGENCE SUMMARY

Army Form C. 2118

(Erase heading not required.)

Place	Date	Hour	Summary of Events and Information	Remarks and references to Appendices
LES BREBIS – Nº 9 Forward Batteries	Feb 1st		Very bad light all day. Hostile artillery quiet. Enemy seen pluming out of the day. 76th BAC reports further work done on saps. All new saps reported by Batteries. 9th and 7th Batteries fired intermittently rounds of H.V. on new trench during the night.	
	Feb 2nd		Quiet day. Nothing of importance to report. 8th Battery fired on enemy trench in M.S.C. during the night. O.P.s reported enemy infantry.	
	Feb 3rd		Quiet day. Bad light. B sections fired on working parties, much ventilators and supplied O.P.s. 17th Battery fired on enemy mortar. Movement unseen in Forge 12. About 8 pm have exploded a mine north of Loos Crassier. Heavy MG firing. Enemy on Pylones and outside Loos Crassier. During night 9th Battery fired on working party in MSC v d with excellent results. A turn was heard to groan. OC Bde (Col. Lowe) proceeded on leave.	
Near 4IR Feb			Major Bayley A.S.O. assumed command of the Lowe Group. Enemy artillery exceptionally quiet. 2022–12 Battery had as an O.P. brickwork. A/m done on new saps & trench. During the night the 8th & 13th Batteries fired during the night on new saps down the LENS road.	

WAR DIARY
INTELLIGENCE SUMMARY
(Erase heading not required.)

Army Form C. 2118

Instructions regarding War Diaries and Intelligence Summaries are contained in F. S. Regs., Part II. and the Staff Manual respectively. Title Pages will be prepared in manuscript.

Place	Date	Hour	Summary of Events and Information	Remarks and references to Appendices
LES BREBIS Fosse 7 Mine	5th Feb		Very quiet day. Excellent light. Night firing on new saps and trenches undoubtedly hindered the work at these place. Very little additional work has been done. A hostile aeroplane was flying with our own aeroplane, Fosse 7 heavily shelled from VERDUN. 7th & 17th Batteries fired on new trenches during the night. At 5 a.m. there was a concentration of fire of all the Corps Guns – each gun firing 1 round on its night line.	
	6th Feb		Very quiet day. 8th Battery fired at O.P. Posn II. 9th Battery fired at our B.P. & caused observers to withdraw. 15th Battery fired at suspected position & ammunition near superior tour. 16th Battery fired on assembly trenches opposite the Copse. 9th & 16th Batteries fired to prevent the enemy saping new saps and trenches, and our guns firing rule – LENS–BETHUNE road. No further work on new trenches south the Copse.	
	7th Feb		Very quiet day. Such light in the afternoon. Batteries registered various points other than those in their zones. 9th Battery test applied three posts on the crest of the hill. 16th Battery report no further work on Sap opposite Souchez Chalk Pit but fresh work 75 x 125 yds NE possibly the staff knew sap. 17th Battery fresh no further work done on sap & trench. 10th J. Copse. During the night 15th Battery fired on sap opposite Chalk Pit and approaches road; 8th Battery on trench south the Copse.	

WAR DIARY or INTELLIGENCE SUMMARY

Army Form C. 2118

Place	Date	Hour	Summary of Events and Information	Remarks and references to Appendices
LES BREBIS MARCH 2001 7.	Feb 7th	8th	Very quiet day. Enemy shelled door 7 with 9cm shells from 12.30 pm to 3 pm - no damage done. During the night 75th Battery fired on new sap opposite Chalkpit and down LENS road - 17th Battery fired on the new trenches & saps south of the Copse. At 4 a.m. we established a mine post south of the southern Chalkpit - 15th & 16th Batteries fired on the communication trenches behind; At the request of the Infantry the 8th Battery opened fire. There was no hostile shelling until 4.20 am which was not vigorous. No new work visible on new trenches south of the Copse.	
	Feb 8th		With the exception of very heavy shelling of the new crater, and slight retaliation for afternoon bombardment, hostile artillery was fairly quiet. At 3.20 pm a bombardment by guns enfilading trenches C and Ntre Opt, Battery guns was taken with 4.00S during the night. This was very successful and every round by 4.00S was observed to fall in the trench. Capture balloon was up most of the day. Wiring of the new trenches by the Germans has continued - Coil wire top wire & Chevaux de Brise. No more wire was noticable. No more wire was seen during sap opposite Chalkpit. Batteries did not fire during the night.	

WAR DIARY or INTELLIGENCE SUMMARY

Army Form C. 2118.

Place	Date	Hour	Summary of Events and Information	Remarks and references to Appendices
Roclincourt Huts O.C. Section 7	Feb 10th		Enemy Artillery was very quiet all day owing to the number [?] aeroplanes up. Ammunition (opposite the Copse) was active at 12.30 pm and 11 pm. 15th Battery fired on it & successfully caused it to stop. No work here on revetting [?] S.N.K. & Copse. 17th Battery fired on new trenches South of Mill Copse during the night, and the 15th fired on to oppose the Copse and down the Zerns road.	
	Feb 11th		Daylight. 1st Battery at 2 M.G. emplacements. Enemy reported digging new trench front line. At 7.30 pm B stores fired a harassing [?] it roads. Dummy night 7 to Battery fired on snipe at M69 x 17 to M.S.C.u.d.	
	Feb 12th		Very quiet day. Batteries fired very little during day. Dummy night 15th Battery fired on new trenches & down road M18a. Round & Battery on trenches & down road M18a.	
	Feb 13th		At 7.30 am German exploded amine a Sommer [?] Harrison's Crater. 15 x 16 Batteries fired on communicating trenches. No movement nor new German trenches. Dummy night 15 & 16 Batteries fired down roads, booking [?] Batteries until 16 & (see [?] presented 15 Battery fired on new trench till midnight.	

WAR DIARY
INTELLIGENCE SUMMARY
(Erase heading not required.)

Army Form C. 2118.

Place	Date	Hour	Summary of Events and Information	Remarks and references to Appendices
Les Brebis Trench Front 7	Feb 14		Germans exploded mine in front of Apex, which one communication trench leads to after. Our party latched till about 9 a.m. otherwise day fairly quiet. When we went up 15th & 17th Batteries immediately fired on their night lines on enemy's front line trenches. 16th Battery fired shrapnel on enemy at request of infantry & Hulluch Station (8th Battery) The loss gun (8th Battery) handed over to 4 GMS C18. With excellent results. During night 17th Battery fired on exposed point in MS C vd.	
	Feb 15th		Very quiet day. Little firing on either side. Germans have not dug much new trenches as they were running there 17th Battery tired on this front intermittently. 9th Battery again descended artillery fire on salient from M 6 d 39 GM 6 643. 8th Battery during night 15 & Battery fired on Safin in M S c vd.	
	Feb 16th		Quiet day. 2nd Battery did distinctly destructive fire of Form C1 on 11 a German O.P. No more Germans seen walking towards new latrines. During night 16th Battery fired 25 rds shrapnel & & attempts M 6 v d & 9th attempts in MS c vd.	

WAR DIARY
or
INTELLIGENCE SUMMARY

Army Form C. 2118.

(Erase heading not required.)

Place	Date	Hour	Summary of Events and Information	Remarks and references to Appendices
	Feb 17th		One notice Trench Battery came into wagon lines on arriving taken over from 147th (?) Bge. The 6th London Bgde R.G.A. moved into rest with the remainder of the 47th London Division to Curlu. The 3rd London Bgde estimated about 1 month drove spent moving through Bernafay Maricourt.	
Curlu	Feb 18th		Batteries arrived late about 12 or 1 o'clock units at different unit commanders.	
Aurel	Feb 19th		On 5 Wagon Lines for training. Bgde on arrived details party	
Bony	Feb 20th		Units of disposal of unit commanders. Various Ordered to move from Bony by Major or General commanding Division to make arrangements for attack.	
Bony	Feb 21st		Proceeded to arrange about 4 miles S.W. Very satisfactory move.	
Aurel	Feb 18th 19th		Units under this own arrangements. Units under their own arrangements. Billeting party went on to Bony.	

WAR DIARY
or
INTELLIGENCE SUMMARY.

(Erase heading not required.)

Army Form C. 2118.

Instructions regarding War Diaries and Intelligence Summaries are contained in F. S. Regs., Part II. and the Staff Manual respectively. Title pages will be prepared in manuscript.

Place	Date	Hour	Summary of Events and Information	Remarks and references to Appendices
Cudel	Feb 20th		Brigade moved to Bonn to undergo training. Brigade arrived at about 2 pm	
Bonn	Feb 21st		Units at disposal of unit commanders. Revived news that our muithears Bonn to complete infantry Brigades proceeds to Coryeupe.	
Bonn	Feb 22nd		Moved to Coryeupe in a snowstorm. Better place than Bonn.	
Coryeupe	Feb 23rd		Arrival at about 11.0 — All batteries paraded in drill order under their own arrangements.	
"	Feb 24th		All batteries paraded in drill order under their own arrangements	
			2nd Lieut McLaddie proceeded on 7 days leave of absence to England (?)	
"	Feb 25th to Feb 29th		These days were spent in training, battery + brigade manoeuvres, Officers rides, gundrill, harness cleaning, staff training + lectures by officers + NCOs.	

R. Lows
Lt. Col.
Cmdg Sixth XXX F.A.B.

44

1/6 London Blo R. Fd

Vol XIII

WAR DIARY
or
INTELLIGENCE SUMMARY

VOL XIII

Place	Date	Hour	Summary of Events and Information	Remarks and references to Appendices
Corques	March 1st 2nd 3rd 4th		Three days were employed entraining, officers riders, etc, up to noon on the Order received late last night to leave billets & proceed to different area. Villages formerly infected with measles. Brigade Orders out & heads down to COECQUES when the 15th Batt London Regiment had initial start. After a certain amount of difficulty the Brigade S March m.ts to old billets with extreme exception. The B.A.C. mvr went to WESTREHEM. Church Parade by Batteries in Girls' School in morning. Potato match in afternoon between 16th London Battery RFA v Headquarters RFA & London 15th Battery 10-2. Whilst transport waders unit Commanders	

WAR DIARY
INTELLIGENCE SUMMARY

Army Form C. 2118.

Place	Date	Hour	Summary of Events and Information	Remarks and references to Appendices
Etaples	Wed 7		15 Gordon Batt'n gave convert to celebrate 1 year service in France.	
		8	Units at disposal of unit commanders.	
		8.30	Units at disposal of Unit commander. Lt G.A.C. gave	
		9	Units his welcome to officers and N.C.O.s in the	
			Struggle at Verdun.	
(Error in date)		9 10	Units at disposal of Unit commander. Billets put forward by together. Rest of the Brigade moved and states no town one's arrived at DIEVAL at 6 p.m.	
		10	Brigade Rest Day. Two patrols (25) up. General Speaking. G.O.C.R.A. & Divisions were present.	
		11.30	Units at disposal of Unit commander. Billets party (?)	
		12	15 Gordon R jned R.F.A. proceeded to its new reserve area and arrived at DIEVAL at 5 p.m.	

Army Form C. 2118.

WAR DIARY
or
INTELLIGENCE SUMMARY

(Erase heading not required.)

Place	Date	Hour	Summary of Events and Information	Remarks and references to Appendices
Dieval	March 13th		Units at disposal of unit commanders. Most of day spent in cleaning up	
	March 14th		Day spent in preparing for tomorrow's march and inspection by G.O.C. 47th Division. 2/Lt M.W. Eddis transferred from Headquarters Staff to 15th London Battery. 2/Lt H.L. Burgin transferred from 15th London Battery to Headquarters Staff to take up the duties of Orderly Officer to C.S.B. Major Rayley, A.S.C. OR left for England. Capt. Cooper assumed command of 15th Lon Bty.	
	March 15		Brigade inspected by G.O.C. 47th Division. Afterwards the S.O. C.R.A. 47th Division inspected its officer Riding Positions. The day units were at the disposal of unit commanders.	
	March 16th		Units at its disposal of unit commanders, went to inspect new unit Mercury commanders went to inspect new unit positions.	
	March 17		Units at the disposal of unit Commanders, a section of the 15th, 16th, 17th Lon RFYs went up to their new position at CARENCY, taking over from 103rd Brigade. 23rd Division.	

WAR DIARY
or
INTELLIGENCE SUMMARY.
(Erase heading not required.)

Army Form C. 2118.

Place	Date	Hour	Summary of Events and Information	Remarks and references to Appendices
Dièval	March 18th		Units at the disposal of Divl Commanders.	
Carency	March 19th		H.Q Staff left DIEVAL for Bois de la Haie. Other sections of batteries went up to new positions.	
Carency	March 20	10 A.M.	1st Bde R.F.A. took over from 103rd Bry R.F.A. (23rd Div.) at 6th Bde HAQ. Brigade Headquarters at mill. (A.S.d.32.) attached to the 6th Bde (Lt. Col Hussey) the whole forming the Centre Group (Lt Col Hussey) is the B/1/6 Battery. Northly Group on left (Lt (U al Peak) Souter,) Centre Group on right (Lt Col Hussey). During the day chiefly between 9 am & 9.30 HM and about 5.30 pm the enemy shelled Ablain St Nazaire with 5.9". CARENCY was also shelled. Enemy were also active with aerial torpedoes about mid-day. The enemy were silenced by our Heavy & Trench mortars. Otherwise all was quiet on this front. His Majesty reconnoitred the lines by aeroplane.	
Carency	March 21		Very little Artillery fire owing to bad light. Returns for a few rounds for registration, otherwise all quiet. Hostile aircraft very active.	
Carency	March 22		Very misty weather. Observation impossible. Very little enemy shelling all day. Lieut Craufurd proceeded Bry Hd Qrs G/1/7 on B/1/7 for instruction.	

WAR DIARY
INTELLIGENCE SUMMARY

Army Form C. 2118.

Place	Date	Hour	Summary of Events and Information	Remarks and references to Appendices
Carency	March 23		1st Lt Newsitt. 6" Howr. Ammn column attached to the 15th & 16th Bn Battery. The day on the whole was quiet. Living field guns were active to-day than yesterday firing about 75 rounds into CARENCY, the shells seemed to come from the direction of Bois de QUERENCY. The 15th Howr. Battery made satisfactory shoot on the Pimple, this has been reported as an observation station. The batteries of the Centre Group did not fire. At Bomont (11th Ldn Bty) proceeded to Lilliers on a course of instruction.	
Carency	March 24		Leave again opened for the 47th Div Artillery. During the day there was very little shelling, the enemy was very quiet. On reverse was weather being very bad. Our wiring parties on the Enemy tired on the road to the E of CARENCY which is used by our infantry for transport. 13/176 Battery replied firing on the cross road in CARENCY. The reply was effective to —	
Querency	March 25		2nd Lt Gordon-Tonhe arrived from England. Capt Cooper 15th Ldn Bty + Lt Hyne Smith (Adjutant) the 6th Ldn Ammunition Column— 47" D.A.C. attached to 16th Battery proceeded to England on ten days leave. Lt Needie for instruction. Night for observation very poor. Enemy artillery more active again. Flew thru the our roads in SOUCHEZ we retaliated again with 4.5". Otherwise all quiet.	

WAR DIARY or INTELLIGENCE SUMMARY

Army Form C. 2118.

(Erase heading not required.)

Place	Date	Hour	Summary of Events and Information	Remarks and references to Appendices
Carency	March 26		Enemy shewed little activity on day. Bavaria fired a few rounds for registration otherwise all quiet.	
Carency	March 27		Enemy were active to day. Q. howitzers fired on our tirfort and communication trenches, our Batteries replied and in each case kept on repeat the hinzewrfer fire diminished. A howr in hiding was observed by the 1" Battery to be in constant use, the is probably a Head quarter of some kind. We fired some by the battery to day was at request of the Infantry. 2nd Lt Gossan attached to the 15" how Battery from the Brigade Ammunition Column S.O.C. Wilson in miles the 11" Battery position. Enemy Artillery throughout the day quiet, having movements again noticed in the houses at hickem. Nothing else on this front to report.	
Carency	March 29	10.15 AM	A.D.V.S. inspected the horses of the Brigade at 10.15 AM. Intermittent shelling of Souchez Valley & Carency with LHV 11mm gun fire. In the afternoon 8 gm on Notre DAME DE LORETTE was shelled with 5.9"+4.2". Otherwise day was quiet quiet. Lt Devin 16 How Bty proceeded on 7 days leave to England.	

WAR DIARY
or
INTELLIGENCE SUMMARY

(Erase heading not required.)

Army Form C. 2118

Place	Date	Hour	Summary of Events and Information	Remarks and references to Appendices
Queuvry	March 30.		ABLAIN & Spur of LORETTE shelled with 5.9 + 4.2. between 12.45 & 3 p.m. 68 shells intermittently about 3 p.m., the shell was mostly active 68 shells intermittently about 3 p.m. There were nine times known flashes over 16th Bty. Then died down. There were nine times known flashes in N.E. direction about 6 p.m., no doubt taking wind. Apart for bc N.E. direction about 6 p.m., no doubt taking wind. Apart for flight. Shelling the day was quiet. Aeroplanes were very active all day. A Taubenfaper demonstration was held at Army Services which 28 Officers & other ranks attended.	
Raneury	March 31st		Army orders were again taken henry. Enemy the Spur of N.D. de LORETTE being shelled on and off throughout the day with 77 m 4.2 + 5.9.3. The 15th Batty successfully experimental will wire and signally between its gun position & Balla Hays. Group O.P. on N.D. de Lorette ready for use. A.D.V.S. expired the home of the 14th Lon Bty and the B.A.C.	

Sig
A. Loius Lt Col.
O.C. 6 London Brigade RFA

44.

To Officer i/c A.G's Office

Base.

Herewith War Diary of 6 London Brigade R.F.A for the month of April.

Vol XIV

Lt Col Bapé ?/?
for OC 6" London ?A?B

Army Form C. 2118

WAR DIARY
or
INTELLIGENCE SUMMARY
(Erase heading not required.)

Instructions regarding War Diaries and Intelligence Summaries are contained in F. S. Regs., Part II. and the Staff Manual respectively. Title Pages will be prepared in manuscript.

Place	Date	Hour	Summary of Events and Information	Remarks and references to Appendices
CARENCY	April 1		15th Bty. reported points behind the German front line from the LORETTE O.P. German still working hard on the PIMPLE. A British aeroplane was brought down by enemy antiaircraft guns at 3:45 p.m. to-day. From 7 p.m. onwards the enemy fired on our transport in CARENCY and East of CARENCY Main Roads.	
CARENCY	April 2		Major London appeared on a court of investigation at the First Army school at AIRE. Lt. Lucas Tooth was killed over the command of the 16th London Bty. Very little artillery activity on either side though our two batteries to the South of CARENCY were very active. At 5.20 p.m. & 7 p.m. one or two batteries [The D.D.R. to A.U.S. 1st Army (enquired the hours firing Origids?] this was on April 3rd of CARENCY were attacked 14th Bty attached B.A.C.	
CARENCY	April 3		Capt. Courtland & Howard Division awarded to 15th London Bty. England. Lt. Woollett & London Bty. A quiet day. Battles numerous enemy aircraft about 9 a.m. we instructed a German aeroplane was shot down in our lines about with effect. a German aeroplane was shot down in our lines about 10 a.m. 15th Bty. surprised by aeroplane in the afternoon.	

WAR DIARY or INTELLIGENCE SUMMARY

(Erase heading not required.)

Army Form C. 2118

Instructions regarding War Diaries and Intelligence Summaries are contained in F. S. Regs., Part II. and the Staff Manual respectively. Title Pages will be prepared in manuscript.

Place	Date	Hour	Summary of Events and Information	Remarks and references to Appendices
CARENCY	April 4th		15th LON BTY fired a 4/t today on enemy's wild infantry, it is reported that when ever we shell the PIMPLE the Germans retaliate on BOUCHEZ. h/h/t was open until for observation. About 7pm & 6pm the 16th Battery shelled the cross road west of where SOUCHEZ was. Fired in the afternoon with Free Gun. Lt Gy German Lt Corps Commander (Lumel Wilson) gave a lecture to officers.	
CARENCY	April 5th		7th Lt Huzzo & 1st order R.A.C. proceed on a course after water phone at St Vineent. The day was more active. Enemy fired 5.9" like many withdrawal trenches for R. battery. The enemy stopped sheering immediately a British aero plane approached their lines. Manoeuvres for much mortars were busily actively.	
CARENCY	April 6th	11:45 AM	Hostile artillery much more active to day. At 11:45 AM 16 Battery engaged an flak line with light heavy trench mortars & fr 2 craters for about a quarter of an hour. At 2:15 PM 1st Battery line covered 60 to 7 on the CARENCY-SOUCHEZ road set a dug about out. Our artillery again carried out an apparent very much active. Our after registration with several & wire butter fire by 16th and else trial set to day. J.	

Army Form C. 2118

WAR DIARY
or
INTELLIGENCE SUMMARY
(Erase heading not required.)

Instructions regarding War Diaries and Intelligence Summaries are contained in F.S. Regs., Part II. and the Staff Manual respectively. Title Pages will be prepared in manuscript.

Place	Date	Hour	Summary of Events and Information	Remarks and references to Appendices
CARENCY	April 7		Lt Lyon Smith returned to duty after 10 days leave. 2nd Lt Davis 16th Lon Bty (attached) returned to duty after seven days leave. The whole day was very quiet, there being practically no hostile shelling. In the morning between 6 am & 9 am hostile trench mortars bombarded our support line. Between 5-15 pm & 6 pm L.H.V. gun bombarded four SOUCHEZ line S.7 and later A.16.d & S.13 & all Bérenfort road N communication trenches at intervals about 220 HE rds were fired. R. halters 8" for later three guns to day.	
CARENCY	April 8		Lt Barnard returned from course at Lillers. Hostile artillery quiet owing to activity of our aeroplanes. The Brough O.P. had some S.7 fire on it in the afternoon. 17th Battery regrets in afternoon while the registration lasted the enemy returned on NOTRE DAME with S.9.	
CARENCY	April 9		Lt Lucas 16th Lon Bty wounded by a premature shell from R.& L. Bty. Major Gordon proceeded on 10 days leave to ENGLAND. Major Clifton 14th Lon Bty proceeded to AIRE for a course at the Heavy Artillery school. Our own hostile artillery now active	

1875 Wt. W 593/826 1,000,000 4/15 J.B.C. & A. A.D.S.5./Forms/C. 2118.

Army Form C. 2118

WAR DIARY
or
INTELLIGENCE SUMMARY
(Erase heading not required.)

Instructions regarding War Diaries and Intelligence Summaries are contained in F. S. Regs., Part II. and the Staff Manual respectively. Title Pages will be prepared in manuscript.

Place	Date	Hour	Summary of Events and Information	Remarks and references to Appendices
CARENCY	April 9 (contd)		today. Our front line trenches were shelled with 4.2 + a heavy trench mortar. On returning fire many rounds in retaliation at the request of the infantry they seem satisfied with the result.	
CARENCY	April 10.		The Pimple was bombarded with heavy & light guns at first with little effect but later on many good hits were obtained. This was in conjunction with a bombardment by the 23rd Division which seemed very effective. The enemy retaliated for the bombardment of the PIMPLE by shelling the SOUCHEZ valley with 4.2".	
CARENCY April 11.			Capt CORSAN 1st Lon Rty proceeded on 7 days leave to ENGLAND. Mr CORSAN 6th Lon R.F.A. attached to 17 Lon Bty. Howitzer artillery very quiet except for trench mortars which were very active between 6.15 p.m. & 6.30 p.m. We replied with some rounds of shrapnel & H.E.	
CARENCY	April 12.		Hostile artillery very quiet until about 5.30 in the evening when our wires were rather heavily shelled with 4.2 & trench mortars. Our batteries fired in	

WAR DIARY
or
INTELLIGENCE SUMMARY

(Erase heading not required.)

Army Form C. 2118

Place	Date	Hour	Summary of Events and Information	Remarks and references to Appendices
CARENCY	April 13.		Whiskerin. Nothing else to report.	
CARENCY	April 13.		Light for attention very good, anchor. Very warm cloudy on day. Receipt from 6 pm to 6.15 pm when the damain on our Right was heavily bombarded by the enemy. Our driver for 1st Army notified our officers 1 men on leave to return to the country by 17th of this month.	
CARENCY	April 14.		1st Bn harrow returned from Trench Mortar course. Very little hostile shelling all day. Between 11.30 am & 12 noon the NORTHERN of the LOOS PYLONS opposite with the midge connecting it with the FURTHERN PYLON collapsed. Nothing else to report.	
CARENCY	April 15.		Major Clyffe returned from 1st Army Lectures course at AIRE. All day was very quiet nothing to report.	
CARENCY	April 16.		Brigade Headquarters moved from hamlet TOP #2 to Bois de le Haic little artillery very active between 4.30 pm & 5 pm 15th Un 12th trenches between SOUCHEZ Village & part line were heavily	

WAR DIARY or INTELLIGENCE SUMMARY

Army Form C. 2118

(Erase heading not required.)

Place	Date	Hour	Summary of Events and Information	Remarks and references to Appendices
CARENCY	April 17		Relieved with 1/4th & 4/3 We retaliated. Major Gordon Reid 18th London Rgt returned from leave to England. In front line trenches were subjected to 5.9 trench mortar + rifle grenade shelling. Trench mortars today thoroughly ever so fired on the PIMPLE. The enemy retaliates with bursting shrapnel. A fire was seen to break out in a house in LENS about 6.30 pm.	
CARENCY	" 18		Enemy artillery very quiet all day. Otherwise not good.	
CARENCY	" 19		Enemy Trench Mortars active about 3.20 pm. We retaliated with 18 pr + 4.5 how. The enemy stopped at once. At 6.25 pm, trench mortars bombarded the enemy front line, the effect appeared to be very satisfactory.	
CARENCY	April 20		2nd Lt Ford 1/6 London Ammunition Column attached to the 1st Ldn Rhy + 2nd Lt Cottam 6th Ldn Ammunition Column attached to the 15th Rhy returned to his unit. The enemy shelled its ZOUAVE VALLEY + M.D. DE LORETTE slopes intermittently all day	

WAR DIARY
or
INTELLIGENCE SUMMARY

(Erase heading not required.)

Army Form C. 2118

Instructions regarding War Diaries and Intelligence Summaries are contained in F.S. Regs., Part II. and the Staff Manual respectively. Title Pages will be prepared in manuscript.

Place	Date	Hour	Summary of Events and Information	Remarks and references to Appendices
CARENCY	April 21.		At 6.25 P.m. the enemy exploded a mine on the left front of the Division on our right.	
CARENCY	April 22		The enemy artillery were very active today. 16" [howitzer?] Btry & R.G. hows. Btry were hurling their 5-9". One hour in R. Bty. was in around its Batteries. About 250 5.9 + 4.2 were fired on these two positions. Observation very bad owing to snow + rain. After the 15" Bty had fired from 9am to 10pm the infantry reported much work in the enemy trenches. Whistles were blown + evidently casualties had been caused.	
CARENCY	April 23		Quiet Power at 10.15 in 16" Bty wagon lines. The N.E.R.A arrived. The enemy [?] were more active today bombarding our front line with Trench Mortars. At 10 am + 11 am our own Reserve whistles. There were at least 7 German observation balloons up to day. 13 G.R.A marched the 15" Bty, O.P. + saw the enemy firing on Pub 6. The CARENCY - SOUCHEZ road was shelled from 12.15 to 1 pm with bursts of 12 shells.	

WAR DIARY or INTELLIGENCE SUMMARY

Army Form C. 2118

Place	Date	Hour	Summary of Events and Information	Remarks and references to Appendices
CARENCY	April 24		Capt Cooper OC. 15th Hour Bty promoted to Major dating from 15/3/16. Ranny again during the morning with 5.9" Observation being very clear. 15th Bty was heavily shelled with 5.9" in salvoes of three nearly all the shells fell just in front of the position. Enemy again active with heavy trench mortars, our 18"pr & Hows retaliated	
CARENCY	April 25		Have again spared. Very wire shelling. We counter to both the trenches limit Trench Mortars. Heavy TM's fire considerable damage. The enemy retaliated with a few 4.2 H.Es.	
CARENCY	April 26		Lt Rignaud proceeded on 7 days leave of absence to ENGLAND. During the afternoon the enemy trench mortars were very active. During the afternoon they appeared to use a new very heavy bomb. At 7.6 pm the enemy sprung a mine the explosion was a large one big column of flame & dust hit the air immediately after the explosion the enemy opened a heavy bombardment of our trenches, our artillery formed an effective barrage. The bombardment lasted about half an hour with less than before for about an hour after. Short times till such firing	

WAR DIARY
or
INTELLIGENCE SUMMARY

(Erase heading not required.)

Army Form C. 2118

Place	Date	Hour	Summary of Events and Information	Remarks and references to Appendices
CARENCY	April 27		Day very quiet. At about 6.30 pm to 7.30 pm the enemy bombarded our lines with very heavy trench mortars, the enemy & the bomby shook the trenches shot-guns. Our howrs & field guns replied to this bombardment.	
CARENCY	April 28		2nd Lt L.C. Coxon & 2nd Lt G.E. Toutz joined the 6th Bn. Cwm Bn. Bombardment starting at ARLAIN & SOUCHEZ VALLEY by 5.9's & 4.2's at 4.30 AM. We exploded a fuse mine just in front of our front line opposite ROBINAUX Trench this is called the Brooklyn crater.	
CARENCY	April 29		A few Trench Mortars were fired in the support lines & communication trenches about 2 pm. Otherwise all was quiet. At 7.10 pm three were (not exactly) on the left of the Creasin a one night, heavy firing Fishing place.	
CARENCY	April 30		2nd Lt Ellis 15th Wky & Lt Gordon Toutz 4th & Lt Gorer 6th Bn R.F.O. proceeded to the 147th Div Arty Corner at Villement. During the day the trench mortars were active & did some good shooting. Aeroplanes shelling of ZOUAVE Valley near Cabrú Wood W.S. At 7 pm the enemy exploded a large mine in front of the CRATER	

WAR DIARY
or
INTELLIGENCE SUMMARY

(Erase heading not required.)

Army Form C. 2118

Place	Date	Hour	Summary of Events and Information	Remarks and references to Appendices
			Company of the CEMTRE PATTN. Heavy firing with flares but the enemy did not attack. We were issued opening of fire. 2" It given 3/c how Brigade RFA reported from England (attached to the 1" Bty.	
			R. Lowe 2nd Lt RFA Ord 6" London 7.FAB.	

47

Vol 15

WAR DIARY

1/1t 236th Brigade R.F.A.
late 1/6 London BAC

May 1st to Aug 31st

VOL XV

WAR DIARY
or
INTELLIGENCE SUMMARY

Army Form C. 2118

Place	Date	Hour	Summary of Events and Information	Remarks and references to Appendices
CAENEY	May 1		Enemy very active between 5.30 & 8.30 pm with a very large minenwerfer firing about 20 rounds into the CENTRE KEEP ZONE. At 2 pm the enemy fired 10 rounds 5.9" on light Railway between 16th & 14th + the CAENEY Station getting 6 direct hits. Everything else on quiet.	
CAENEY	May 2		Lt Col Price N.S.O. Commanding the 6" on 7.A.B., Capt Edwards V.O. & Lt Walker 6" on R.G.A. proceed on 7 days leave to England, the former to him days leave. At 7.45 pm our artillery opened fire on the Centre Kaken reporting a mine going up. This report proved later false, the sound startled firing. Major Gordon D.S.O. 16" on R.By attached command of RIGHT GROUP	
CAENEY	May 3		Everything quiet all day till 4.45 pm. At 4.45 pm we exploded 3 mines in front of the night & centre retrenchments. Three large craters was formed how known on the Northern, Middle & Southern craters. Our heavy & light artillery bombarded the enemy front support lines. After the explosion for three hours to secure the infantry to occupy t	

WAR DIARY or INTELLIGENCE SUMMARY

Army Form C. 2118

Place	Date	Hour	Summary of Events and Information	Remarks and references to Appendices
CARENCY	May 4		consolidated the crater. The evening retaliation was steady till 4pm & was by no means excessive. After 10pm. the night was very quiet. Our 15" pm fire is this clip, firing 12 rds.	
CARENCY	May 5		The day passed off fairly quiet, very little shelling taking place. In the activity the infantry had a little difficulty with its loving in the middle crater. 2 Lt Van Buyen 4/5 Lan T.H.R. reported & is attached to 16" Btry. Lt Barnard returned from leave & took command of 15" [on May] 3 [?] Lt Burnett returned from [torror] [ortorion] courts. On day very quiet. At 7:15pm we bombarded the enemy front line trenches behind his craters to enable our infantry to work on further. 19 of craters. At 7.40 pm message came to defend the 17 Corps on our right, three batteries switched & that it a barrage. It appears that the attack was only a small bombing one & all was quiet again by 9.15pm.	

WAR DIARY
or
INTELLIGENCE SUMMARY

(Erase heading not required.)

Army Form C. 2118

Place	Date	Hour	Summary of Events and Information	Remarks and references to Appendices
RARENCY	May 6th		The Advant of Brigade headquarters moved to Trevieres. the Carter 6" How & Am took over duties of Enquires to Right Group. 8" Am Hrs headquarters took over from 6" Am & Hrs Headquarters.	
Trevieres	May 7th		Colonel Elley commanding 6" How & Am. took over command of Right Group from Major Gordon D.S.O. 16" Am Btty	
Trevieres May 8th				

Army Form C. 2118

WAR DIARY
or
INTELLIGENCE SUMMARY
(Erase heading not required.)

Instructions regarding War Diaries and Intelligence Summaries are contained in F. S. Regs., Part II. and the Staff Manual respectively. Title Pages will be prepared in manuscript.

Place	Date	Hour	Summary of Events and Information	Remarks and references to Appendices
ACHEVILLERS	May 9th		Capt Low, OC. 6" Lon B.A.C. this section & 1" Lon N/g proceeded on 7 days leave to England.	
FREVILLERS	May 10th		Inspection by the A.D.V.S. of Nk Passing wagon lines.	
FREVILLERS	May 11th			

WAR DIARY
or
INTELLIGENCE SUMMARY

(Erase heading not required.)

Army Form C. 2118

Place	Date	Hour	Summary of Events and Information	Remarks and references to Appendices
PROVILLERS	May 12		Capt. Edwards S.O. Lt. Weller 1/Lon R.a.e returned from 7 days leave of absence to ENGLAND.	
PROVILLERS	May 13th			
PROVILLERS	May 14th		Lt. Blackwell 1S. Lon Bty & Capt. Luendon 2/6 Lon Bty proceeded on seven days leave of absence to England. 2 NCOs & privates to London 1 Bty. Col. Lowe returned from leave.	
PROVILLERS	Aug. 15th			

WAR DIARY
or
INTELLIGENCE SUMMARY
(Erase heading not required.)

Army Form C. 2118

Instructions regarding War Diaries and Intelligence Summaries are contained in F.S. Regs., Part II. and the Staff Manual respectively. Title Pages will be prepared in manuscript.

Place	Date	Hour	Summary of Events and Information	Remarks and references to Appendices
FREVILLERS	July 16			
FREVILLERS	July 17		At present, 6" Hz R.A.e Howitzers to 13" hr My R.a.e split up between batteries & H.Q.a.a. 6" Hr Hz Firs. now weed 2.9.6 Rypos R.A. with the batteries eccept 15". 0.2.26. 16" R.226. 9"=r 226. The 2nd Hr Howitzer now in the Nivipur now called D.226 My.	
FREVILLERS	July 18			

WAR DIARY or INTELLIGENCE SUMMARY

Army Form C. 2118

Place	Date	Hour	Summary of Events and Information	Remarks and references to Appendices
FARBUS	May 19		Capt. Foss OC. 6"Hr R.G.A. is transferred to C/226 Bty. 2Lt. J.E. Cotton 6"/60 R.G.A. transferred from 2/2c Bty to 6/226 Bty. 2Lt Green transferred more NTY.	
FRANVILLERS	May 20		2Lt Hudson transferred from C/11 R.G.A. to B/236 Bty but is attached to 6/226 Bty for one week.	B/236
MARY	May 21		Col Low took over command of North Group at 11 am. Very heavy enemy shelling of zone 9/236, 9/226 & Bttn Hq. from 5.30 am to 12.30 pm on the ammunition very active on our front, enemy fire. Shelter was reported on enemy Railway Infantry + main roads in CHERISY + ARRAS at 3.30 pm enemy shelled a heavy	

WAR DIARY or INTELLIGENCE SUMMARY

Army Form C. 2118

Place	Date	Hour	Summary of Events and Information	Remarks and references to Appendices
CHENEY	May 22		The Louth Jeery shelled communication trenches front + support lines of the 8th NIGHT Battn LEFT Brigade + also the Night Brigade. At about 8 pm the enemy used lachrymatory shells on leading front run as well as 5.9", 16" on my that a direct hit on No 1 gun wounding five men. About 9:30 enemy attacked trenches of the front + support lines of Night Brigade (140) + front line of 4th company of Night Battn left Brigade. A bombing attack was organised + bombs + however enemy cleared part of trenches of Night Battn were retaken this relieved off about 3.30 am. Lt BARNARD 18/276 My promoted Captain. Lt Van den Bergh 1/276 My, Lieu Klein to LEFT Battn Night Brigade Reported much my activity not near our front part of line trenches till 11.50 pm I took enemy text from Zichts, + then artillery opened + many burst in LOUTH valley. MCLATAN. + CARTNEY	

Army Form C. 2118

WAR DIARY
or
INTELLIGENCE SUMMARY
(Erase heading not required.)

Instructions regarding War Diaries and Intelligence Summaries are contained in F.S. Regs., Part II. and the Staff Manual respectively. Title Pages will be prepared in manuscript.

Place	Date	Hour	Summary of Events and Information	Remarks and references to Appendices
			FLORETTE heights were heavily shelled with 9.9" & 6". Our trenches the day have extensively hopped up & steady fire on enemy front & support line (Kruelers). 34' Regime ? 9.A. on Division wheeled to Right Group.	
CARENCY	May 23.		Intermittent shelling during the day by Batteries in CARENCY, ABLAIN + on LORETTE. At 4 pm our artillery opened a slow bombard meet of the enemy new front line. Infantry movement till about 6.25 pm when they lifted on to (?) the German front line. The enemy replied by barraging Zouave valley, Railway, every avenue all night, very heavy shell. 3:30 am 24/5/16.	
CARENCY	May 24		Our artillery very active throughout the day carrying on a slow bombardment of the enemy front & support line. Enemy artillery replied with 5.9 round about every fortam. There was no infantry attack at all.	

1875 Wt. W593/826 1,000,000 4/15 J.B.C. & A. A.D.S.S./Forms/C. 2118.

WAR DIARY
or
INTELLIGENCE SUMMARY

(Erase heading not required.)

Army Form C. 2118

Place	Date	Hour	Summary of Events and Information	Remarks and references to Appendices
CARENCY	May 25		C/176 Bty had two hits on Enemy dug out. Killing three Sergts + wounding 2 Lt Green + one Sergt. Fires on rock side much reduced. During the afternoon Divisional Headquarters in Chateau DE LA HAIE was shelled with 4.2". During the night 25"-26" 47th Div Infantry relieved by 2nd Div Infantry.	
CARENCY	May 26		Lt Col Lowe D.S.O. commanding Right Group handed over command to Lt Col Curry of 34th Brigade RFA. 2nd Division. 276 Brigade RFA moved to rest billets at VALHUON.	
VALHUON	May 27		B/276 + C/176 were relieved by batteries of 34th Brigade RFA + went into rest billets at HUCLIER + ANTIN. A/176 remained attached to line MAISNIL-BOUCHE to dig gun pits at ABLAIN M. 0/176 remained in action.	
VALHUON HUCLIER BARLIN	May 28		D/176 + C/176 Batteries moved wagon lines to NOYELLES.	
BARLIN	May 29		Brigade Headquarters B/176 + C/176 moved to BARLIN.	
BARLIN	May 30		2 Lt Hudson of the 2nd Roman D/176 proceeded on 7 days leave to England.	

Army Form C. 2118

WAR DIARY
or
INTELLIGENCE SUMMARY

(Erase heading not required.)

Instructions regarding War Diaries and Intelligence Summaries are contained in F. S. Regs., Part II. and the Staff Manual respectively. Title Pages will be prepared in manuscript.

Place	Date	Hour	Summary of Events and Information	Remarks and references to Appendices
BARLIN	May 31st		B/236 C/236 & D/236 in 1st Army reserve — ready to move at one hours notice.	

H.C. Lowe
Lt Col R.F.A.
Commanding 236th Brigade R.F.A.

WAR DIARY or INTELLIGENCE SUMMARY

Army Form C. 2118

236 Bde R.F.A. Vol 16

Place	Date	Hour	Summary of Events and Information	Remarks and references to Appendices
BARLIN	June 1			
BARLIN	June 2		Capt Guyman B/1 East-Anglian R.F.A. reported its arrival to C/236 Battery.	
BARLIN	June 3			
BARLIN	June 4		R.G.R.A. IV Corps, inspected the horses of the B/236 +C/236 batteries	
BARLIN	June 5		B/236 + C/236 Batteries inspected by the R.G.R.A. IV Corps. Relief of A/236 battery went into action at ABLAIN.	
BARLIN	June 6		S.O.C. 47 Division inspected the HQrs. Line of RFC/236 Battery. 2 Lt Bowyer HQ staff proceeded to England on seven days leave. Relief from Paris Gazette dated June 5th Military honours— Lt Lewis "Laden Brigade R.F.A. - Military Cross — R.S.M. Hood - D.C.M. O/Noie — HQ staff military medal — Old trenches NE of Bty - Military Cross.	
BARLIN	June 7th		OC Batteries went to inspect gun position.	

WAR DIARY
or
INTELLIGENCE SUMMARY
(Erase heading not required.)

Army Form C. 2118

Instructions regarding War Diaries and Intelligence Summaries are contained in F.S. Regs., Part II. and the Staff Manual respectively. Title Pages will be prepared in manuscript.

Place	Date	Hour	Summary of Events and Information	Remarks and references to Appendices
BARLIN	June 8th	8:15	A/C/236 Batteries dugging reserve gun positions near VERDREL.	
BARLIN	June 9th	9:15	Gt. Major ave inspected D/236 Battery.	
BARLIN	June 10th	10.		
BARLIN	June 11th		Church parade at BARLIN	
BARLIN	June 12th	12:30	B.C's went to reconnoitre positions of batteries of 23rd Division. Capt Kindell B/236 Bty proceed to 7 days leave to England. Col Love D.S.O. appointed M. Nightingale. Nightingale consists of the following batteries. A.P.C./237 Hdy. A.D.E.D./236 R.F.A.	
BARLIN	June 13		2/Major to Hdqrs returning from leave.	
BARLIN	Aug. 14.		Sectors of batteries moved up into action. A forward O.P.s of N.D. DE LORETTE. B/236 lieth me hill H/236 G western slopes of BOIS de PETIT BERTHONVAL. C/236 le Pape. DE NOULETTE. D/236 du Bois DE NOULETTE.	

A/K - NOULETTE. C/236 le Bois DE BOUFIGNY

1875. Wt. W593/826 1,000,000 4/15 J.B.C. & A. A.D.S.S./Forms/C. 2118.

Army Form C. 2118

WAR DIARY
or
INTELLIGENCE SUMMARY
(Erase heading not required.)

Instructions regarding War Diaries and Intelligence Summaries are contained in F.S. Regs., Part II. and the Staff Manual respectively. Title Pages will be prepared in manuscript.

Place	Date	Hour	Summary of Events and Information	Remarks and references to Appendices
BARLIN	June 15		Remainder of batteries moved up into action. Brigade HQ Staff moved to house in DOYELLES All guns on our front. Lt Pritchett capt 237 Bty RFA available RIGHT CENTRE	
ATK NOULETTE	June 16		2nd Bde both over command of NIGHT group from CRE 102 Brigade. Batteries registering; except for a few S.O.S. test's until midnight. All was quiet on our front at 10.30 pm a large mine exploded to the South foreseen by heavy artillery & machine gun fire.	
ATK NOULETTE	June 17		Lt Petrie e/176 Bty evacuated to England. Some three Road between ATK NOULETTE + BULLY GRENAY. Great aerial activity at 12 noon 9 enemy planes passed over ATK NOULETTE in direction of HERSIN.	
ATK NOULETTE	June 18		High up good for observation. Mrs Brown fair 38 an	
ATK NOULETTE	June 19		Flight moves up - fire on our front gun batteries installed Weather later fine Enemy aeroplanes more active. M726 nine gun fired 36 rds. M727 Mjr change in Position	
ATK NOULETTE	June 20		Major Cooper Mine Mjr Thayer Clifton At 737 Bty nominal	

WAR DIARY or INTELLIGENCE SUMMARY

Army Form C. 2118

Place	Date	Hour	Summary of Events and Information	Remarks and references to Appendices
			In continuation. 14/7 Bgr Jonny 1/2 M.G. awarded the Military medal by the Commander in Chief under authority from H.M. The King. IV Corps O.No. 943. Enemy trench mortar again very active in the morning on No. 2 Sub-Sec. 1st Bn. Leinsters. Shews with fair results. Our own trench mortars replied the german wire.	
AIX NOULETTE	June 21		There was much trench mortar activity about 12 noon. The enemy trench mortars were also very active on on the W. buried 1600 yards killing 2/Lt Gatrip Ery #37 Rife attached 9/76 T.M. Battery, wounded 2/Lt Kemble, O.R. 18/227. My action as Liaison officer to No 5 7 Bn T.T.V. our T.M. as great groups the day before to enemy wire in front title. Wished to meet Share and this chaps in relation. G.O.C. Division sent a message to the officers concerned then work. There was again a lot of aerial activity. Lt Kimber & 2nd Lieut. Tolerley totally lots dead of wounds the same night.	

WAR DIARY
or
INTELLIGENCE SUMMARY

(Erase heading not required.)

Army Form C. 2118

Place	Date	Hour	Summary of Events and Information	Remarks and references to Appendices
AIX NOULETTE	Jun 22		Very little shelling today. Enemy put 6.4.2 on Battery B/237 position. High velocity curved observation from a bank of enemy aeroplanes flew over AIX NOULETTE Nr Aix position. Very low. Lunch about two hours after followed by our planes. The following Officers arrived from England:— 2 Lt G.N. Cochrane posted to C/176 Bty 2 Lt Miles posted to C/176 Lt E.A. A.B. went in place to D/176 Bty.— 2 Lt Gordon Toomby attached to C/176 injured his wrist. 47th D.A.C. Lt Pilkitch aft 237 Bde R.F.A. Reserve group H.Q. & Lt Tausley newly Officer 237 Bde attached to Bde H.Q. One of the guns of A/216 T.M.B. had a premature. One man was killed & 2 wounded.	
AIX NOULETTE	Jun 23		All quiet. Hostile aeroplane very active. B/223 Bty commanded by Major Turner joined Reserve Flight Group. Position taken by A/237 Bty.	

WAR DIARY or INTELLIGENCE SUMMARY

Army Form C. 2118

Place	Date	Hour	Summary of Events and Information	Remarks and references to Appendices
AIX NOULETTE	June 24		(South of) on edge of NOULETTE WOOD. All carriers of this party stored wire cutting on Hun's own. 1/47 TM BATTERY (Lt Brown) fired 50 cm wire system & repulsion of enemy wire cutters. Wind serene slowly coming from westerly. Lt Hutton attached to 1/47 TM Battery. A gun of 1/47 TM B blew up firing its 185th on charge of its gun.	
AIX-NOULETTE	June 25		Divisional artillery continued wire cutting in conjunction with T.M. batteries. Enemy TMs active at times during the day but stopped when fired on by our howitzers. Telephone activity much less owing to the weather. Found 1 heavy bombardment not worth of ANGRES, South about 12.30 pm.	
AIX-NOULETTE	June 26		Wire cutting throughout the day. Enemy field mortars were active on our front but were silenced by our batteries. At 11.30 pm a sudden opened a heavy bombardment of enemy trenches on VIMY RIDGE. Enemy's Rauly was fairly heavy for a time	

WAR DIARY or INTELLIGENCE SUMMARY

Army Form C. 2118

Place	Date	Hour	Summary of Events and Information	Remarks and references to Appendices
AIX NOULETTE	June 27		and by it and night practically ceased, but for long on the about 12.45 am - at 11.45 pm exactly similar stacks of affairs were observed opposite the Loos Salient, very heavy fire from the lines heard & infantry confined themselves chiefly to bombs & machine gun fire.	
AIX NOULETTE	June 27	18[?]	Artillery + T.M. fire was cutting all day. At 11.45 pm desultory artillery spent a bombardment along the whole of Divisional front which covered of this gas was let off at 1.20 am artillery fire became white + at 1.25 am infantry raided German lines at points there were not know. The enemy retaliated very heavily with 5.9 + heavy minenwerfers on our front line also a few shell on roads leading into AIX NOULETTE. All was quiet again by 2.30 am. The was discharged from the AVOHES SECTOR. The artillery barrage was excellent + very heavy.	
AIX NOULETTE	Aug 28		Poerivin sniped in wire cutting lights very heard for otherwise during the morning. About 9.45 pm enemy artillery very active in KOOS sector. Capt Bayus Cpr's May went in rear of Frounsent.	

1875 Wt. W593/826 1,000,000 4/15 J.B.C. & A. A.D.S.3./Forms/C. 2118.

Army Form C. 2118

WAR DIARY
or
INTELLIGENCE SUMMARY
(Erase heading not required.)

Instructions regarding War Diaries and Intelligence Summaries are contained in F.S. Regs., Part II. and the Staff Manual respectively. Title Pages will be prepared in manuscript.

Place	Date	Hour	Summary of Events and Information	Remarks and references to Appendices
Mt A. NEULETTE	June 29		A very high wind made wire cutting very difficult owing to the movement of the ground by the BOIS EN HACH which our S.O.S., Chre & Blue Rhys trench posts were is very difficult. Fire was returned a few for wire cutting in Keyher else arrived from England, but went at once to field ambulance again at 9.10 ↓ 2 trenches opened shot out any interior forward front of Vimy RIDGE, Enemy replied with about 4" barrage.	
AIX NOULETTE	June 30		Wire from G.H.Q. 3rd & 4th Armies launched attacks at 7.20 am this morning in conjunction with French which is far sumpoising. Batteries were cutting barbfour entirely much reduce the feeling.	

H.F. Crowe
Lt.Col. R.F.A.
O.C. 236th Brigade R.F.A.

30/6/16

1875 Wt. W593/826 1,000,000 4/15 J.B.C. & A. A.D.S.S./Forms/C. 2118.

47th Divisional Artillery

236th Brigade   R. F. A.

JULY, 1 9 1 6

Army Form C. 2118

WAR DIARY of 236th Brigade R.F.A.

INTELLIGENCE SUMMARY

(Erase heading not required.)

July 1916

VBC 17

Instructions regarding War Diaries and Intelligence Summaries are contained in F.S. Regs., Part II. and the Staff Manual respectively. Title Pages will be prepared in manuscript.

Place	Date	Hour	Summary of Events and Information	Remarks and references to Appendices
AIX-NOULETTE	July 1		A very quiet day. German aeroplanes displayed slightly more activity. After 17/236 Bty were cutting wire enemy triple fences	
AIX-NOULETTE	July 2		2 Lt Gwen C/236 Bty moved from here in advance to his battery. A quiet day – twenty retaliator [shells] so wounding ten but one of 17/236 Btys.	
AIX-NOULETTE	July 3		Batteries wire cutting. B/237 battery shared with A + E at about 8 am. One gun was damaged. Enemy shelled battery positions in the AIX NOULETTE - BOULYONCHY road all day between 5.9" + 4.2". Huron mouth was attacked about 4 pm. It is to be every battery up to mine. A very large way was effectively fire followed. Another way was expected at 12.30 am. At 1.45 am our artillery opened a strong barrage in self. on 9. A raid by 15 km N+E of [illegible] to relieve a BOISON HACHE. Raid lasted twenty minutes. Result at present not known. Enemy retaliation was much heavier than in the round one. All quiet again by 2.30 am.	

1875 Wt. W593/826 1,000,000 4/15 J.B.C. & A. A.D.S.S./Forms/C. 2118.

Army Form C. 2118

WAR DIARY
or
INTELLIGENCE SUMMARY
(Erase heading not required.)

Instructions regarding War Diaries and Intelligence Summaries are contained in F. S. Regs., Part II. and the Staff Manual respectively. Title Pages will be prepared in manuscript.

Place	Date	Hour	Summary of Events and Information	Remarks and references to Appendices
AIX NOULETTE	July 4		Enemy active in ANGRES SECTOR this morning with Trench mortars. Otherwise all quiet.	
AIX NOULETTE	July 5		Observation impossible - all quiet on the front	
AIX NOULETTE	July 6	2nd Lt MILES c/m Mastery proceeded on TRENCH MORTAR course. During the early morning Trench mortars were active on SOUCHEZ in retaliation enemy different ourring to bad weather.	
AIX NOULETTE	July 7		All quiet. 2nd Lt Worker transferred (temp) to 1/4 TM Bty.	
AIX-NOULETTE	July 8		All quiet.	
AIX-NOULETTE	July 9th		Col Peel took over command of RIGHT GROUP from Col Lowe - Col - left HQ with HQ staff moved to new billets in the rear. All quiet on the front. During night enemy lights & rockets were stellar in conjunction with ½ hrs heavy artillery. All quiet on this front.	
AIX NOULETTE	July 10			
AIX-NOULETTE	July 11		Enemy artillery about 6 pm on L.Main trg. Our how retaliated on enemy support line allen a few rounds enemy stopped firing	

1875 Wt. W593/826 1,000,000 4/15 J.B.C. & A. A.D.S.S./Forms/C. 2118.

WAR DIARY
INTELLIGENCE SUMMARY

(Erase heading not required.)

Army Form C. 2118

Place	Date	Hour	Summary of Events and Information	Remarks and references to Appendices
AIX-NOULETTE	July 12		Officers & men of 163 Division attached to 1/7 Royal Bn for information. However carried out trench strafe on enemy trench. Heavy enemy fire on positions & dumps. Hostile minenwerfer has fired heavy trench mortars.	
AIX-NOULETTE	July 13		Artillery carried out a barrage on road dump & trenches 1/P & G Bty fired 20 rounds on AVION DE MIRABELLE scoring several hits. Much heavier shell fire from 2.30 pm to 4 pm covered by fire from 18 pdrs.	
AIX-NOULETTE	July 14		Trench mortars were active. Covered by fire from 18 pdrs — 6 & 4 pm. Enemy retaliated (on our wire cutters) on the STRAIGHT - HUNTRENCH & BOSH WALK. Our artillery retaliated strongly & enemy ceased firing.	
AIX-NOULETTE	July 15		Wire cut by TMs & 18 pdrs during afternoon — Enemy wire was cut yesterday on the STRAIGHT & BOSH WALK. Otherwise all quiet.	

Army Form C. 2118

WAR DIARY
or
INTELLIGENCE SUMMARY
(Erase heading not required.)

Instructions regarding War Diaries and Intelligence Summaries are contained in F.S. Regs., Part II. and the Staff Manual respectively. Title Pages will be prepared in manuscript.

Place	Date	Hour	Summary of Events and Information	Remarks and references to Appendices
AIX-NOULETTE	July 16		TRENCH MORTARS were active in afternoon from 4.30 pm to 5.30 pm at 1 mm. night of 16-17. 20th London Regiment carried out a raid on enemy lines at small salient north of BOIS-EN-HACHE. He raid was supported by active artillery fire with 2" mortars + Stokes mortars - enemy retaliation was slight consisting of a few 4.2" shells + Minen Werfers - infantry opposition from close trenches was entered + dug-outs were bombed a machine gun was destroyed out casualties were slight. All was quiet again by 1.45 am.	
AIX-NOULETTE	July 17		Nothing to report. All quiet.	
AIX-NOULETTE	July 18		Except for slight shelling of Petrin Trench + the enemy everything was quiet. 14th 1st Inf. Regt. relieved by 63rd Division.	
AIX-NOULETTE	July 19		All quiet.	
AIX-NOULETTE	July 20		Quiet all day - enemy blew up mine by houses exam air 10.30 pm.	

WAR DIARY
or
INTELLIGENCE SUMMARY

Army Form C. 2118

(Erase heading not required.)

Place	Date	Hour	Summary of Events and Information	Remarks and references to Appendices
AIX NOULETTE AIX NOULETTE AIX 1000 METRE	July 21st July 22nd July 23		All quiet - nothing to report. M. Rating's fire on enemy trenches from 2 pm to 6 pm. Whereabouts of 5th Div artillery cannot be established at gun positions per battery. enemy were quick to retaliate on our support line.	
HERSIN	July 24		2 Lt Wallace returned from TM course. During the course he was sent to the NEUVE CHAPELLE front - to take command of a T.M. battery during the operations there.	
HERSIN	July 25		Orders received for Brigade to move to SAINS-LES-PERNES.	
HERSIN + SAINS-LES-PERNES	July 26		The Brigade left HERSIN commencing on instructions for cayer for battery to leave over to 316 & 2 Bde R.F.A. Marched to SAINS LES PERNES via BARLIN - HOUDAIN - DIVION - CAMBLAIN-CHATELAIN + PERNES. The BRIGADE was inspected by the B.G.R.A at BARLIN. Bde arrived at SAINS LES PERNES by 5.30 pm.	
SAINS-LES-PERNES	July 27		Batteries at disposal of battery commanders.	
SAINS-LES-PERNES	July 28		Batteries at disposal of Battery commanders	
SAINS-LES-PERNES	July 29		Batteries commenced arriving at SAINS LES PERNES from detr.n	

WAR DIARY
INTELLIGENCE SUMMARY

Army Form C. 2118

Place	Date	Hour	Summary of Events and Information	Remarks and references to Appendices
SAINS-LES-PERNES	July 29		(continued) after having our 6.3" 6" Howitzers Officers NCOs men of T.M. Bty report at SAINS-LES-PERNES.	Y/47
AUBROMETZ	July 30		Bde moved to AUBROMETZ — Staff went from SAINS-LES-PERNES at 4.10 am and arrived at AUBROMETZ at 12.30 pm marching by way of TANGRY - HESTRUS - WAVRANS - BEAUVOIS - LINZEUX - FILLIEVRES - a halt was made at WAVRANS for water. The 47th Division is attached to 3rd ARMY from 30 inst.	
AUBROMETZ	July 31		Batteries at disposal of battery commanders — Rev. Heywood + representatives of each battery inspected the gun pits just put out of action at Pte 50 mm E. 21st Division which are just put out of action at Pte 50 mm E.	

R. C. Lowe
LT-COL. R.F.A.
COMDG. 236 BDE. R.F.A.

47th Divisional Artillery.

236th BRIGADE.

ROYAL FIELD ARTILLERY

AUGUST 1 9 1 6

Army Form C. 2118

78th Brigade RFA WAR DIARY August 1916

INTELLIGENCE SUMMARY
(Erase heading not required.)

Vol 18 Page 1

Place	Date	Hour	Summary of Events and Information	Remarks and references to Appendices
AUBROMETZ to BEAUVOIR RIVIERE	Aug 1st		Brigade marched to BEAUVOIR RIVIERE. Brigade started at 3.45 pm marched by way of RUIRE-au-BOIS - NOEUX-WAVRANS - Bde arrived at BEAUVOIR RIVIERE by 7 P.M. Bde was inspected by B.G.R.A. at NOEUX.	
BEAUVOIR RIVIERE	Aug 2nd		Batteries at disposal of Battery Commanders.	
BEAUVOIR RIVIERE	Aug 3rd		Batteries at disposal of battery Commanders in the afternoon a lecture [illegible] officers was with great success. In the evening a band & concert was held. Col Helmsley 21st Londons Bn sent the whole band which was a great success, the concert ended at 10 pm	
BEAUVOIR RIVIERE	Aug 4th		Batteries at disposal of battery commanders.	
BEAUVOIR RIVIERE	Aug 5th		Brigade marched to VITZ-VILLEROY + VILLEROY-BARAUDE, "B" Battery, "D" Battery at the latter, Brigade marched off at 4.45 am arrived at VITZ-VILLEROY at [illegible] am [illegible] by AUXI-LE-CHATEAU + WILLENCOURT	

WAR DIARY
or
INTELLIGENCE SUMMARY
(Erase heading not required.)

Army Form C. 2118

Page 2

Place	Date	Hour	Summary of Events and Information	Remarks and references to Appendices
VITZ-VILLEROY	Aug 6		R&R carried out a minor attack to advance their position by 2.35 afternoon. Attack proceeded according to plan & the new position was occupied by 3.0 that evening.	
VITZ-VILLEROY	Aug 7		Platoon at defined locality. Commanders.	
VITZ-VILLEROY	Aug 8		Entraine at the head of the battery commanders.	
VITZ-VILLEROY	Aug 9		Divisional Field Day. Troops issued at BEAUMONT H.Q. at SOUFFLES & offrs & men formed cup, surrounded by hostile forces to take up positions in neighbourhood of CHAUMONT after advance. X.I been in action till 2.30 pm returning to Billets in evening.	
VITZ-VILLEROY LANCHES	Aug 10		Brigade moved to further front near LANCHES. Start was made from VITZ-VILLEROY at 6 am & arrived at LANCHES at 12.30 pm marching by WILLENCOURT - BERMATRE - ARGENVILLES - BEAU METZ - RIBEAUCOURT. A halt was made at ARGENVILLE for water.	

1875 Wt. W593/826 1,000,000 4/15 J.B.C. & A. A.D.S.S./Forms/C. 2118.

WAR DIARY
or
INTELLIGENCE SUMMARY
(Erase heading not required.)

Army Form C. 2118

Page 3

Place	Date	Hour	Summary of Events and Information	Remarks and references to Appendices
LAHERES & HAVERNAS	Aug 11		Bty. Abn. moved to HAVERNAS - Start was made at 6.30 am route - NEUFMENIL - CANAPLES. Arrived at HAVERNAS at 9.15 am.	
HAVERNAS	Aug 12		Bde. moved to BEHENCOURT - Bde. marched off at 12 noon + arrived at BEHENCOURT at 6 p.m - route - PLESSALES - VILLERS-BOCAGE - MOLLIENS AU BOIS - MONTIGNY. Bty. + Battery commanders proceeded to look at her battery positions near MAMETZ WOOD reached by 23 Divn Divnl. H.Q.	
BEHENCOURT & BOTTOM WOOD	Aug 13		C/Battery & sections of A, B & D Batteries move up to action at Bottom Wood. Remainder remain at Behencourt	
BOTTOM WOOD	Aug 14		Remaining sections of A B & D Batteries move up to action at Bottom Wood. Gun Wood & Gn Mason injured through G.S. wagon overturning.	
BOTTOM WOOD	Aug 15		Batteries fired 4.6" Infantry Brigade in trenches. Quiet day. Work done on position. Quiet day except for German shelling at intervals WELSH ALLEY and	
	Aug 16		70th AVENUE when all O.P's are. Practice barrage at 4 p.m. Batteries shelled SWITCH LINE on right of tramway running to MARTIN PUICH during the night.	

Army Form C. 2118

WAR DIARY
or
INTELLIGENCE SUMMARY
(Erase heading not required.)

Page 4

Place	Date	Hour	Summary of Events and Information	Remarks and references to Appendices
BOTTOM WOOD	Aug 17		Quiet day until about 3 p.m. Morning spent in registration. Lt. GRABURN C/236 Battery was wounded in the trenches. Battery opened an intense barrage 200 yds over the SWITCH LINE and infantry made (unsuccessful) attack along SWITCH LINE towards tramway. Germans made full counter attack near tramway which was repulsed. No firing during the night by batteries. At 8.55 a.m. a heavy barrage was put up by our batteries 200 yds over the SWITCH LINE and formed with 47 Div Arty a double barrage.	
	Aug 18		At 2.45 p.m. heavy barrage on SWITCH LINE on Right of TRAMWAY. Smoke discharged on our front. 1st Division attacked intermediate LINE on our Right. Enemy S.O.S. barrage in our front were kept up at odd intervals on division outs. From 8.30 p.m.	

Army Form C. 2118

Page 5

WAR DIARY
or
INTELLIGENCE SUMMARY
(Erase heading not required.)

Place	Date	Hour	Summary of Events and Information	Remarks and references to Appendices
BOTTOM WOOD	Aug 19		Tracks and trenches leading to MARTIN PUICH. From midnight 18/19th fire was continued at intervals to 7.30 a.m. Quiet morning and quiet afternoon. Nothing during the night.	
	Aug 20th		From midday fired on MARTIN PUICH and surroundings. At 10 p.m. and at intervals during the night batteries searched back to MARTIN PUICH for a line 400 yds over our SWITCH LINE and west of TRAMWAY.	
	Aug 21st		During night 20/21st B/236 Battery was shelled with Gas shell losing 2 men killed, 2 wounded & gassed. 5 German aeroplanes came over at about 9.20 a.m. & dropped 6 bombs in the neighbourhood of the wagon lines. During the afternoon D/236 Battery fired on Martinpuich. MAJOR POLLARD went up in a balloon and took the light too bad for clear observation.	
	Aug 22nd		Very quiet day. At 2 h - 5.10 p.m. and 8.25 p.m. C our batteries bombarded new German trench in front of Martinpuich. At 1.55 pm 5.15 pm & 8.20 h D/236 Battery fired salvoes into MARTIN PUICH.	

WAR DIARY
INTELLIGENCE SUMMARY

Army Form C. 2118

Page 6

Place	Date	Hour	Summary of Events and Information	Remarks and references to Appendices
BOTTOM WOOD	Aug 23		Quiet day. Very little firing by batteries. A/236 had 4 casualties. One very bad. The remainder very slight. C/236 Battery had one man wounded.	
	Aug 24		Quiet in the morning. B/236 went out of action with A/236 Battery to leaving only 16 men & 1 officer with A/236 Battery; this is a new system of reliefs with their guns. Hostile artillery provided greater activity in the afternoon. MSD wires on our right (?) slashed and locations adjoining very lively with heavy shell. later in the evening A/236 Battery was shelled with gas shell. Attack was a failure.	
	Aug 25		Brigade carried out harassing fire as ordered by Div Arty. Fairly quiet day. Hostile aircraft rather more active. One of our aeroplanes was forced to descend in K.29 thereby entirely destroyed, but was broken up in course and difficult	

WAR DIARY or INTELLIGENCE SUMMARY

Army Form C. 2118

Page ?

Place	Date	Hour	Summary of Events and Information	Remarks and references to Appendices
BOTTOM WOOD	Aug 26		Army about evening. Hostile artillery activity was somewhat below the average. Hostile artillery displayed activity today against our movement positions harassing valleys with heavy shell fire, short periods with no small intensity. The valley south of Mametz B ordered west of Bottom Wood & Shelter Wood were also heavily shelled. Otherwise the day was fairly uneventful except that the Division on our right (15th Div.) fired after 200 yds S of the Intermediate Line. Hostile aeroplanes on the number of 15 carried out a small reconnaissance over the number of 5.	
	Aug 27		DEATH VALLEY and its environs about 5 p.m. Battery 236 Brigade carried out a continuous bombardment on German front line. Markach (not shown). B/236 Battery took over from A/236 Battery in accordance with the programme of reliefs instituted by the G.O.C.R.A. 47 Division. At about 11:50 a.m. a heavy hostile bombardment was put on VILLA WOOD, and the N.W. corner of MAMETZ WOOD. At about 2.15 pm the supposition of B/236, A/236 & the 235 Bde positions were violently shelled with heavy howitzers. 3 men of B/236 were buried but were	

1875 Wt. W593/826 1,000,000 4/15 J.B.C. & A. A.D.S.S./Forms/C. 2118.

WAR DIARY
INTELLIGENCE SUMMARY
(Erase heading not required.)

Page 8

Place	Date	Hour	Summary of Events and Information	Remarks and references to Appendices
	Aug 29		Shrapnel again and enemy somewhat suffering from slight shell shock. The Brigade fired continuously throughout the day on barrages. Major W. COOPER A/236 Battery RFA proceeded to Field Ambulance sick. Brigade line continuously throughout the 24 hrs. Hostile artillery was moderately active compared with the previous day. Capt R. Gunton Warburton came to attached to 0/236 Battery; 2/Lt PEARSON and 2/Lt TABOR from the 4)ᵉ DAC were yesterday attached to their battery for instruction, while Lt CH DEWAEL was attached to C/236 Battery from 4/7 DAC. Faulty pistoling. Continuous barrage kept up all day on the frontline in front of the infantry our infantry dug round MARTINPUICH. At midnight our	
	Aug 30		INTERMEDIATE LINE. Heavy rain interfered with work. Our battery barraged as before. 136 prisoners were obtained from the INTERMEDIATE LINE, 4 Officers, 2 N.C.O's and 130 prisoners. These passed down WELCH ALLEY between the hours	

WAR DIARY
or
INTELLIGENCE SUMMARY

Army Form C. 2118

Page 9

Place	Date	Hour	Summary of Events and Information	Remarks and references to Appendices
BOTTOM WOOD	Aug 31		3 and 6 p.m. Major CAPT R.A. CORSAN A/236 Battery rejoined unit after a stay in hospital. Brigade kept up continuous harassing artillery activity particularly with gas shell. Brigade Headquarters were shelled with gas shell from about 10 p.m. till about 11 p.m. No damage was done. Relatively quiet day. A and B/236 Batteries were heavily shelled with lachrymatory and poison shell.	

P.C. Lew
LT-COL. R.F.A.
COMDG. 236 BDE. R.F.A.

Army Form C. 2118

WAR DIARY or **INTELLIGENCE SUMMARY**

236th (Howitzer) Brigade R.F.A.

September 1916

Page 1

Place	Date	Hour	Summary of Events and Information	Remarks and references to Appendices
BOTTOM WOOD	Sept 1		Continuous barrages kept up by Brigade all day cumulating in 8 rounds who dropped out about mid-day but were relieved with 8 guns. They took over positions later barrages were taken on by C/236 Battery until relieved by the 238 Brigade. One man was wounded & one or two others when waters (intentionally?). Enemy artillery very active. Severed to change positions the section of A/236 Battery	
	Sept 2		Section of A/236 moved to alongside C/236 Battery. Heavy artillery began their bombardment for the attack of the 3rd, 14th and 15th Corps.	
	Sept 3		In the morning the Australians captured MOUQUET FARM. About 12. noon 1st Division occupied their objectives in WOOD wood. At 12 o'clock the 14th Corps captured GUILLEMONT and the 15th Corps captured GINCHY. The French took CLERY and reached within 1500 yards of COMBLES. Batteries took in intense feint bombardments prior to the attacks mentioned above.	

Army Form C. 2118

WAR DIARY
or
INTELLIGENCE SUMMARY
(Erase heading not required.)

Page 2

Place	Date	Hour	Summary of Events and Information	Remarks and references to Appendices
BOTTOM WOOD	Sept	4th	Relatively quiet day on our front. One man of B/226 Battery wounded by a premature from one of the 235 Brigade Batteries. The 7th Division attacked GINCHY. At 3.10 p.m. Batteries fired an intense bombardment on hostile Batteries for a few minutes.	
	Sept	5th	Batteries fired on MARTIN PUICH and its neighbourhood during the day in accordance with programme. Fairly quiet day. Further hostile through batteries Combles & Cléry.	
	Sept	6th	A quiet day, however enemy artillery exploited the programme of their shoots thoroughout the day. There are reports of their enemy 500 yds of enemy trench near COMBLES. Personnel were today counted arracks which were relieved. Major COOPER returned to take Command of A/226 Bty.	
	Sept	7th	A quiet day. Batteries carried out programme of special shoots. C/226 Bty began to dig new position near BAZENTIN-LE-PETIT WOOD. French attacked south of the SOMME & took fortified parts of BERNY- & western half of VERMAN DOVILLERS.	
	Sept 8.		A quiet day. Batteries carried out programme of special shoots — at 6.45 p.m. 1st Division in accordance energy trenches in High Wood. 47th Divisional Battery co-operated with a nature	

WAR DIARY or INTELLIGENCE SUMMARY

Army Form C. 2118 — Page 3

Place	Date	Hour	Summary of Events and Information	Remarks and references to Appendices
	Sept 9th		bombardment for 15 minutes then fired on trenches to N.W. of HIGH WOOD. 1st Division at first took their objective but shifted back on account of their flanks being exposed. A few prisoners were taken.	
	Sept 10th		A quiet day until 4.45 pm when 1st Div attacked trenches in HIGH WOOD & to the EAST of HIGH WOOD. CANADIAN DIVISION also attacked trenches to N.W. of MUNSTER ALLEY. 47th Div ARTY co-operated with an intense bombardment for 15 mins on trenches in front of MARTINPUICH. 1st Div took their objectives to N.E. of HIGH WOOD. took some prisoners. CANADIANS took all their objectives by prisoners & one machine gun. – 15 Corps took HOP ALLEY – 14th Corps took GUINCHY. 2.35 & 2.36 Bdes came under command of C.R.A. 47th/15th Division. – B&D Bty moved Bretons W.B. new positions – B Bty in LOWER WOOD. C Bty S. of BAZENTIN-LE-PETIT WOOD & D Bty in BAZENTIN-LE-PETIT. Group O.P. in 10th AVENUE was heavily shelled with 5.9's during the afternoon.	

Army Form C. 2118

WAR DIARY
or
INTELLIGENCE SUMMARY
(Erase heading not required.)

Page 4

Instructions regarding War Diaries and Intelligence Summaries are contained in F. S. Regs., Part II. and the Staff Manual respectively. Title Pages will be prepared in manuscript.

Place	Date	Hour	Summary of Events and Information	Remarks and references to Appendices
BOTTOM WOOD	Sept 11th		Batteries moved numerous two batteries into new positions all fairly quiet on the front	
Bottom WOOD	Sept 12		HQ came under command of B.C.R.A. 47th Div. Front HIGH WOOD supporting 47th Div INFANTRY. Reserve vigilant fires + HIGH WOOD.	
Bottom WOOD	Sept 13.		Batteries carried out harasp active enemy lines + en HIGH WOOD.	

1875 Wt. W593/826 1,000,000 4/15 J.B.C. & A. A.D.S.S./Forms/C.2118.

Army Form C. 2118

WAR DIARY
or
INTELLIGENCE SUMMARY
(Erase heading not required.)

Instructions regarding War Diaries and Intelligence Summaries are contained in F. S. Regs., Part II. and the Staff Manual respectively. Title Pages will be prepared in manuscript.

Place	Date	Hour	Summary of Events and Information	Remarks and references to Appendices
BOTTOM WOOD	Sept	14	Fairly quiet day. Batteries fired a barrage all night (13-14). Registration carried out during the day. Bombardment for 23 minutes beginning from 7 p.m. Fairly quiet day except there was a certain amount of shelling by the enemy. The heavy artillery bombarded High Wood.	
"	"	15	At 6.20 a.m. all our artillery bombarded violently the selected German positions and the 4 Army Offensive commenced. The D. divisions on our Left & right (50 D & N.Z.) made satisfactory progress. The right (Battalion of the 140 Brigade) made progress but the Left Battalion and the 141 R.B. were held up at the start by machine gun fire. At 8 a.m. the artillery again bombarded the enemy front line in HIGH WOOD after which an heavy bombardment the artillery lifted the INFANTRY again attacked & captured the wood chiefly by working round the flanks. A line was then dug running more or less E & W in front of N.E. corner of the wood. At 6.15 p.m. the 23 & 24 attacked the second objective with the 1st Regt on their right. The 2nd Objective was not taken but a new line was dug about 250 yds in front of HIGH WOOD.	

Army Form C. 2118

WAR DIARY
or
INTELLIGENCE SUMMARY
(Erase heading not required.)

Page 6

Place	Date	Hour	Summary of Events and Information	Remarks and references to Appendices
15th cont'd			Were employed F.O.O's. to go forward + find out positions of INFANTRY. A/276, B/276, C/276 Btys moved up during the night to new positions about 500 yds to N.E. of BAZENTIN-LE-PETIT. During the night the enemy shelled BAZENTIN-LE-GRAND + valley running N.W. + S.E. with gas + tear shell. The whole Bn was fairly quiet on this front. Lt Lort B.S.O. to 276 Bde R.F.A. was Liaison Officer to 44th Inf Bde. Lt Blackwell A/276 Bty was awarded the Military Cross.	
MAMETZ WOOD Sept 16	Sept 16		Bde HQ moved to MAMETZ WOOD. The waggon lines moved to BOTTOM WOOD. The day was occupied with enemy in the enemy's lines. Many targets were taken on by us as a result of observation by Major F.O.O. The night passed fairly. Waggon lines moved up to BOTTOM WOOD.	

Army Form C. 2118

WAR DIARY
or
INTELLIGENCE SUMMARY
(Erase heading not required.)

Page 7

Place	Date	Hour	Summary of Events and Information	Remarks and references to Appendices
MAMETZ WOOD	Sept. 17		There was a certain amount of heavy shelling on front but NO INFANTRY action. Lt WHITTEN B/176 Bty was wounded while up at observation station. 2/Lt Searle B/170 Bty slightly wounded but still at duty.	
MAMETZ WOOD	Sept 18.		Our artillery shelled certain parts of the enemy front & prevented him flying stores in in 34 b.12 in the STARFISH LINE. Our INFANTRY made a further bombing attack about 8.30 pm which partially succeeded.	
MAMETZ	Sept 19		Our artillery carried out bombardments according to programme at different periods & in support of Infantry. About 5pm enemy made counter-attack against our infantry in Drop Alley. Our artillery opened fire on S.O.S. lines at once on artillery was reported quiet.	

Army Form C. 2118

Page 8

WAR DIARY
or
INTELLIGENCE SUMMARY
(Erase heading not required.)

Place	Date	Hour	Summary of Events and Information	Remarks and references to Appendices
MAMETZ WOOD	Sept. 20th		Batteries fired on FLERS during the day & on Fleeting targets. 1st Aus: Infantry relieved 47th Aus. Infantry during the night. The weather gradually improving. F.O.O.s continue reconnoitre. The point trench & Howitzer battery fired all night into ENTRECOURT L'ABBAYE.	
"	Sept. 21st		At 3.25 A.M. S.O.S. Signal given. False alarm. At 3.55 A.M. batteries ceased firing. At 10.30 A.M. D/236 fired a burst of 50 rds on row in FLEERS LINE No. S.E. of ENTRECOURT L'ABBAYE. At 11.30 A.M. & 1.30 P.M. 18pdr batteries fired 15 H.E. Shrapnel into ENTRECOURT L'ABBAYE, & 10pdr batteries fired continuously during the night 10pdr batteries fired continuously on FLEERS LINE at 100 rds an hour.	
"	Sept. 22nd		At 10.30 A.M. howitzers batteries commenced firing 50 rds an hour on FLEERS LINE M.29.b.12. & M.23.C.Y.O. (ceased firing at 4.45 pm). At 1 pm transport was seen on BAPAUME-LE SARS road M.6 c.+ M.11.b - heavies informed. Our Infantry (1st Aus) Welsh Regt - occupied PRUE + STARFISH trenches. Patrols sent out in front as far as 700 yds without meeting any resistance.	

WAR DIARY
or
INTELLIGENCE SUMMARY

Army Form C. 2118

Page 9

Place	Date	Hour	Summary of Events and Information	Remarks and references to Appendices
MAMETZ WOOD	Sept 23		Fairly quiet day. Battery did very little firing. The enemy was similarly quiet throughout the afternoon, their artillery being almost entirely silent. At night Battery fired a few rounds on a gunners working party digging a trench.	
	Sept 24		Fairly quiet day. Battery did very little firing except my battery. Hostile artillery very little. B/236 Battery relieved C/236 Battery. A/236 Battery was in action at night at 8.20 pm the 1st Division launched a local attack on the FLERS LINE which proved abortive. Battery fired moderately at 12.30 p.m. the enemy resumed the offensive. The N.Z. Division attacked along the FLERS line & secured their objective with very little trouble. They joined hands with	
	Sept 25th		NEW ZEALANDERS in GOOSE ALLEY. The NZ Division on our right secured all its objectives; our troops securing GRID TRENCH in front of GUEDECOURT, LES BOEUFS, (the NORTH) of MORVAL. The FRENCH secured FREGICOURT and RANCOURT. Battery kept up continuous fire all day on the barrages ordered by A.7 D.A. at night	

WAR DIARY
or
INTELLIGENCE SUMMARY

(Erase heading not required.)

Army Form C. 2118

Page 10

Place	Date	Hour	Summary of Events and Information	Remarks and references to Appendices
MAMETZ WOOD	Sept 26th		D/236 Battery was shelled with lachrymatory & other shells suffering 2 casualties. More or less uneventful day on our front. The CANADIAN CORPS on our left captured THIEPVAL and 1500 prisoners. B Battery assisted by an intense bombardment at 12.35pm for a few minutes on the hostile trenches. At about 7pm D/236 Battery was again shelled. 2/Lt STEPHENSON being wounded & 1 man killed & 5 others wounded. MAJOR POLLARD was slightly wounded in the head but remained at duty. At 11.30pm 1st Division assaulted hostile trench in M29 & but failed chiefly owing to losing their way.	
	27th		47th Division relieved 1st Division in HIGH WOOD sector. day. Batteries lined was shelled except for registration purposes considerably on defensive barrages. There were no infantry operations but counter artillery was fairly active	
	Sept 28th		Fairly quiet day. C/236 Battery staff relieved A/236 Battery staff. It was decided	

WAR DIARY
or
INTELLIGENCE SUMMARY

Army Form C. 2118

Page 11

Place	Date	Hour	Summary of Events and Information	Remarks and references to Appendices
	Sept 29.		during the afternoon that D/236 should change their position & these reached by D/27's Battery R.F.A. Fairly quiet day, Batteries fired on enemies transport.	
	Sept 30		Very quiet day until 5:30 pm when the 141 by Brigade assaulted the hostile trenches in M23c & d & M29 a & b (Pheasdin). They failed to capture their objective. Batteries fired an intense barrage on hostile trenches prior to objectives. D/236 Battery moved in early morning to SQ 823. Hostile artillery fairly active on our trenches in the morning & afternoon. Little anti-aircraft guns very active against our aeroplanes. Major General Sir Charles BARTER & relinquished command of 47 London Division. Batteries fired on transport but there was no infantry action on our front.	

R.C. Owen
Lt. Col.
Commanding 236 Brigade R.F.A.

WAR DIARY or INTELLIGENCE SUMMARY

Army Form C.2118

236 Bde R.H.A.

Place	Date	Hour	Summary of Events and Information	Remarks and references to Appendices
MAMETZ WOOD	Oct 1		At 7 a.m. D/236 began to bombard hostile trenches in & near EAUCOURT L'ABBAYE. Batteries fired a short intense bombardment (runs) at 10/7 a.m. till 10.15 a.m. At 3:15 14/14/ th. assaulted & took EAUCOURT L'ABBAYE in conjunction with on our right. Then encountered hostile fire (but the 26th Rea Infantry on their right) another Battn attacked but the situation still remained obscure.	
	2nd		2 new Battns attacked & partly rectified the situation on the left flank. B 1 section of A/236 & 1 of B/236 moved up to new position A/236 being in the Starfish Valley 200 yds east of sunken road from earlier round (High Wood (M35c5.4) & (5236) near Tank Trench (M36a0.7). Several wagons of the batteries of A/236 was running east of High Wood down the STARFISH LINE. Our gun Sgt stuck on trench in attempt on old position. Hence only 3 guns of brigade in new good event to move.	
	3rd		Position: A/236 Bty 9 Staff returned to B/236 Bty Position 6 hrs. sols/actively shelled up EAUCOURT L'ABBAYE definitely captured & in day-out & should be silent. The wagons that stuck were all German hand & 3 mm guns brought down to the new position station down & dusk. Fairly quiet day.	

WAR DIARY or INTELLIGENCE SUMMARY

Army Form C. 2118

Page 2

Place	Date	Hour	Summary of Events and Information	Remarks and references to Appendices
MAMETZ WOOD	Oct 4		Very quiet day on our front; no infantry action at all. A/237 Batty & C Batty had no guns in new position & B Batty has 4. Light very bad, but some registration done by the batteries.	
	Oct 5		Rained most of the day. Decided to move H.Q. to new position at S10c 4.6 on road running from LONGUEVAL – CONTALMAISON ROAD to EAST CORNER of HIGH WOOD. Hostile artillery active on the 14a, NE of HIGH WOOD. Nothing of any great importance.	
BAZENTIN-LE-GRAND (HIGHWOOD (EAST) ROAD (S10c 4.6)	Oct 6.		Brigade H.Q. Moved to new position on east side of HIGHWOOD (S10c 4.6) from LONGUEVAL – CONTALMAISON ROAD. The C/236 Batty was shelled in their new position with 5.9 and 8" and had to evacuate it. Gnr Green E.J.B. was killed and one wounded (Sgt ? hour). Two or Three other men bruised but were seen fully duty-out and remained at duty. Batteries fired on ordered barrages. A/236 Battery relieved C/236 Battery in their position with B/236 Battery & their horses. At 10.45 p.m. 47th Division ordered A/236 to send N.C.O. to sign for GIRD LINE & BUTTE DE WARLENCOURT. The 137th Batts all left platoons & when objectives & after several unsuccessful attacks with a few parties who did manage to get to the outer lip of the attack was in a whole unsuccessful any little ground was saved. Batteries fired continuously on barrages ordered by Div.Arty.	
	Oct 7		Lt J. F. GAYMER proceeded to Field Ambulance still suffering from effect of being wounded by bullets howich in Contamination road.	

Lt J.F. GAYMER
2/Lt D.D. WALLACE A.D.S.S.

WAR DIARY or INTELLIGENCE SUMMARY

Army Form C. 2118

Page 3

Place	Date	Hour	Summary of Events and Information	Remarks and references to Appendices
BAZENTIN LE GRAND — BAZENTIN HIGHWOOD ROAD	Oct 8	8ᵃ	236ᵗʰ Bde RFA were relieved by 237 Bde at RFA, A/236, D/236 Battery remained in action with 237 Brigade R.F.A.; D/235 Battery was taken over in entirety by 236ᵗʰ Brigade RFA, all batteries took up their waggonlines in BOTTOM WOOD except C/236 Battery which took over C/237 gun position near MARLBORO' WOOD and kept in charge of the Light guns of 47 Div Arty. D/235 Battery acts as Light Howitzer battery. Brigade Head waggon lines moved to 237 Brigade Headquarters near MAMETZ.	
MAMETZ	Oct 9	9ᵃ	The enemy shewed guns + howitzers passed through our hands.	
"	Oct 10	10ᵃ	No events of any importance. C/236 Battery widely shewed itself at old position at BAZENTIN-LE-PETIT WINDMILL and took ammunition up to the 237 Battery positions.	
"	Oct 11		Nothing of any importance.	
"	Oct 12	12ᵖ	Battalion parties proceeded to BEAUCOURT the 47 Div Arty being relieved by the 9ᵗʰ Div Arty. The 51ˢᵗ Bde RFA (A Corps) took

WAR DIARY
or
INTELLIGENCE SUMMARY.

Army Form C. 2118.

Page 4

Place	Date	Hour	Summary of Events and Information	Remarks and references to Appendices
MAMETZ	Oct 12		Own form the 236 Brigade RFA. Lt Col A.C. LOWE D.S.O. proceeded on leave of absence to England.	
	Oct 13		Preparation for relief. The Brigade left wagon lines at BOTTOM WOOD at 4:30pm arriving at BEAUCOURT at 1.30am	
BEAUCOURT	Oct 14		Spent the day at BEAUCOURT. Billeting parties proceeded to TALMAS.	
TALMAS	Oct 15		Brigade marched to TALMAS. Billeting parties proceeded to AMPLIER.	
AMPLIER	Oct 16		Brigade marched to AMPLIER.	
AUBROMETZ	Oct 17		Brigade marched to AUBROMETZ. Billeting parties proceeding ahead of column. The Bedford Yeomanry were in the town but after a little trouble the Brigade got in very comfortably.	
BERGUENEUSE	Oct 18		Brigade marched to BERGUENEUSE. Billeting parties proceeding ahead of column. Best villages in hands of troops. Billeted in	
CREQUES	Oct 19		Billeting parties again rode on ahead of the column. Brigade marched to CREQUES near AIRE-SUR-LA-LYS.	
(BELGIUM) (S/WATOU)	Oct 20		Brigade marched into billets near in BELGIUM about 5 miles W.S.W. of POPERINGHE & about 1 mile S. of WATOU on the WATOU - ABEELE ROAD.	

WAR DIARY
INTELLIGENCE SUMMARY

Pop'S

Place	Date	Hour	Summary of Events and Information	Remarks and references to Appendices
BELGIUM (Salt Water)	Oct 21		One section of each battery moved up to relieve the 10th, 11th, 12th, 14th Batty's & 104th Howitzer Battery belonging to the 2nd Australian Div Arty. One battery of the 238th Brigade was left & the 236 Brigade for this purpose.	
ZILLEBEKE BUND	Oct 22		Remaining sections moved up into action and Bde H.Q. 236Bde was attached to 47 Div and form part of a composite artillery group covering 23rd Division. LT. COL A.S. LOWE D.S.O is in command of RA, 23rd Div, in rather the composite group representing same, LT G. LYON-SMITH also being at RA 23rd Div. MAJOR A.C. GORDON DSO is in command of RIGHT Bde consisting of 236 Fd. RFA. and B/238 Battery RFA with HQ at ZILLEBEKE BUND. RAHQ at RENINGHELST and 47 RA HQ at HOOGRAAF.	
	Oct 23rd Oct 24th		Nothing of any importance. Batteries registered. Very little firing. A certain amount of movement in our our zone which extends from Hull (3700) CLONMEL COPSE to just north of 2WA BTE LEE N Batteries going through in order from the north A/236, B/236, C/236, A/238. Very little activity. C/238 added to RT. BRIGADE. This battery commanded	
	Oct 25			

WAR DIARY
INTELLIGENCE SUMMARY

Army Form C. 2118.
Page 6

Place	Date	Hour	Summary of Events and Information	Remarks and references to Appendices
ZILLEBEKE RUND			by MAJOR DIGBY. LEFT BRIGADE consists of remainder of 180B & 12P Awdr. the command of MAJOR STEBBING. RT DG HQ shifted to LILLE GATE	
LILLE GATE	Oct 26		Combined movement of attack by the enemy from about 12 noon to 3 pm. Batteries fired in retaliation. Nothing else of much importance.	
	Oct 27		Very quiet day. Batteries only fired in retaliation. BELGIAN INTERPRETER attached 6th Brigade. The front interpreter M. CHAPAIR returned after his away some weeks with a Frenel Corps Headquarters. Very quiet day until about 2 pm when the hostile movement from the western activity between affectively silenced by our Howitzer Battery.	
	Oct 28			
	Oct 29 Oct 30		Nothing of very great importance. Some hostile movement. Gnl Fraser called arty to memory. Nothing of any importance occurred. Very little hostile activity over also. artillery intervene movement activity. Quiet day. Very little firing by batteries except for a little retaliation on c/180 Corps went nomad Batteries...	
	Oct 31			

[signatures]

236th Bde RFA November 1916

Vol 2

WAR DIARY or INTELLIGENCE SUMMARY

Place	Date	Hour	Summary of Events and Information	Remarks and references to Appendices
YPRES LILLE GATE	Nov 1		Quiet day with work. Considerable trench mortar activity on our right. Batteries fired in retaliation only.	
"	2		Light trench mortar activity on our front or regiment. Some trench mortar and artillery activity displayed on our front about 1 p.m. Batteries D/236 battery fired in retaliation. In the night	
"	4		Quiet day until about 8.30 p.m. when there was heavy hostile mortar activity on the right portion of our front (DAVISON STREET, WINNIPEG ST, CRAB CRAWL and SANCTUARY WOOD). Batteries fired in retaliation and eventually stopped the enemy's fire.	
"	3		At about 4.30 p.m. enemy fired some trench mortars on (CRAB CRAWL) but was stopped by the retaliation of C/180.	
"	5		Fairly quiet day. Some movement on roads in the batteries only fired in retaliation.	
"	6		Pretty much the same, B/236 spotted 4 new minenwerfers in afternoon. It was decided that D/236 Brigade should be reorganised into 2 six gun batteries and 2 four gun 4.5 How batteries	

Army Form C. 2118.

WAR DIARY
or
INTELLIGENCE SUMMARY.
(Erase heading not required.)

Instructions regarding War Diaries and Intelligence Summaries are contained in F.S. Regs., Part II. and the Staff Manual respectively. Title pages will be prepared in manuscript.

Place	Date	Hour	Summary of Events and Information	Remarks and references to Appendices
YPRES	Nov 7		Practically nothing happened all day	
LILLEBATH	" 8		A little shelling took place on the German side but very little happened otherwise.	
	" 9		Maj-General Gorring came round the Batteries in the afternoon. Very quiet day and only about 5 minenwerfer were fired by the enemy all afternoon only from CLONMEL COPSE.	
	" 10		Reorganisation Battery came into effect. Battery at Noon, with enemy's retaliation. Day very quiet except for some light minnenwerfer fire by enemy at night.	
	" 11		Nothing quiet. At 8 pm enemy opened fire on CRAB CRAWL with TM? trifle grenade. We retaliated sharply but enemy kept on at intervals until 5.35 pm.	
	12		O.C. 128 Trench Mortar Battery went round and inspected in morning to advise on drainage and points in trenches. Visited Valeric OP. also visited new observation of O.P. on verge. Situation normal until 3pm when T/M activity opened from the light intended Late Lusen enemy did not give up until 5.35 pm in spite of sharp retaliation	

T2134. Wt. W708—776. 500000. 4/15. Sir J. C. & S.

WAR DIARY
or
INTELLIGENCE SUMMARY

Army Form C. 2118.

Place	Date	Hour	Summary of Events and Information	Remarks and references to Appendices
Ypres	12/1/16	6 p.m.	Had visitors 12/1/16. Major P.J. Shaffer went to 3rd/3rd on relief of G.R.A.	
	13/1/16	6 p.m.	Visibility good. Shelling as usual in Comparatively inactively of Hostile T.M.? Fog lifted on thickened. Several working parts. A/26 burriedrepeato of 2nd Sub Group. Our aeroplane active: one hostile came over 5 p.m. but soon sheared off.	
	14/1/16	10 p.m.	During morning intermittent shelling of SANCTUARY WOOD, MAPLE COPSE, LILLE GATE, YPRES with M.M. T.M.? Batteries fired in reply. 12 noon Gun limber again. At 2 p.m. hostile T.M.? active a light flotsam speed to our zone at 4.5 p.m. We retaliated with 50-45. + 80 15 p.m. in sharp bursts. The enemy fell our 5 p.m. F.O.O. then seen T20A94 dressed in blue uniform disappeared. Six men in gap J16 1055. Stokes Mortars dropped with 18 r.a. as they turned back along sap. Considerable movement of men in huts on road T21A17 - T27A05. Squad of men seen at TOWER HAMLETS but disappeared quickly.	
	15/1/16		Mortars, light & heavy switches by actually firing and exchange of fire probably. Div Zone. Day generally quiet. Bombardment of M.O.V.T provoked lively retaliation. At 2.30 hostile aeroplane humbly destroyed, manoeuvred Archive Our machine flew almost unmolested 1500 feet over I 26, 27 MAPLE COTTAGES New survey work at I9a & 14 v.I 30 & 30 in progress. Retaliation zone after new battle Phase Supple Offensive sapping operation, retaliate in line as probably	

WAR DIARY
or
INTELLIGENCE SUMMARY

Army Form C. 2118.

Place	Date	Hour	Summary of Events and Information	Remarks and references to Appendices
	16/11/16		being to damp our front line trench round House Slope & Ship Rabbit. Weather excellent. Enemy unusual distinct shelling. Hostile aeroplane again active during afternoon. Level crossing I.14.d.45 & Shrapnel Corner Hell Fire Corner Zillebeke shelled with 77s & 15cm. Enemy 15cm T.M. generally unusually active. Proper bombardment of I.30.c.9.0 fell through owing to failure of communication.	
	17/11/16		Several T.M. emplacements registered. At 11.30 A.M. bombardment of I.30.6.80 branch carried out by No.26 T.M.B. After 3 rds were fired it being cleared No shoot very satisfactory shoot. Several hits obtained and four bomb stores of wood revetment being thrown into the air. Shew up the work wrecked. S8 Pound fired all rounds for first fire. Visibility poor generally. 4.2 gun active & showing a marked spot. Some activity with T.Ms. a bit S side. New M.G. by the Dump. Remainder of S.W.O.T.	
	18/11/16		4.30 by 18 pr Heavies. Pamba no retaliation. 4.6 Heavies did. Register for special operation carried out in evening but T.M. retaliation active all day. At 10.15pm Enemy T.M. retaliated but stopped at once on our firing between CLONMEL COPSE. 3.50pm T.M. active again. Retaliation at first ineffective because	
	19/11/16			

T2134. Wt. W708-776. 500000. 4/15. Sir J. C. & S.

WAR DIARY
INTELLIGENCE SUMMARY

Place	Date	Hour	Summary of Events and Information	Remarks and references to Appendices
Ypres	30/11/16		too dispersed. Send retaliation wells grouped. Hows & T.Ms effectively silenced enemy. Enemy T.Ms fired from about TIGER 27.30.b.60. B&D carried Registration on new works. D/236 report hr work at his points. Enemy shelled I.27.d.9.8 for first time for about 3weeks, but except for slight T.M. activity at 3pm day was quiet. D report 3/27.b.blah visibility bad all day which was quite.	
	2/11/16		Raid attempted at 11.30 pm on CROSS TRENCH against T.27.d.45.55 failed owing to wire not being completely cut by the Bungalow Tulle. Contricrs reports Belt Down. 18 Sep Artillery Barrage had almost immediately to lift it again. This was done very quickly in each case communication being excellent. Full programme was carried out by Artillery after abandonment of raid. went to all wire for CRAB CRAWL being broken. The remainder barrage appeared to be very effective. Enemy retaliated with T.Ms only on trenches & 9mm behind. Batteries engaged A/80, B/236, C/236 C/188. M/236. Retaliation of 12 pr Battery took place at WOOD 21, thus: Right Section C/236 to B/236. Left Section C/236 to A/236. B.9. N.S. continued to their rates. No made formal enquiries for C/236 under B major time.	

WAR DIARY
or
INTELLIGENCE SUMMARY

Army Form C. 2118.

Place	Date	Hour	Summary of Events and Information	Remarks and references to Appendices
Ypres	22		Visibility bad and day quiet. At 5.30 P.M. a party of 12 Germans came over opposite Cross Roads C.9.c.6.1. and attempted to throw bombs. These all fell short & they retired into C.I.3.	
	23.		Enemy began their Counter Bombardment programme in the morning. 10.30 A.M. Enemy Wolfe his custom about 30 bombs on our trenches. I.01 d.5.3 & I.24d.5.4. group of pinmp and Scheme 2 for Bombardment of T.M.S. was ordered at 10.50. Left B & Glenor. did not fire but C/180 carried out programme. Heavy because annoyed at 11.20 opened a heavy T.M. fire on our trenches. Retaliation Scheme 2 ordered again. The time all batteries fired and at 12.30 enemy was silenced for the day. No Right Group zone enemy T.M.s were very active from 1.45 to 2.15 P.M. from S.W. out to DUMP. This he put R.30 3pm 5.45 P.M. will subdue by 4.3 pm. Retaliation officially ordered but S.O. A.S.C. 3.20 insist that O. Battery should draw it on return.	
	24.		Hostile T.M.S became active 2.50. Scheme 2 was ordered. Enemy fire as	

WAR DIARY
or
INTELLIGENCE SUMMARY.
(Erase heading not required.)

Army Form C. 2118.

Place	Date	Hour	Summary of Events and Information	Remarks and references to Appendices
Ypres	24		He appeared to retaliate for Sheeme's further right. At 3.50 Scherens was ordered from offectus, but almost immediately a heavy Barbard. burst both on front KNOLL ROAD to the Dump & the enemy having TH 4.2's & 7.7m.m. Divn on Right Retaliated in its Sector just by 4.45 p.m.	
	25		Infantry Officers ordered to A&B Batteries for the direction. Bulletin did not file observation being bad.	
	26		Morning very quiet until 11 A.M. when 5 - 59's fell near BLAUPOORT FARM. Gas Shell fire upon at 12.30. Heavier with fires South bearing from a Battery suspected to have remained fire. Retaliation shoot made from T.28 D.S.8, approx at a band of VERBRANDENMOLEN HILL to cover AR.A.A6.11 OD, OBS + Yeomany P. Ridge. from 10 A.M. 1 P.M. the Dump hir shelled with high S.g. at one round per minute.	
	27		C/130 dispersed working party at T.19.39.1. Between 11.25 a.m. & 12.15 p.m. D/225 registered by aeroplane. Usual scattered hostile Shelling. Fine day but low cloud interfere with aeroplane observation.	

Place	Date	Hour	Summary of Events and Information	Remarks and references to Appendices
Ypres	27		Reorganisation came into force at noon. 9/236 officially disappeared 523 the Battery known as 9/236 ceases to be. Ammunition Parties 9/226 B.C. Though it remained Custodial as before.	
	28		Shells for powered observation today very quiet. 9/80 fired & round of blast reported by F.O.O.	
	29		2.50pm – 3.30pm Hostile T.M.'s became active against T.30.A. believe it was enemy trench was filled in. heavy thr approved by Artillery. SANCTUARY WOOD but in twelve by our L.A.G.T.M. Shoots were provided on eastern suspender line Enemy to DMC, tia., trench, part, phones.	
	30		9/236 Dispersal for special operator. 9/236 dispersed to all batteries firing at T.195.E.9 gas hombs. 11.30 am 4.9 How. was active along OBSERVATION RIDGE and down to VALLEY COTTAGES. Visibility fair to our throughout.	3

Army Form C. 2118.

Vol 22

WAR DIARY
or
INTELLIGENCE SUMMARY.
(Erase heading not required.)

CONFIDENTIAL

WAR DIARY

of the

235th Brigade, Royal Field Artillery

from Dec 1st 1916 — Dec 31st 1916

Army Form C. 2118.

WAR DIARY
INTELLIGENCE SUMMARY.
(Erase heading not required.)

Instructions regarding War Diaries and Intelligence Summaries are contained in F. S. Regs., Part II. and the Staff Manual respectively. Title pages will be prepared in manuscript.

Place	Date	Hour	Summary of Events and Information	Remarks and references to Appendices
YPRES	Dec 1st		236 Bde RGA still covering the 23rd Division for Special operations. Heavy and 15 batteries registered. Heavy visual observation impossible. Enemy Artillery & T.Ms. were very quiet. At 12.30 p.m. a raid was	Our map references Our ZILLEBEKE Ed. 3. E. 1/10.000
	Night 1st/2nd		attempted by the 11th SHERWOOD FORESTERS on S.P. at I.30. b. 15.20: this was not successful	and Sheet 28 1/40,000
	Dec 2nd		No firing. Much mist	
	Dec 3rd		Batteries did not fire. Visibility bad. Ov. T.Ms were active, both heavy and medium. The enemy did not retaliate. At 3 A.M. in the morning the Observing Officer reported T.Ms active. At 2.30 AM a successful raid was carried out at I.19.c.15.55. Our damage silenced the enemy fire.	
	Dec 4th		Visibility good. All batteries carefully checked map and overranges. Considerable enemy subsequent fire behind the enemy line. Working parties were dispersed by A/236 Battery. 2 salvos falling amongst them — after this no further movement was observed. "Barrage Z" by half 47th Division, was ordered at 3.1pm — successful.	

WAR DIARY or INTELLIGENCE SUMMARY

Army Form C. 2118.

Place	Date	Hour	Summary of Events and Information	Remarks and references to Appendices
YPRES	Dec. 5th		Visibility good in the morning. D/226 Battery registered a single gun at I.20.b.95.95. Working party at J.14.b. fired on and dispersed, a direct hit was obtained on a wheelbarrow they were using. T.M's active. A salvo of trench mortars between 1.15 & 1.30pm and 3.30pm and 3.35pm. Scheme 4 was ordered and silenced the enemy fire at 3.40pm. Increased hostile artillery activity behind our lines – L'Ecole, ZILLEBEKE village & Station were shelled with 4.2's. YPRES Square, Station crossing and MENIN road shelled with 4.2's at 5pm. Direct hits by S.G's were obtained on ZILLEBEKE Lake duck boards, HELLBLAST CORNER and the BUND.	
	Dec. 6th		Visibility fair. Morning quiet. Hostile T.M's opened fire as typical on CRAB CRAWL & WINNIPEG St. at 1pm. Scheme 2 successfully silenced them.	
	Dec. 7th		Morning quiet. At 2pm T.M's active on I.30.a. Scheme 4 was effective in silencing them. Visibility bad – owing to the mist. An enemy stationary engine was heard working near STIRLING CASTLE. Another was heard at 4pm behind BODMIN COPSE.	

WAR DIARY
or
INTELLIGENCE SUMMARY.
(Erase heading not required.)

Army Form C. 2118.

(3)

Place	Date	Hour	Summary of Events and Information	Remarks and references to Appendices
YPRES	Dec 8th		Visibility again bad. At 1.25pm hostile weapons T.Ms opened fire on WINNIPEG St - Scheme 2 was ordered. Counter-battery fire before the scheme (with Heavy Artillery) was put into force - but the enemy did not persist. Enemy Artillery inactive.	
	Dec 9th		During the morning considerable enemy movement was seen CASTLE at J.13.d.4.5 & at TOWER HAMLETS. When parties were fired on and dispersed. Engine again heard as leaving tanks from I.24.d.7.71. A/230 battery carried out carft registration on guns. Hostile fire 5.9(how) battery firing on DICKEBUSCH was observed 140°?(true) from I.24.d.7.3. Four rows flash to sound, 12½ seconds. Five edges observed. A large tower-like edifice about 40ft high. Construction ?poles with 3 looped strands roundthem, true bearing 32° from I.24.d.70.35. It has no platform working parties at J.13.d.30.15. 3 time disposed by A/235 battery with casualties. Hostile balloon up towards 8pm. At 9pm a hostile hostile aeroplane came over BLAUWE PORT Farm. Lewis battery fired on it but was not seen again a few were shelled.	

T2184. Wt. W708-776. 500000. 4/15. Sir J. C. & S.

Army Form C. 2118.

WAR DIARY
or
INTELLIGENCE SUMMARY.
(Erase heading not required.)

Place	Date	Hour	Summary of Events and Information	Remarks and references to Appendices
YPRES	Dec 12th		Visibility very poor. None of the trench mortars fired. Enemy also very quiet. During the morning the 2nd Army Commander visited all batteries and trench mortar posts. What he saw.	
	Dec 13th		Unusual enemy activity. At 9 am enemy T.M's opened fire from between 2 & Contoured intermittently until 12 noon. A 7" trench mortar of C Sup. this fire. At 1.40pm enemy made special bombardment of C Sup. About 2pm hostile T.M's was again active and spread down towards HEDGE STREET. Trench mortars at once put in operation after which there was no further activity.	
	Dec 14th		Morning - hostile At 3pm Division on our right bombarded Hill 60 & the SALIENT - we co-operated on the front. Enemy retaliated at 3.25 pm. D/23b shewed a heavy T.M. Shewed was opened live _ this seemed to have was effective. Much movement seen on TOWER HAMLETS road.	
	Dec 15th		An eventful day. From 7 am to 9.40 am enemy bombarded whole of trench system, paying especial attention to but front HEDGE ST to CANAL. TRENCH mortars retaliated vigorously. Considerable damage done to our trenches.	

Army Form C. 2118.

WAR DIARY
or
INTELLIGENCE SUMMARY.
(Erase heading not required.)

(5)

Place	Date	Hour	Summary of Events and Information	Remarks and references to Appendices
YPRES (continued)	Dec 15th		At 7pm the enemy commenced another bombardment this time accompanied by artillery "barrage" all batteries stood to about 40 gunners advanced against Sap 5. S.O.S. rockets were fired and our barrage opened which the rocket was sent in the air. This barrage came down on the enemy in No Man's Land and inflicted casualties. The enemy at once left our trenches and returned to his own. No more Germans attempted to reach the parapets. No General Dead Germans were left in our trench & on the parapets. No casualties were suffered.	
	Dec 16th		Enemy Artillery fairly active in back area. Rifle grenades beyond our Right. D/236 Batty fired 106 rounds at 3.30pm in cooperation with planes of Division in an "Cgw" (4th?) Aeroplanes active on both sides.	
	Dec 17th		Very quiet day. Poor visibility.	
	Dec 18th		Again very quiet. Batteries calibrated	
	Dec 19th		At 9.50 A.M. D/236 Batty fired an 4 dispersed contact park. At 3.15 p.m. M/236 fired on new M.G. emplacement on D.P at J.19.C.10.65 for interest	

Army Form C. 2118.

WAR DIARY
or
INTELLIGENCE SUMMARY.
(Erase heading not required.)

Instructions regarding War Diaries and Intelligence Summaries are contained in F. S. Regs., Part II. and the Staff Manual respectively. Title pages will be prepared in manuscript.

Place	Date	Hour	Summary of Events and Information	Remarks and references to Appendices
YPRES (Continued)	Dec 19th (continued)		effect. A lot of work is being done here.	
	Dec 20th	10 AM to 11.30 AM	Enemy bombarded our trenches with T.M.s however he retaliated. S/236 firing 120 rds. Heavy + Counter Groups Cooperated. G.O.C. 23rd Division asked for a further bombardment at 3.30 pm - this was carried out on enemy front supp. or line opposite STEWART STREET & considerable damage was done to the enemy's works.	
	Dec 21st		Day normal. Slight artillery activity on usual places. 18/236 trench deepened a working party.	
	Dec 22nd		Our front was very quiet all day. Considerable activity on our right. At 2.30pm about 77mm battery was seen in action from S. Peter's St. 1762. This battery shells Yeomanry Post + Observatory Ridge (tree) from 1.29.d.6.1.	
	Dec 23rd		Day was quiet except for slight activity from TM was outposts working parties seen and dispersed by our fire.	
	Dec 24th		Enemy artillery activity on Railway Dugouts + Duckboards. Counter Batteries engaged his battery shelling these places & enemy ceased fire at 5 pm.	

T2134. Wt. W708—776. 500000. 4/15. Sir J. C. & S.

WAR DIARY
or
INTELLIGENCE SUMMARY

Army Form C. 2118.

Place	Date	Hour	Summary of Events and Information	Remarks and references to Appendices
YPRES	Dec 25th		XMAS DAY. All very quiet during the morning. D/236 batty fired at intervals throughout the day on working parties at J.20.d.77 firing 36 rounds. A/6 firing on two occasions. Stretcher parties were seen & finally a large horse ambulance drawn up & after [illeg] the Bordeaux at ZILLEBEKE & YPRES SQUARE were shelled with 4.5 how and A2s repeatedly.	
	Dec 26th		Very quiet all day. Observation balloons to two Battery Commanders of relieving Brigade — 103 Bde RFA — came up early. At 10 am a German fighting aeroplane came over our lines & shot down one of our planes near GORDON HOUSE. The four sections of the 103 Bde returned reliefs for actions as soon as it will be dark enough.	

WAR DIARY
or
INTELLIGENCE SUMMARY.
(Erase heading not required.)

Army Form C. 2118.

(8)

Place	Date	Hour	Summary of Events and Information	Remarks and references to Appendices
Ypres	Dec 27th		Slight trench mortar activity in the morning 4.5 hours. The remainder of the day was quiet. Completion of relief - the remaining 2 sections of each battery moved in. Relief was completed by 9 pm when command of Ypres sector, Artillery Group was handed over to O.C. 103 Bde R.F.A. 23rd D.A. During the day the remaining ordnance wagons moved to rest billets at WINNEZEELE & OUDEZEELE. Lt Col R.C. ADYE D.S.O. assumed command of the brigade from Lieut. Col of Lowry Smith retired to advance Brigade Major of Lowry Group R.A.	
WINNEZEELE	Dec 28th		Brigade in billets at WINNEZEELE & OUDEZEELE. All moves were 9.9." under Cover	
"	Dec 29 30 31st		Refitting Sector Commanders' inspections Xmas festivities held late, owing to the fact that the relief was taking place on the 25th & the day after.	

M.Lo...
Lt Col RA
Cmdg 236 Brigade R.F.A.

236 Bde RFA.

1917

Index..............

SUBJECT.

No.	Contents.	Date.
	YPRES, 1914 — Cavalry Corps Dispositions, 21/X/ — 11/XI/1914	21 Oct. 30 Oct. 1 Nov. 5 Nov. 11 Nov.

J S
Southern Devon
Church April 1919

236th Brigade R.F.A. WAR DIARY January 1917

Army Form C. 2118

Vol 23

Place	Date	Hour	Summary of Events and Information	Remarks and references to Appendices
1917 WINNEZEELE	Jan 1st		Batteries with exception of C/236 battery in action but left gun of D.A. Continued training in Reserve Area. 2/Lr A. Morton Coke posted to L B/236 batty.	
	Jan 2nd to 10		} Training Continued	
	Jan 21			
	Jan 11th		D/236 Batt. went up into action.	
	Jan 15th		Lt Col A.C. Lowe D.S.O. leaving 236th Brigade, assumed command of 116 Brigade	
	Jan 1st		BIRTHDAY HONOURS Major P.J. Clifton (now B/235 batty) — D.S.O. 2/Lt J.C. Corran — Military Cross Lt Col A.C. Lowe D.S.O. (commanding) } mentioned in Dispatches Lt G. Lyon Smith (Adjutant) }	
	Jan 21		236 Brigade R.F.A. relieved 238 Brigade R.F.A. and known as Left Group. 47 D.A. covering Hill 60. and the front from I35a20 40 to I29d0050	

WAR DIARY
INTELLIGENCE SUMMARY

Place	Date	Hour	Summary of Events and Information	Remarks and references to Appendices
YPRES	Jan 21st		The Infantry in the Line covered by Left Group was the 140th Brigade. Right Battalion 7th London Regiment and the Left Battalion 8th London Regiment. On the Left Flank the 23rd Division with the 7th Brigade in the line and on the Right flank 142 Brigade. 47th Divn Infantry. One section of the Batteries of the Brigade relieved 238 Brigade on the night of 20/21 January and the remaining sections relieved on the night of the 21/22nd. The relief was complete at 7.35 pm. At the same time there was taking place a reorganization of the 47th D.A. was taking place in which the 238 Brigade was split up. Some of the Batteries going to the 41st Division with others were used to bring the Batteries of 235 + 236 Brigades to six gun batteries. C/238 Battery (18 pr.) was transferred in its entirety to make C/236 Battery. While the previous C/236 (4.5 How) was sent to 41st Divn Less one section which was absorbed in A/236. Left Group. Consists of :— A/B/C/ D/236 Batteries V.47. Trench mortar Battery. 2 inch Heavy. V.47	

Army Form C. 2118.

WAR DIARY
or
INTELLIGENCE SUMMARY.
(Erase heading not required.)

Place	Date	Hour	Summary of Events and Information	Remarks and references to Appendices
YPRES  1917	Jan 22nd		The Brigade checked zero lines and registrations, A Job S.O.S was received by the Batteries of the Brigade and the lines averaged 2 minutes. Lt Lyon-Smith left for England on Jan 21st 1917. Lt Canham his medical duties yet. M.O. Haskell R.F.A.(S.R) Acting Adjutant. On the night of 22/23 1st Battalion relieved 7th Battalion and 13th Battalion relieved 8th Battalion	
	23rd		Bombardment of enemy front line system and communication trenches by the Division in conjunction with the M.A. was carried out. The Enemies retaliation to this Bombardment was slight. The effect of the Bombardment was good as his front and communication trenches were admittedly knocked about. Lt Hillair 1 Fr Battery (wounded), (the Park Y.T.M.B. wounded). Casualties. The lines above.	
	24th		We were received by the Brigade. The previous list S.o.S. No test S.o.S.	
	25th		Improvement over the previous test S.o.S. Hostile artillery (77mm 4.1 cm and 5.9 cm) bombarded B/76 Battery and D/76 at Woodcote House and vicinity with about 300 rounds causing 4 casualties (3 in "D" and 1 in "B") all slight. 3 direct hits were obtained on pits but only 1 gun was put out of action. A barrage was put on fishes kondestrait followed at 4 x 75 metres.	

WAR DIARY or INTELLIGENCE SUMMARY

Army Form C. 2118.

Place	Date	Hour	Summary of Events and Information	Remarks and references to Appendices
YPRES	Jan 26th		Our Artillery registration and calibration 2 red S.O.S.'s were received and the average time was about 1 minute. Casualties 1 otherrank. 2/Lt L.G. Tansley R.F.A. assumed the Adjutancy and 742 M.B. Nashall became N.C.O. for	
	27th		The four Batteries of the Brigade in conjunction with the 1 and V Bties of Trench Mortars and the Batteries of R.G.A. Group and Corps Heavy Artillery carried out a bombardment lasting from 1.12 noon to 7.30 PM onto the hostile trenches on the 167 Group front with special reference to enemy O.P.s. 2nd Lt O. Payne (late 123 Howr Bty) posted to D/236 with effect from 26/1/17	
	28th		The Batteries of the Group took part in a Test S.O.S. at 8.9 PM C/236 Battery at LANGHOF FARM was shelled during the day.	
	29th		2nd Lieut R.S. Ayers transferred from 235 Brigade R.F.A. to C/236 Battery with effect from todays date. C/236 Battery and vicinity was shelled during the afternoon with 300 to 400 rounds — no casualties	

Army Form C. 2118.

WAR DIARY
or
INTELLIGENCE SUMMARY.
(Erase heading not required.)

Place	Date	Hour	Summary of Events and Information	Remarks and references to Appendices
YPRES	Jan 30"		Two test S.O.S. calls were fired on by the Group, one at 12.10 AM and one at 3.12 AM. Y Battery never returned sufficient to fire and must be damaged somewhere. Enemy firing on Battery Posn of 38 Mtn now with the Group working on visual reinforcement positions.	
	Jan 31"		All quiet	

R L Lowe
Maj. LRA.
Cmdg 236th Brigade R.F.A.

Confidential

Vol 24

WAR DIARY
OF
236 BRIGADE RFA

1-2-17 to 28-2-17

WAR DIARY
or
INTELLIGENCE SUMMARY.
(Erase heading not required.)

Army Form C. 2118.

Place	Date	Hour	Summary of Events and Information	Remarks and references to Appendices
YPRES	Feb 1st		Enemy Artillery very active - ended on Buck areas and Batteries. A Bty SOS called was received by the Troops at 9.11 PM and all Batteries tried 2nd artillery two minutes. 2nd Lt D.S. Culverwell was transferred from C/256 Battery to the A/ "D" Bde. with effect from 31/1/1.	
	Feb 2nd		The G.O.C. Division visited B, C and D Batteries at midday.	
	Feb 3rd		V Trench Mortar Battery bombarded the enemy's frontline across the RAILWAY CUTTING with 60 rounds - no retaliation of importance.	
	Feb 4th		Bombardment of small area of enemy's trenches EAST of the SNOUT at 3 PM - lasting until 4 PM - by Corps Heavy Artillery and 4.5 Howitzer Battery including D/236 which fired 180 rounds. Moderate Trench Mortar Battery with 35 rounds and A Battery shelled enemy OPs during the bombardment. Much damage done - enemy retaliated with eight guns only. Relief by X Trench Mortar Battery of V Battery in the Line. 2/Lt F.A. de B. Neal (D Bty) evacuated sick.	

WAR DIARY
or
INTELLIGENCE SUMMARY.
(Erase heading not required.)

Army Form C. 2118.

Instructions regarding War Diaries and Intelligence Summaries are contained in F.S. Regs., Part II. and the Staff Manual respectively. Title pages will be prepared in manuscript.

Place	Date	Hour	Summary of Events and Information	Remarks and references to Appendices
YPRES	Feb 5th	6ᵃ	2nd Lt H.V. Ramsey attached to F.A. on T.3.17 whilst on 47 D.A. course. D/236 Howitzer Battery from 2.40 to 3.40 P.M. continued bombardment with 2.3" D.A. and Corps Heavy Artillery onto area of trenches immediately SOUTH of "STIRLING CASTLE" on 25 DM front. C/236 Battery fired 100 rounds in enfilade through enemy's wire carrying bombardment of T.4 not EAST of the "SPOIL". All quiet. Registration by battery.	
		7ᵃ	2nd Lt H.V. Ramsey proceeded onto Personnel Area, not Aeroplane Co-operation work. Cart by D/236 Battery to Conduit Battery horse. Small enemy work suspected.	
		8ᵃ	enemy machineguns concealed by truck mortar Battery with 60 rounds - many direct hits obtained.	
		9ᵃ	At 8.30 P.M. the enemy Trench heavy strafed fire on old Battalion front. Corps Batteries replied accurate also was asked for increasing to SOS fire at 8.50 in answer to SOS call from Rgt / Battalion. The hostile fire soon died down.	

Army Form C. 2118.

WAR DIARY
or
INTELLIGENCE SUMMARY.
(Erase heading not required.)

Instructions regarding War Diaries and Intelligence Summaries are contained in F. S. Regs., Part II. and the Staff Manual respectively. Title pages will be prepared in manuscript.

Place	Date	Hour	Summary of Events and Information	Remarks and references to Appendices
YPRES	Feb. 10		The Field Marshall Commander-in-Chief awarded the French decoration "Medaille Militaire" to Corporal N.R. Noel HQ Staff. At 2 P.M. D/236 4.5 Howitzer Battery set out on 1 hours bombardment by all C/235 and 41st Div Field Howitzers area opposite trenches of left Battalion of Right Brigade AD in. A registration by aeroplane by D/236 Bty was also attempted and 3.30 P.M. 2nd Lt T. Ballantyne C/236 Battery was evacuated to 8 Btys.	
	Feb 11		Conference of C/Zargo our Battery Commanders. First salvoy C/236 wiring alter.	
	Feb 12		D/236 Battery fired 200 rounds in a counter bombardment on 23rd Div trenches all counted howizers. X Trench Mortar Battery commenced wire-cutting on the left Battalion front and fired 57 rounds. Remander of C/236 Battery went out of action and handed over position to B/104 Battery which is the 3rd party of BJ235 in rest at WINNEZELE. C/236 took over wagon lines of B/235 in rest at WINNEZELE.	

T2134. Wt. W708—776. 500000. 4/15. Sir J. C. & S.

Army Form C. 2118.

WAR DIARY
or
INTELLIGENCE SUMMARY.
(Erase heading not required.)

Instructions regarding War Diaries and Intelligence Summaries are contained in F. S. Regs., Part II. and the Staff Manual respectively. Title pages will be prepared in manuscript.

Place	Date	Hour	Summary of Events and Information	Remarks and references to Appendices
YPRES	Feb 14th		B/236 Battery commenced semi-circular apposite Report Rectilium front. X Trench Mortar Battery continued and were not 30 rounds	
	15th		A/236 and B/236 Batteries continued on the enemy wire with the normal allotment of 200 rounds a day. D/236 fired on an wire penetration scheme at 3.45 an registration with murders of 23rd & 41st Divs and Heavy Battery on - Hill 60. X Trench Mortar Battery fired 60 rounds into enemy wire. 2nd N.V. Overton and Lewis Metcalfe attached to A & D Batteries respectively for 14 days instruction (from R.D.H.)	
	16th		All Batteries of the Group (except D/236) and including X Trench Mortar Battery, which fired 50 rounds, continued the	
	17th		things were today - many papo mult. were willing by A/236 and B/104 Batteries continued average of 200 rounds a day being fired by each Battery. X Trench Mortar Battery fired 100 rounds out the wire.	D/236 tot A
	18th		wire cutting continued successfully by all Batteries.	D/236 tot A

WAR DIARY
or
INTELLIGENCE SUMMARY.
(Erase heading not required.)

Army Form C. 2118.

Place	Date	Hour	Summary of Events and Information	Remarks and references to Appendices
YPRES	Feb. 18th		part in an area bombardment with all other heavy Batteries at 2.30 P.M. — 180 rounds fired — XTMBty fired 60 rounds. Enemy's trenches much damaged and quiet for the last few days bombardment.	
	19th		C/236 Battery came into action in position immediately behind Infantry Brigade HQ & using Battery to Potijzelhoek. Firing continued by A.B./236 Bties and 9/04 on Brun Ave "NATURAL" with the Howitzer Bact guns on Sinus Cross. R Trench Mortar Battery group fired 60 rounds.	
	19th		180 rounds of enemy fire.	
	20th		18pdr Batteries continued normal use culting wire enemy Hd Trench Mortar Battery also much damage hostile tour and many rifle with & minnerwurf shells. At 5 P.M. was Zero time for Cape Wappet raid carried out by Right Brigade front of 3rd Division. A dummy raid was much by Inftry of Inftren of mines and bombardment on the Hill	

WAR DIARY or INTELLIGENCE SUMMARY

Army Form C. 2118.

Place	Date	Hour	Summary of Events and Information	Remarks and references to Appendices
YPRES	Feb. 20th (cont'd)		C.O. Selected the Sluice Farm Dill Bellewaarde Left Group banged northern boundary of sound area and therefore took Parel. Approx 7.25 P.M. Read light signal 113 Prisoners and 4 machineguns being found by 8 Batalion. 2/Lieut. M.O. Mitchell A/236 By (Att. HA.) acted as liaison officer with centre meeting party. 6600 rounds of 18 pdr ammunition, 100 rounds of 4.5" Howzr, and 450 rounds 2" Trench Mortar ammunition were used by LEFT GROUP in the Read operations from 13" not exceeded. All quiet — no immediately retaliation by the enemy for the Raid.	
	22nd		2/Lt H. Duvos rejoined Brigade from Hospital (3236 By). Enemy aero projected from barrage on his line by Stafford.	
	23rd		2/Lieut. P.F. Oxley posted to C/236 from 47 DAC with effect from 21st inst. C/236 "Battery" anti-aircraft anti/two personnel area and mach guns.	

WAR DIARY
or
INTELLIGENCE SUMMARY.
(Erase heading not required.)

Place	Date	Hour	Summary of Events and Information	Remarks and references to Appendices
YPRES	Feb 23rd (cont'd)		temporarily under orders of 5th A.A. Corps, 41st Division Artillery.	
	24th		After very successful raid by 41st Division C/236 Battery goes back to rest - during raid to NUNEZEELE	
	28th		2nd Lt Metcalfe 2nd Bn returns to 47th DAC after attachment. 2nd Lt Hellier attached from 47th DAC to D/236 Battery to of tonight. R.F. 10a.m. 1st off. R.F.A.	OR 336 1st R.F.A.

Army Form C. 2118.

236th BRIGADE RFA.

Vol 25

WAR DIARY
or
INTELLIGENCE SUMMARY.
(Erase heading not required.)

Place	Date	Hour	Summary of Events and Information	Remarks and references to Appendices
YPRES	March 1st		Heavy shelling of A/236 and B/236 Batteries in the afternoon. Direct hits on Dugouts & Dump caused a few casualties. The Gas and vicinity of Group H.Q. also shelled — one wounded in H.Q. Visual signalling this morning — whilst telephones closed down from 10 P.M. to 2 P.M. Batteries fired on S.O.S. at 10 P.M. — no attack.	
	2nd		A/236 Battery again heavily shelled. Batteries on small allotment.	
	3rd		Probable Enemy O. only discovered the taking for a bright sky. Batteries fired from 9 P.M. until 12 P.M. about 120 rounds each. No retaliation was received.	
	4th		Enemy actively shelled our back areas during the evening.	
	5th		Working parties from 104 Brigade RFA and 47th D.A.C. attached to Batteries of the Group for work on the improvement & redemption	
	6		2nd Lieut T. Balvaulgon evacuated to Hop Coud and struck of the Strength with effect from 5-3-17.	
	7th		All quiet on Group front.	
	9th		D/236 Battery fired on Counts Battery target with aeroplane observation.	

Army Form C. 2118.

WAR DIARY
or
INTELLIGENCE SUMMARY.
(Erase heading not required.)

Instructions regarding War Diaries and Intelligence Summaries are contained in F. S. Regs., Part II. and the Staff Manual respectively. Title pages will be prepared in manuscript.

Place	Date	Hour	Summary of Events and Information	Remarks and references to Appendices
YPRES	March 9th	(cont'd)	B/236 Battery fired 130 rounds on enemy wire. Several snipers shewn by the enemy.	
	11th		A/236 Battery fired about 70 rounds wirecutting. Greater activity — lots Bulut machines shewhaud over YPRES.	
	12th		Major Pollard OC D/236 to Field Ambulance sick. R/236 Battery successfully dispersed large working party behind enemy lines. Major Pollard evacuated owing Journal Area — also 2nd Lewis.	
	13th		2/Lt S Taylor appointed C/Captain whilst 2nd in command D/236.	
	14th		Major A.C. Gordon DSO OC B/236 Battery assumes command of 235th Brigade R.F.A. and is struck off the strength of this Brigade from today's date.	
	15th		The enemy batteries active today especially 8" — our Batteries retaliated at request of infantry.	
	16th		B/104 Battery fired 140 rounds in wirecutting — much intermittent retaliation by the other batteries.	
	17th		Capt. R.A. Corsan M.C. A/236 O4 appointed to command B/236 Battery	

T2134. Wt. W708—776. 500000. 4/15. Sir J.C. & S.

WAR DIARY
or
INTELLIGENCE SUMMARY

Army Form C. 2118.

(Erase heading not required.)

Place	Date	Hour	Summary of Events and Information	Remarks and references to Appendices
YPRES	Mar. 17th (cont.)		with Effect from 16th inst. vice Major Gordon D.S.O. D/236 Battery deals counter-battery shoot with aeroplane observation	
	18th		D/236 fired on Counter Battery Target — A&O Btries fired at request of Infantry — D/236 also fired all night on German Battery suspected of moving.	
	19th		Batteries retaliated to enemy firing on 14th Battalion during the morning. 2nd Lieut G. Jaques posted to D/236 Battery from 1/1st Div. T.A.	
	20th		C/236 Battery first section relieved one section of B/142 to carry from Corps Reserve, and took over B/235 Wagon lines.	
	21st		Remaining sections of C/236 Battery relieved remaining section of B/142. A/236 Battery fired 10 rounds retaliating and B/236 Battery fired 120 rounds in retaliation to enemy shelling.	
	22nd		X Trench Mortar Battery fired 50 rounds on HILL60 and rifle new craters blown by the enemy. Work was heard during the night and X Battery again fired into craters.	
	23rd		Enemy actively bombarded in retaliation by T.M's early this morning. Our Batteries replied and X Trench Mortar Battery again fired on craters	

WAR DIARY
or
INTELLIGENCE SUMMARY.
(Erase heading not required.)

Army Form C. 2118.

Place	Date	Hour	Summary of Events and Information	Remarks and references to Appendices
YPRES	Mar 24th		From 8 A.M. until 11.30 C/236 Battery was heavily shelled and the gunner killed and two others wounded. The shelling was repeated at intervals during the day and an ammunition dump blown up. At 6 P.M. after heavy trench mortar activity the S.O.S. went up to the right of Group zone and was reported on Group zone Batteries opened fire on S.O.S. but situation almost immediately cleared and "cease-fire" was given. A small enemy raid had been stopped on left Battalion front. Captain H. Carey-Morgan C/236 Bty posted to command B/236 Bty with effect from this date and Captain R. H. Cozens M.C. B/236 Battery posted to A/236 Bty. D/236 carried out a successful counter battery shoot - Stunning direct hits on hostile gun pits. Enemy batteries very active.	
	25th			
	26th		X.T.M Battery fired on enemy craters to good work	
	27th		2nd Lt. H.W. Stevens and 2nd Lt. H.S. Grover attached from 47th DAC to A&C Btys	

WAR DIARY
or
INTELLIGENCE SUMMARY.

Army Form C. 2118.

Place	Date	Hour	Summary of Events and Information	Remarks and references to Appendices
YPRES	Mar. 27ᵗʰ		respectively for fortnight instruction. D/236 Battery fired 180 rounds in conjunction with Heavy Artillery and other 4.5 How Batteries on field gun opposite Roulers/Belfort. C/236 Battery having shelled gdam during the morning — two direct hits on a parapet — no casualties. Major Hood, OC C/236 goes on leave (special).	
	28ᵗʰ			
	30ᵗʰ		B/236 Battery fired 150 rounds in wrecking enemy dugouts with A/236 Battery fired on German O.Pees inspecting enemy positions. C/236 Battery system shelled this morning, special duty.	(Major Cooper R.A./236)
	31		2ⁿᵈ Lt E.A. de.B. West rejoined from hospital. T/D236 Battery Ballistics returned during the day and X Trench Mortar Battery position craters.	

P. Lowe
Lt. R.A.
Cmdg 236ᵗʰ Brigade R.F.A.

Army Form C. 2118.

236 Brigade RFA

April 1916   236 Bde FA

No 26

WAR DIARY
or
INTELLIGENCE SUMMARY.
(Erase heading not required.)

Place	Date	Hour	Summary of Events and Information	Remarks and references to Appendices
YPRES	April 1st		Wrecelling in preparation for raiding operation started by Mio Group; A/236 fired 150 rounds, B Battery 110, C Battery 120 on the wire. D/236 fired 180 rounds on area opposite Division on Mic BH in celebration with this Brigade old Heavy Batteries & Trench Mortar Batteries fired in retaliation and moved from front to rear more front Battery positions for offensive action started upon by Batteries of 115 New Battery positions for offensive action started upon by Batteries of 115 Group — 12 positions have the completed.	
"	2nd		Wrecelling was carried out on front of high wire by Stokes and trench mortars. D/236 Battery fired in an area "Bombardment" 160 rounds and A/236 Battery fired at intervals during the night on this area.	
	3rd		C/236 Battery fired 44 rounds in wrecelling and X T.M. Battery 60 rounds. A/236 Battery fired during the mortar the area of bombardment yesterday.	
	4th		On wire cutting A Battery fired 170 rounds, B Bty 104, C Bty 133, and X Bty 25 good results being obtained. D Battery fired on area bombarding and X T.M. Battery 107 and C Battery 136	
	5th		Wrecelling was continued today A Bty firing 119 rounds, B Battery 221	

T2134. Wt. W708—776. 500000. 4/15. Sir J. C. & S.

WAR DIARY
or
INTELLIGENCE SUMMARY.
(Erase heading not required.)

Army Form C. 2118.

Place	Date	Hour	Summary of Events and Information	Remarks and references to Appendices
YPRES	April 5th	(contd)	A Battery afternoon reported in the morning was shelled at about 6.30 - Two fuse pits were blown in by 5.9's and two other rounds and one Sergeant wounded.	
"	6th		C/189 Battery (Army Field Brigade) came into action in Potijze East of B/236 as reinforcement Battery for the Group. Nothing fired 100 rounds, B/189 76, C Bty 152 and D Battery 108 but in our contribution in Group zone. X TMBy also fired 57 rounds. C/189 Battery reported Batteries carried out intense wire cutting this morning, firing 130. B/189 155, C Bty 20 rounds	
	7th		Zero time for Daylight Raid 8 P.M. 18th Battalion carried this out on same front as Right Brigade Front - as the Raid in February and a heavy barrage by 2½ divisional artilleries accompanied by dummy raids on German line on Hill 60 and STE101. Enemy fire fairly heavy and caused a number of casualties. 19 prisoners taken. O.C. left Group acted as Liaison officer with G.O.C. 141 Infantry Bde.	

Army Form C. 2118.

WAR DIARY
or
INTELLIGENCE SUMMARY.
(Erase heading not required.)

Instructions regarding War Diaries and Intelligence Summaries are contained in F. S. Regs., Part II. and the Staff Manual respectively. Title pages will be prepared in manuscript.

Place	Date	Hour	Summary of Events and Information	Remarks and references to Appendices
YPRES			and Major Pollard OC D/236 Battery with no liaison with OC Post	
	8th	2.11 AM	OC B/236 Battery posted to 66th Division	
			During the round Artily fire 909 rounds, B.By 984, C.By 898 and D.By 434	
			OC 102 Brigade R.F.A. arrived & took over Group, relief of Batteries not yet begun.	
	9th		Left Group now under tactical command of 23rd Divisional Artillery and covering 23rd Divl Infantry, but still covering HILL 60 front. After much nothing of our lines all day the enemy at 6.35 P.M. opened a heavy barrage along Divisional front particularly on the whole battalion S.O.S. went up at 6.44 and Batteries of 236 Brigade opened barrage immediately. Shelling of Cross in right and Divisions on left, but took to turned a Battery out right Brigade front after ten minutes. Enemy trench barrages on this Brigade front completely held up by our barrage fire and found to have been confined until about 8 P.M. on dead ground in "No Mans Land". Enemy continued until about 8 P.M. at	

WAR DIARY
or
INTELLIGENCE SUMMARY

Army Form C. 2118.

Place	Date	Hour	Summary of Events and Information	Remarks and references to Appendices
YPRES	April 9th (cont'd)		reports that 3960 rounds being fired by the Group inspite of Batteries being all shelled with 5.9 s and 4.5 pro shell. One 4.5 Howitzer totally damaged – no other damage or casualties except slight gas poisoning two Sikhs.	
	10th		Lt. A.F. Yencken (B By) Struck off the Strength on evacuation to England. All quiet today – all front trenches including Battery OPs have been demolished and materials for putting looked for by enemy.	
	11th		First section went out of action tonight and switched to the wagon lines. First section marched to WINNEZEELE and OUDERZEELE and billets. Remaining sections went out of action tonight and C Group handed over defence of front to OC 102 Bgade RFA. 23 Dvn. A,B,C,D Batteries 102 billets over Battery positions on rds. 48 CP from Batteries g/236 Brigade. 104 Army Field Artillery Brigade took over all wagon lines.	
	12th		A & B/236 Brigade H.Q. Brigade in WINNEZEELE and billets and C&D/236 Batteries at OUDERZEELE.	

Army Form C. 2118.

WAR DIARY
or
INTELLIGENCE SUMMARY.
(Erase heading not required.)

Instructions regarding War Diaries and Intelligence Summaries are contained in F. S. Regs., Part II. and the Staff Manual respectively. Title pages will be prepared in manuscript.

Place	Date	Hour	Summary of Events and Information	Remarks and references to Appendices
	April			
WINNEZEELE	15th		Major W. Cooper OC A/236 Battery returned from Special leave.	
&	16th		Drill Order Inspection of Batteries by BGRA. Each Battery	
OUDERZEELE			inspected separately. A & B at WINNEZEELE - C & D at OUDERZEELE	
			Major Ward OC/B/236 Battery returned from leave.	
			Classes in Gunnery and Signalling in each Battery were being carried on	
	18th		OC Brigade to HQ. 47th Divisional Artillery as acting CRA. in absence of CRA. on leave. Major BULLARD OC D/236 Battery to command Brigade in absence of OC.	
	19th		Summaries of evidence in case of 2nd/Lt WISEMAN D/236 remanded for F.G.C.M. on 15th inst. taken.	
	20th		Marching order parade of C & D Batteries - inspected by HQ Brigade (Major C.A. POLLARD DSO)	
	23rd		Gas demonstration by Chemical Adviser 187 Div. from near OUDERZEELE A 187.06. guns of C/236 Battery and 2 4.5 Howitzers of D Battery brought but failed in the gas cloud ORA. and all unreliable	

Army Form C. 2118.

WAR DIARY
or
INTELLIGENCE SUMMARY.
(Erase heading not required.)

Instructions regarding War Diaries and Intelligence Summaries are contained in F. S. Regs., Part II. and the Staff Manual respectively. Title pages will be prepared in manuscript.

Place	Date	Hour	Summary of Events and Information	Remarks and references to Appendices
	April			
WINNEZEELE &	23rd (cont.)		Officers and NCO's of Brigade attend Kentings parties of Exercise in the line relieved by similar parties	
OUDEZEELE	25.		Marching order parade of H.Q. Bde and A/236 and B/236 Batteries at 9.30 a.m. Inspection by Bde Commander - a good turnout.	
	28.		Captain R.A. Cosan M.C. A/236 went to command C/102 Battery on return vice Major Britton killed.	
	29.		Colonel A.C. Love resumed command of Brigade on return of B.G.R.A. from leave and Major C.A. Pilaud relinquished command. Brigade Officers Jumping competition held at 5.30 pm and won by 2nd Lt G. JAQUES B/236 Battery.	
	30.		Brigade Sections Jumping competition and rides. During period under instruction Gunnery has been carried on daily with Battery Staffs - gun drill, laying, fuze setting, signalling with flags, lamps in arms and across stations, riding schools + competitions in turnout.	

H.L. Love Lt Col.
236 BRIGADE R.F.A.
Commanding

Army Form C. 2118.

236th Brigade RFA WAR DIARY
INTELLIGENCE SUMMARY.
(Erase heading not required.)

May 1917

Vol 27

Place	Date	Hour	Summary of Events and Information	Remarks and references to Appendices
WINNEZEELE & OUDEZEELE	May 1st/2nd		Brigade subsections completion for General licrement war by B/236 Btn with A/236 Btn 2nd	
	3rd		First section of Batteries left for positions in the line. Rest billets taken over by 104 Brigade RFA	
	4th		Remaining sections of Batteries and Headquarters staff and its section on the BLUFF and CANAL sectors, immediately South of YPRES and with their Batteries of 235th Brigade remaining in formed CHATEAU GROUP, covering the section of 47th Divisional front. Lt Colonel W.B. GRANDAGE VC 235 Brigade RFA remained in command of Group with HQ Staff 236th Brigade. Two 2nd French Mortars Batteries and one 9.45 Trench Mortar also formed part of Group.	
YPRES	5th		Lt Colonel A.C. Lowe DSO. wanton leave to ENGLAND. Major C.H. POLLARD DSO. assuming temporary command of Brigade. Lieut VC LUCAS VC posted to B/236	
	6th		Heavy shelling of roads and back areas by enemy and much counter battery work by him.	
	7th		Shelling on whole area by the enemy increased	

Army Form C. 2118.

WAR DIARY
or
INTELLIGENCE SUMMARY.
(Erase heading not required.)

Instructions regarding War Diaries and Intelligence Summaries are contained in F. S. Regs., Part II. and the Staff Manual respectively. Title pages will be prepared in manuscript.

Place	Date	Hour	Summary of Events and Information	Remarks and references to Appendices
YPRES	May. 7th (cont)		G.O.C. Division inspected Brigade Major Lines. One NCO and horses of D/256(H)(?). Bombardment of enemy works, railways and communications by every form of 5 minutes. The Army at whose surface for two periods of 5 minutes each at 8.45 and 11.15 PM carried out. The Corps Stokes Mort. and firing an average of 350 rounds per Bden 19/y and 200 per 4.5 Howitzer. Enemy guessed by this retaliation.	
	8th		G.O.C. Division inspected Brigade H.Q. and Batteries during the morning. Still much artillery activity, and bombardment of dumps by the enemy.	
	9th		Enemy active with trench mortars and artillery on trenches during the day — much retaliation by our batteries. Firing increased and heavy bombardment opened at 9.10 P.M. S.O.S. was sent up and Batteries barraged on Group front and on Thaley portion on Right until 10 P.M. Enemy attempted raids on two parts of the front true with little success.	

Army Form C. 2118.

WAR DIARY
or
INTELLIGENCE SUMMARY.
(Erase heading not required.)

Place	Date	Hour	Summary of Events and Information	Remarks and references to Appendices
YPRES	May 10th		Another heavy bombardment, chiefly on the York was opened at 3.45 P.M. and Batteries barraged for half an hour. Much counter Battery work and many targets of guns in action fired on. 2/Lt C.B. Payne struck off the strength of the Brigade on transference to R.F.C.	
	11th		Renewed enemy artillery activity. Vicinity of Group HQ shelled all the morning and the HQ5 Chateau was registered and heavily bombarded from 11.30 a.m. to 2.30 a.m. and partly destroyed — no casualties. D/236 Battery also heavily shelled — one gun and pit and ammunition blown up and completely destroyed and another gun turned — from 5 P.M. to 5.30 P.M. — No casualties.	
	12th		Enemy artillery active — howitzer Batteries retaliated on counter-battery targets. C/236 Battery shelled.	
	14th		Lieut Colonel H.B. GRAYNDAGE commanding the Group died of wounds this morning and 2/Lieut L.J. HELIAR (Orderly Officer 236th Brigade) was killed	

WAR DIARY
or
INTELLIGENCE SUMMARY.
(Erase heading not required.)

Army Form C. 2118.

Place	Date	Hour	Summary of Events and Information	Remarks and references to Appendices
YPRES	May 14th		6th AA SWAN CHATEAU. Major CAPOWARD Temporary Groups commander. Large working parties formed from 104th A.F.A. Brigade for work on offensive positions	
	15th		Lieut Colonel NICHOLSON 104th Army F.A. Brigade arrived & took over command of Group. Battery positions for offensive action specially allotted to Brigade. Wire cutting started.	
	16th		Headquarters 236th Brigade went out of section to Napier Line.	
	17th		Command of Group definitely handed over – all HQ staff now at Napier Line.	
	18th		One section of A/236 Battery relieved by one section A/104 and went to Napier Line.	
	19th		Remaining sections of A/236 relieved by A/104 – and one section put into new offensive position.	
	20th		One section of B/236 Napier Line on relief by one section B/104 Pit. Telephone exchange for HQ Brigade established in new Headquarters at BEDFORD HOUSE. Capt. CEGERTON-WARBURTON posted to B/236 Battery.	
	21st		Remaining sections of B/236 relieved and one section went into new position. Lieut LUCAS M.C. with F.O.O. party to 142 Inf. Bde for practice in training area.	

Army Form C. 2118.

WAR DIARY
or
INTELLIGENCE SUMMARY.
(Erase heading not required.)

Instructions regarding War Diaries and Intelligence Summaries are contained in F. S. Regs., Part II. and the Staff Manual respectively. Title pages will be prepared in manuscript.

Place	Date	Hour	Summary of Events and Information	Remarks and references to Appendices
YPRES	May 23rd		Preliminary instructions for offensive action issued. Batteries all working on positions and wire cutting with super gun.	
			Lt Colonel A.C. Lowe arrived back from leave to England and took over command	
	24th		of Brigade from Major C.A. Petard (temporarily holding it).	
	25th		First section D/236 Battery in action in new position. Target –	
			All Batteries 236 Brigade (two single Bty) in our position tonight – completion of fire ammunition dumps at guns now taking place.	
	27th		Heavy shelling of all roads tonight by the enemy and ??? gun ???. D/236 shelled – one Bombardier killed and six men wounded and ammunition dumps blown up. Firing with fan alarms continued until morning 28th.	
	28th		All 18 pdr Batteries now have completed dumps on ammunition. 1800 rounds. Roads again shelled by the enemy, one driver A/236 killed and one wounded and two horses killed. Several other men slightly wounded.	
	29		D/236 Battery completed dumps of 6600 rounds. A.D. Staff went up ??? cut	

WAR DIARY
or
INTELLIGENCE SUMMARY.
(Erase heading not required.)

Army Form C. 2118.

Place	Date	Hour	Summary of Events and Information	Remarks and references to Appendices
	May			
YPRES	30th		action. D/236 Battery heavily shelled. "C" Group, consisting of A, B, C, D/236 and D/119 as counter battery, formed under command of Lt Colonel AC Lowe DSO. 64th Army Field Artillery Brigade attached as a sub-group (D Group) Bde Head-quarters where remains of BEDFORD HOUSE in YPRES—ZILLEBEKE Road. "C" Group's offensive zone immediately North of YPRES—ZILLEBEKE canal. Batteries all to the East of Headquarters and within close distance — in new positions.	
	31st		Night firing commenced by the Group. Intercepting by "A and C" Batteries. Night firing by "B" Battery and retaliation by all Batteries for raid, to take place near municipality court of CANAL. One driver "C" killed.	

AC Lowe Lt Col RA
Commanding 236 Brigade RFA.

236th (Canadian) Brigade R.F.A. (T.F.)

WAR DIARY

INTELLIGENCE SUMMARY.
(Erase heading not required.)

Army Form C. 2118.

47 D.A. / June 1917 Vol 28

Instructions regarding War Diaries and Intelligence Summaries are contained in F. S. Regs., Part II. and the Staff Manual respectively. Title pages will be prepared in manuscript.

Place	Date	Hour	Summary of Events and Information	Remarks and references to Appendices
YPRES	June 1st		Batteries continued wirecutting. Practice barrage from 3.30 PM to 4 PM fired on by all Batteries on Group. Offensive zone – smoke shell being used. Night firing and neutralization of wire by "B" Battery in addition.	
	2nd		Wirecutting continued in cooperation with Trench Mortars and harassing fire carried out on tracks and communication trenches. D/236 Battery bombarded five forward enemy gun positions. In reply to all day bombardment by our heavy batteries the enemy retaliated with a few rounds on Batteries and Group HQ. Staff Sergt. MASTERS and one gunner killed and two Sergts. wounded in A/236. Lieut. A.F. BUCKNELL A/236 Battery slightly wounded – moving in back area – believed killed. Later found to have been killed.	
	3rd		Usual heavy firing on enemy roads and communication and wire. Batteries fired all day on roads etc. and counter Battery work with gas-shell carried out during the whole night by howitzer batteries. HQ shelled by gas shell vicinity for two hours during the	

WAR DIARY
or
INTELLIGENCE SUMMARY.
(Erase heading not required.)

Army Form C. 2118.

Place	Date	Hour	Summary of Events and Information	Remarks and references to Appendices
YPRES	4th	night	Conference of BMRA and Group Commanders at "C" Group Headquarters. One gun of C/236 knocked out and destroyed by direct hit during heavy shelling of D/236. B/236 in rear range fire all day. Slow round bombardment at 10 p.m. by all Batteries on enemy trenches.	
	5th		Much firing during the night. C/236 had two howitzers destroyed. Three startling barrages by "C" Batteries during the day. Also a practical barrage at 3 p.m. carried out. Lt Col A C Lowe DSO of "C" Group went up as Liaison officer with 142 Infantry Brigade at the BLUFF. Patrol raids carried out during the night. BEDFORD HOUSE zone shelled.	
	6th	2.30 a.m.	D/236 and C/236 fired on enemy barrage. Barrage on enemy to final objective fired in very heavy shelling of all Batteries all day by the enemy with 8" and 5.9" shell. A/236 had two guns destroyed. B/236 had two badly damaged and C/236 had also two guns put out. Ammunition blown up.	

WAR DIARY
or
INTELLIGENCE SUMMARY.
(Erase heading not required.)

Army Form C. 2118.

Place	Date	Hour	Summary of Events and Information	Remarks and references to Appendices
YPRES	June 6th		Jackson and 1070 rounds of ammunition blown up. All 4½" guns of C Battery wounded. A and C Batteries were both flagged to reach positions by one hours. Owing to heavy injuries B Battery failure of mules. Stopping tractor and failed to complete creeping barrage. B/236 could carried out counter-battery work all night. 2½" M.F. Alley to prepare as general officer.	
	7th		Zero time for offensive by the II Army state HILL 60 and HYTSCHAETE and MESSINES ridges 3:10 a.m. At first man all artillery opened heavy barrage which continued to creep forward as infantry advanced for 10 hours until all objectives were gained, and ridge remained in our hands. "C" Group formed the centre of the six groups covering the Divisional front and the barrage crossed the CANAL South of which the final Group protective barrage was placed. Lieut V.C. LUCAS M.C. (A/236) acted as F.O.O. with Brigade Forward	

WAR DIARY
or
INTELLIGENCE SUMMARY
(Erase heading not required.)

Army Form C. 2118.

Place	Date	Hour	Summary of Events and Information	Remarks and references to Appendices
YPRES	JUNE 7th		Station and died of wounds. Lieut H. ELLIOTT acted as Independent FOO with continuous wave wireless set. Captain W.J. BARNARD (BP36) acted as Group Observing Officer. The FC Brigade continued firing as Senior Liaison Officer. A large number of "NF" calls were received and D/236 did retaliation neutralisation of Batteries, and firing on enemy troops on the embankment. At about 6 P.M. barrage carried out on SOS lines but no infantry action by Mt. enemy. New Observing Post established.	
	8th		Registration of Batteries on new zero lines. Otherwise enemy very quiet. 2nd Lieut H.C. BURGIS rejoined the Brigade and to A/236 from ENGLAND.	
	9th		D Group - subgroup to the Brigade moved the Bulleting forward and Zone temporarily taken over by this group. Brigade fired on SOS V call from 7pm to 8 pm - but no change in	

Army Form C. 2118.

WAR DIARY
or
INTELLIGENCE SUMMARY.
(Erase heading not required.)

Instructions regarding War Diaries and Intelligence Summaries are contained in F. S. Regs., Part II. and the Staff Manual respectively. Title pages will be prepared in manuscript.

Place	Date	Hour	Summary of Events and Information	Remarks and references to Appendices
YPRES	10.		Situation. Various hurricane retaliations carried out during the night. The O.C. Brigade still acting as liaison forward. Heavy Officers with two Battalions of Right Brigade at WHITE CHATEAU supplied by the Brigade. Spasmodic shelling of Batteries all PM.	
		From 10.45 to 11.20	Batteries opened fire on S.O.S. barrage in reply to heavy bombardment by the enemy. No counter attack on our front. MAJOR N. COOPER W/236 wounded at duty.	
	11.		Shelling of Batteries and Group HQ by heavy howitzers from the North. "A" Battery Officers mess cut, Lieut MITCHELL slightly wounded at duty.	
	12.		Increased enemy firing by two Batteries.	
	13.		The O.C. Brigade returned to Group Headquarters from liaison duty forward with S-141st Infantry Brigade HQ. Group came under the command of 2/Divisional Artillery and zone changed to one immediately North of CANAL. Wagon Lines moved to day from this occupied for 5 months to a position at MILLEKRUIS near LA CLYTTE. W/236 Battery shelled at about 5 P.M. — one gun damaged.	

WAR DIARY
or
INTELLIGENCE SUMMARY.

(Erase heading not required.)

Army Form C. 2118.

Place	Date	Hour	Summary of Events and Information	Remarks and references to Appendices
YPRES	June 14th		Batteries occupied new Observing Stations on HILL 60 today and registered on new front North of CANAL. At 7.30 pm attack renewed by 24th Division on remaining portion of SPOIL BANK and it developed into BATTLE HOOD and the German front line further South. Batteries fired on German front line and tried on small protective barrage — 15 rounds. Attack successful.	
	15th		Group of 236 Brigade Batteries came under tactical command of 41st Divisional Artillery at 8 am this morning. Zone changes to South of CANAL. A/236 Battery shelled during the morning — one gun put out of action. SOS call at 5.0 PM after heavy shelling. Much counter-battery work by enemy — A and B and D Batteries also fired on two more SOS calls at about 7 PM. and 9.30 PM. Battery commanders reconnoitred new battery positions at ST ELOI.	
	16th		Move of Batteries to new positions cancelled by CRA 41st Division — orders received to go into rest. Responsibility of Brigade for defence of the	

Army Form C. 2118.

WAR DIARY
or
INTELLIGENCE SUMMARY.
(Erase heading not required.)

Instructions regarding War Diaries and Intelligence Summaries are contained in F. S. Regs., Part II. and the Staff Manual respectively. Title pages will be prepared in manuscript.

Place	Date	Hour	Summary of Events and Information	Remarks and references to Appendices
YPRES	June 17th		Front saved at 6 P.M. Shelling by enemy of Belling positions and district during the night. Batteries cleared out of positions commencing at 2 a.m. and withdrew to hidden tube near at MILLENPUSS near LA CLYTTE	
LA CLYTTE	18th		Brigade HQ established in room huts at 7 a.m. Preparation of metals trip BGRA. - Col. NOEL + HQ Staff received Inspection of horse lines by BGRA. Inspection of metals Victoria Military.	
	20th		Training in Gunlaying, Fuze setting and gundrill commenced by numbers and all spare men. Ammunition still being moved from old positions to new. Concert - totally B. Battery.	
	22nd		Subalterns officers riding commenced under instruction of 2nd Lt GRAVES	
	23rd		Inspection of horse lines by Adeson on Horsemastership X Corps. Brigade concert this evening a great success. The BGRA and Staff were present. 17th DAC. and 235th Brigade helped in the programme.	
	24th		Church parade as usual 7 a.m. Lecture on Horsemastership by Army X Corps to all Officers, Sergts, Corporals, Veterinary Sergts and farriers of the	

Army Form C. 2118.

WAR DIARY
or
INTELLIGENCE SUMMARY.
(Erase heading not required.)

Instructions regarding War Diaries and Intelligence Summaries are contained in F. S. Regs., Part II. and the Staff Manual respectively. Title pages will be prepared in manuscript.

Place	Date	Hour	Summary of Events and Information	Remarks and references to Appendices
LA CLYTTE	24th (contd)		Brigade BGRA was present and also inspected horse lines. Captain C.W. EGERTON-WARBURTON transferred from A Battery to 47" DAC and Captain T.H. FLYNN posted to A/236 from 47th DAC.	
	25th		Lieut C.B. TYSON returned from hospital and attached for duty A.B. Battery	
	26th		Practices for Athletic Sports and for Boxing Tournament begun	
	28th		Brigade Boxing Tournament held at 3PM and at 5PM. Tugong Bay, Major E.H. MARSHALL D.S.O. C/235 Brigade	
	29th		OC 21st Battalion London Regiment lends band to the Brigade for four days to play at Brigade Sports, concerts &c.	

R. Lowe Shaw
commanding 236 Brigade RFA.

Army Form C. 2118.

236th Brigade R.F.A.

WAR DIARY
or
INTELLIGENCE SUMMARY. July 1917

WO 29

Place	Date	Hour	Summary of Events and Information	Remarks and references to Appendices
LACITTE	July 1st		Brigade still in rest at MILLEKRUIS near LACITTE	
	2nd		Moon lines and neighbourhood shelled twice during the night at 1.30 am and 4 am. 5 horses of A Battery killed and one driver of B Battery severely wounded. A Brigade to the Vimi to see new Headquarters. Athletic Sports held this afternoon, won by band of 21st Battalion A & first success.	
	3rd		Athletic Sports Covert during the evening.	
"THE BLUFF" YPRES	4th		Advance parties from Batteries & Brigade with relieve take over communication ed. Brigade relieved 235th Brigade R.F.A. in action taking over zone in positions South of CANAL and YORK East of STEDI evening zone immediately front/BATTLE HQ in Brigade HQ in command of 236 and 104th Brigades. Batteries and known as BATTLE WOOD GROUP — 6/18th and 2 4.5 Howitzer Batteries evening of 4th Infantry Bde. Registration carried out. Much scattered shelling by the enemy especially in neighbourhood of Camp HQ in the Spoil Bank and round Batteries all night.	
	5th		A/104 Battery shelled from 7 PM to 8 PM — one ammunition dump blown up.	
	6th		All Batteries now again in action very large ammunition dumps blown up. 7/Lt W.G.B. THOMPSON struck off the strength on evacuation to England.	

Army Form C. 2118.

WAR DIARY
or
INTELLIGENCE SUMMARY.
(Erase heading not required.)

Instructions regarding War Diaries and Intelligence Summaries are contained in F.S. Regs., Part II. and the Staff Manual respectively. Title pages will be prepared in manuscript.

Place	Date	Hour	Summary of Events and Information	Remarks and references to Appendices
"THE BLUFF" YPRES	July 7th		Much heavy shelling by the enemy along the whole front during the night. Batteries of the Group retaliated at 1.30 am, 2.15 am and 2.25 am. At 2.40 S.O.S. was sent by two Batteries and barrage opened. The enemy had rushed a post of Left Battalion which took one prisoner. Slow barrage fire continued for an hour.	
			Meeting of Battery Commanders. Each Battery allotted one position to work on and stock with large ammunition dumps with views to forthcoming operations. Portions allotted to 236 Brigade immediately S.W. of the BLUFF.	
	8th		Post in Left Battalion line regained during the night. Batteries retaliated for usual enemy shelling. C and D/236 shelled this evening by means of an area bombardment - 3 other ranks of C Battery killed.	
	9th		General enemies battery work by the enemy and shelling of working parties. One man killed and one wounded in A/236 Battery. 9 P.M. Zero hour for opening of barrage by B, C, and D/236 Batteries. Genie the Haute of a barrage covering an actual advance further south. Raids carried out and prisoners taken &c &c. Divisional front. Batteries ceased firing 10.40 P.M.	

T2134. Wt. W708—776. 500000. 4/15. Sir J. C. & S.

Army Form C. 2118.

WAR DIARY
or
INTELLIGENCE SUMMARY.
(Erase heading not required.)

Instructions regarding War Diaries and Intelligence Summaries are contained in F.S. Regs., Part II. and the Staff Manual respectively. Title pages will be prepared in manuscript.

Place	Date	Hour	Summary of Events and Information	Remarks and references to Appendices
"THE BLUFF" YPRES	July 10th		1 Signaller killed and 6 others wounded by shellfire at VOORMEZEELE – at A/236. Battery. Still much enemy "crumbs" being brought up by light railway train – nearly 10,000 rounds a night.	
		11.15	Wheeling on those Group Ford commanded by Fields. Counter-Battery operation with aeroplane cooperation carried out by D/236 By.	
		12th	Positions in which Batteries have been putting handed over to 10th and 11th Australian Brigades for continuation of work. Dumping of ammunition continued – also wireshing carried out.	
		14th	Searching of shellholes in front of Battery zones and general harassing fire carried out during the day. Heavy shelling of tracks, Group HQ etc by gas shell during the night and batteries returned once to enemy shelling. 1 Other rank of C and 1 other rank of D wounded.	
		15th	1 Other rank of C wounded. Harassing fire and wireshing continued. 9/189 Battery were in BATTLE WOOD GROUP instead of C/101 Battery. The Military Cross presented by Divisional Commander to Captain J. BRAND B/236, 2/Lt C. WILKINSON D/236 and 2/Lt P. FOXLEY G/236 for gallantry	

T2134. Wt. W708—776. 500000. 4/15. Sir J. C. & S.

WAR DIARY
or
INTELLIGENCE SUMMARY.
(Erase heading not required.)

Army Form C. 2118.

Place	Date	Hour	Summary of Events and Information	Remarks and references to Appendices
THE BLUFF YPRES	July 15th (contd)		in the field during the burst of the battle of June 7th. The MILITARY MEDAL was presented to the following Other ranks Sergt W.G. PHILPOTTS B/Bty, Sergt W. BRADLEY D/Bty, Sergt R. CARTER D/Bty, Sergt F.N.O. LIPPIATT C/Bty, Bomb A.V.N. DALE A/Bty, 9/Bdr S. DARE B/Bty, 2/Bdr W. RUCKETT B/Bty, Gnr CH. BRITT A/Bty, Dvr H.A. CRYSTAL B/Bty, Gnr C. COOK B/Bty, Dvr S.B. SYMONS B/Bty, Dvr H.C. OYSTER A/Bty, D/GR. BOYDEN A/Bty, Gnr R.C. GRIFFIN B/Bty. The enemy again shelled all tracks and Detachments of Group Hqrs.	
	16th		well—gas shell during the night. Harassing fire by three Batteries and unrelenting. Many calls for retaliation during the night and one S.O.S. call at 10.30 p.m. when all Batteries of the Group fired for 20 minutes. the attack by the enemy. From 11.30 p.m. to 3 a.m. 17th continuous shelling of Battery positions. Group Thurgmates and tracks by gas and Lachrymatory and H.E. shell.	
	17th		9/236 Battery heavily shelled from being knocked — 4 O.R. killed	

Army Form C. 2118.

WAR DIARY
or
INTELLIGENCE SUMMARY.
(Erase heading not required.)

Instructions regarding War Diaries and Intelligence Summaries are contained in F.S. Regs., Part II. and the Staff Manual respectively. Title pages will be prepared in manuscript.

Place	Date	Hour	Summary of Events and Information	Remarks and references to Appendices
"THE BLUFF" YPRES	July 17th (cont)		and 2 O.R. wounded. A B and D Batteries fired at 9.50 P.M. & 10.50 P.M. in response to Bavarians ask. Retaliers by Division and Beyond. In the night.	
		2210	V.C. Ross P/236 lightly wounded and shell shock. 1/H.C. POUND-CORNER R.E. attached H.Q. C.F.A. (gnr) and 1 O.R. from H.Q. K.F.A. (gnr)	
	18th		The usual counterbattery concentration shoots carried out by the two D Batteries in the Group. Also usual harassing fire and worrying continued.	
	19th		1 O.R. of C Battery wounded today. Harassing fire at night commenced – The Group firing about 150 rounds during the hours.	
	20th		Several concentration shoots on Batteries and much harassing fire carried out. 1 O/Murrans killed and 2 others wounded in D Battery. Considerable arm shelling by this enemy all day and all night. Brigade H.Q. also delayed with assaults by shellfire, and their dug-out destroyed.	
	21st		Brigade H.Q. moved from The BLUFF tunnels to VICTORIA MINE SHAFT at St ELOI Craters and handed over to 189th AFA Brigade H.Q. who became	

Army Form C. 2118.

WAR DIARY
or
INTELLIGENCE SUMMARY.

(Erase heading not required.)

Place	Date	Hour	Summary of Events and Information	Remarks and references to Appendices
SZELOI	21st		BATTLE WOOD GROUP now becoming CHATEAU GROUP are of this artillery Group. Covering the Right Brigade 41st Division (Under command of A Battery (temporarily lent to BLUFF GROUP) B and C Batteries, D Battery doing China Bellewarde. A and B/47 Brigade. Visits in Old HQ by Corps Commander, Divisional Commander & B.G.R.A. 41st Division.	
	22nd		Shrewdleg by D/236 with trench relief guy carried out. Bollocratics of D Battery wounded. Lieut. T. BALLANTYNE billed 6 A Battery Batteries shelled thor Jackson and B Shrupnel billed and I wounded in D Battery. Pickin terrace in commissier with 2 and fired on by A/47. B Battery heavy shelled early this morning - two guns and 2000 round of ammunition put out of action. One other truck wounded (Gov.)	
	23rd		Only Barrage for 40 minutes Jordan by B & C Batteries Covering a rail by the 140th to Railway Brigade at 10pm.	
	24th		One new gun of J B Battery and one of C Battery hit and put out of action. B Battery with one gun in action only. Taken off normal zone.	

T2134. Wt. W708-776. 500000. 4/15. Sir J. C. & S.

Army Form C. 2118.

WAR DIARY
or
INTELLIGENCE SUMMARY.
(Erase heading not required.)

Instructions regarding War Diaries and Intelligence Summaries are contained in F. S. Regs, Part II. and the Staff Manual respectively. Title pages will be prepared in manuscript.

Place	Date	Hour	Summary of Events and Information	Remarks and references to Appendices
STLOI	25th		B and C Batteries at 1 P.M. and 4 P.M. took part in combined bombardments of special points and were shelled in return. 8 Battery continued with harassing fire throughout night. Visit by GOC 41st Division.	
	26th		Harassing fire on enemy shell holes and practice barrage carried out by batteries of the Group. At 10.50 S.O.S. was reported after heavy enemy shelling and fired on by C Battery and battery of 47th Brigade. No infantry action took place.	
	27th		D/119 Battery and D/236 Group. D/236 fire for ??? each night. On patrols carrying out tonight fired harassing fire and S.O.S. lines for The night. Night firing increased. Lieut R.B. OLLMAN 9236 awarded Military Cross	
	29th		C/236 Battery and D/236 Battery took shelled this afternoon. Some of the guns on reserve brought up into action	
	30th		The remainder of reserve guns and howitzers brought up into action and reported. Barrages checked with flank batteries. 2nd Lieut J.C. ???? evacuated to England.	
	31st		ZERO TIME for Offensive by 2nd and 5th Armies 3.50 am Barrage from West	

Army Form C. 2118.

WAR DIARY
or
INTELLIGENCE SUMMARY.
(Erase heading not required.)

Instructions regarding War Diaries and Intelligence Summaries are contained in F. S. Regs., Part II. and the Staff Manual respectively. Title pages will be prepared in manuscript.

Place	Date	Hour	Summary of Events and Information	Remarks and references to Appendices
STEEN	July 31st (cont'd)		Fired on by CHATEAU GROUP consisted of B/236, C/236 and A/147 on a creeping barrage and B/147 and D/147 on standing barrages D/236 doing continuous counter-battery work with push pull. Decrease of fire ordered at 8.30 am decreasing after half an hour. Further details to complete objectives covered at 11.30 am. Machine guns and dynamite holding up the advance by (22nd and (23rd Syfretty Brigades fired on by Batteries of Group, Reristcu Barrage at slow rate finally stopped at 5.30 pm. C/236 continuing fire on Group front in bursts. About 1100 rounds fired. MCO in B/236 wounded. Counter attack imminent at 9.30 pm and protective barrage placed for 30 minutes. Total casualties to the Brigade during operations from July 4th onwards:— 2 Officers wounded, 14 Other ranks killed, 3 Other ranks died of wounds and 27 Other ranks wounded.	

H. C. W. Lt.Col. R.A.
Commanding
236th Brigade R.F.A.

236th Brigade R.F.A.

Army Form C. 2118.

WAR DIARY
or
INTELLIGENCE SUMMARY.
(Erase heading not required.)

August 1917

Vol 30

Place	Date	Hour	Summary of Events and Information	Remarks and references to Appendices
ST ELOI	Aug 1st	4.20 AM	Zero Hour for further attack by 122nd & 123rd Inf. Bdes. 41st Divn. moon to slaughter line. HOLLEBEKE now occupied. Creeping barrage fired on by Batteries in the same manner as on Z day (31st July) and for ordinary Night firing programme carried until 7 am. All quiet during the day. Night firing programme carried out and machine guns engaged.	
	2nd		Reconnaissance and shoots on enemy machine guns carried out. Operations hampered by bad weather. Special night firing programme still in force.	
	3rd		Heavy shelling opened at 3 am and at 3.7 am SOS calls were received all along the line and batteries fired on barrage line until 4.30 am. No infantry action developed.	
	4th		One OR of C/236 Battery killed.	
	5th		Batteries of Brigade heavily shelled early this morning and up to noon. At about 5 am the enemy attacked and in spite of barrage in attack got into HOLLEBEKE I and POLKA FARM. Infurso attack counter attacked and driven out. Another attack was made at 9.25 pm but SOS was seen and attack was entirely stopped by barrage.	

WAR DIARY
or
INTELLIGENCE SUMMARY.
(Erase heading not required.)

Army Form C. 2118.

Place	Date	Hour	Summary of Events and Information	Remarks and references to Appendices
S'207	Aug 5th		4 other ranks of C/236 wounded. First Sections of A/147, B/147 and D/119 moved out — the two former to cat- training over respectively to sections of A/236 and B/236 at the DAMMSTRASSE position	
	6th		Relief of A/147 and B/147 by A/236 and B/236 completed, and also of D/119. CHATEAU GROUP now consists of 236 Brigade only.	
	8th		One Other rank of D/236 wounded. Night firing barrages carried out by all Batteries during the night. C/236 much shelled all night.	
	10th		Batteries fired on Barrage this morning, zero hour 4.35 am, B an hour covering an advance of posts on Divisional front and are in conjunction with an attack by II Corps on the left.	
	11th		The C.O. Brigade to Cunnay Hope course at STOMER	
	12th		D/236 Battery during an attack by the Division on the left carried out a gas shell counter battery bombardment for half-an-hour at 4.25 am. Concentration shoots by all batteries again carried out at times prearranged times.	

Army Form C. 2118.

WAR DIARY
or
INTELLIGENCE SUMMARY.
(Erase heading not required.)

Instructions regarding War Diaries and Intelligence Summaries are contained in F.S. Regs, Part II. and the Staff Manual respectively. Title pages will be prepared in manuscript.

Place	Date	Hour	Summary of Events and Information	Remarks and references to Appendices
SELOI	Aug. 13		Three other ranks of D/236 wounded (gas). CO returned from Course at SCHAP.	
	14		Concentration shoots and SOS rounds per night still fired.	
	16		All 18pdr Batteries fired a barrage & an hour and D/236 fired on enemy battery targets in conjunction with a other attack by the 5th Army. One Shoot 4.45 a.m.	
	18		Road firing carried out. One section of B/236 Battery relieved by one section of A/119 this evening. Caused D Batteries shifted during the whole morning - one howitzer damaged by shell fire.	
	19		Remaining sections of B/236 went out of action.	
	20		First sections of A, C and D Batteries withdrew to wagon lines in the evening.	
LA CYTTE	21		CHATEAU GROUP ceased to exist at noon today and Brigade HQ with OC Brigade withdrew & wagon lines - remaining sections of A, C and D Batteries withdrawing later in the day. Concentration in wagon lines complete by 9 p.m. Major A.C. POLLARD OC D/236 evacuated wounded (gas).	
	22		Brigade (Batteries marching independently) relieved to X Corps reserve	

Army Form C. 2118.

WAR DIARY
or
INTELLIGENCE SUMMARY.
(Erase heading not required.)

Instructions regarding War Diaries and Intelligence Summaries are contained in F. S. Regs., Part II. and the Staff Manual respectively. Title pages will be prepared in manuscript.

Place	Date	Hour	Summary of Events and Information	Remarks and references to Appendices
	Aug.			
BOESCHEPE	22nd		In BOESCHEPE area marching at 8.30 a.m.	
	24th		Inspection by II Army Commander of personnel and horses of the Brigade near BOESCHEPE	
(YPRES)	28th		Brigade moved 45th Brigade in action opposite GLENCORSE WOOD on the MENIN ROAD front. Batteries relieving as follows A/236 - 1st By RFA ; B/236 - 3rd By RFA ; C/236 - 5th By RFA; D/236 - 57th By RFA ; four Group tins on position. Brigade now part of "A" Group under command of OC 86 RFA Brigade on left. Personnel Area of II Corps 5th Army.	
HOOGE	29th		Major Lees of the Brigade moved up to Mess of 45th Brigade area OUDERDOM at 8.45 a.m.	
	30th		Major NEWBOLD OC C/236 Battery wounded. One OR B/236 wounded. One NCO A/236 wounded. One OR C/236 wounded.	

W. G. [signature]
Commanding 236 Brigade R.F.A.

236th Brigade R.F.A. September 1917 Army Form C. 2118.

WAR DIARY
INTELLIGENCE SUMMARY.
(Erase heading not required.)

Place	Date	Hour	Summary of Events and Information	Remarks and references to Appendices
HOOGE	Sept. 2nd		The Brigade in action near HOOGE on the MENIN ROAD came under the tactical command of "B" Group 47th D.A. commanded by Lieut Col. A.C. GORDON D.S.O.	
	4th		The Brigade commander still on leave — Major W. N. COOPER in command. All Batteries heavily shelled — 1 O.R. D/236 killed and 1 other rank D/236 wounded and one other rank C Battery wounded. Colonel A.C. LOWE D.S.O. commanding the Brigade promoted to rank of B.G.R.A. 66th Division.	
	6th		Two other ranks B Battery wounded	
	7th		One other rank A Battery wounded	
	8th		Major H.C. MORGAN transferred from B/236 to command C/236 with effect from 31st Aug. Capt. W.J. BAGNARD M.C. to command B/236 with Lieut WARDERON (B/235) as Captain with effect from 1st and 2nd Sept respectively. Lieut B. AYERS posted from C/236 to H.Q. 235 Bde. R.F.A. Lieut H.T. CUTHBERT posted from A/2 D.A.C. to D/236. and Lieut C.B. TOSON attached.	
	9th		Forward parties of 11th Australian Brigade arrived — take over waggon lines and first sections relieved at gun positions tonight. 1 other rank E Bty wounded	

Army Form C. 2118.

WAR DIARY
or
INTELLIGENCE SUMMARY.
(Erase heading not required.)

Instructions regarding War Diaries and Intelligence Summaries are contained in F. S. Regs., Part II. and the Staff Manual respectively. Title pages will be prepared in manuscript.

Place	Date	Hour	Summary of Events and Information	Remarks and references to Appendices
	Sept			
HOOGE	10th		Billeting parties proceeded to new billeting area at CROIX-DE-POPERINGHE near BAILLEUL. Remaining sections of Batteries relieved by 11th Australian Brigade — concentration of Brigade in Nepool Lines.	
BAILLEUL	11th		Brigade marched at 9 a.m. from Nepool Lines at OUDERDOM with sections of Batteries at 200 yard intervals via LA CLYTTE and LOCRE to new area at CROIX-DE-POPERINGHE. BGRA inspected tail of march. Concentration of Brigade completed by 12.15 p.m. Visit this evening by GENERAL A.C. LOWE late Brigade Commander before his departure to take up Command of 66 DA.	
	12th		Entrance parties from Batteries to positions. Guns only of all Batteries started at from 2 p.m. to 3 p.m. arriving on new positions before dark. A and B Batteries South of CANAL and just SOUTH of "BLUFF" and SPOIL BANKS respectively; C and D Batteries on old German lines immediately EAST of "BLUFF". A Battery under command "D Sub-Group (Col. AMBURY)", B and D under "E Sub-Group (Lt Col A.C. GORDON); C under "F Sub-Group"; all Sub-Groups under LEFT GROUP (Commander Brig Gen. STANLEY CLARKE 7th DA)	

WAR DIARY
or
INTELLIGENCE SUMMARY.
(Erase heading not required.)

Army Form C. 2118.

Place	Date	Hour	Summary of Events and Information	Remarks and references to Appendices
"BLUFF" YPRES	Sept 13th		All being under orders of 19th Divisional Artillery. Front covered by Batteries is the EAST of CANAL	
	14th		On this march killed and two wounded in D Battery on new position. Lieut Colonel R.H. BOHRING arrived and posted to command Brigade. Major W. COOPER relinquished temporary command of Brigade. 1 other rank wounded in both A and C Battery. Registration carried out by Batteries.	
	15th		Major W. COOPER to KEMMEL (Rescision Notes) with Signal Offrs tactics. Reconoit Officers with 57th Infantry Brigade. 2 other ranks of A Battery wounded. Practice Barrage carried out by Batteries at 8 a.m.	
	16th		A practice barrage on army front carried out — Batteries firing 40 minutes at 10am. One other rank of A Battery wounded. Two barrages — at 7am and 5 p.m. — Carried out by Batteries and a certain amount of noise Battery day and night firing by D Battery. 11. C. WILKINSON M.C. rejoined D Battery from Base (his operation (sick))	

Army Form C. 2118.

WAR DIARY
or
INTELLIGENCE SUMMARY.
(Erase heading not required.)

Instructions regarding War Diaries and Intelligence Summaries are contained in F. S. Regs., Part II. and the Staff Manual respectively. Title pages will be prepared in manuscript.

Place	Date	Hour	Summary of Events and Information	Remarks and references to Appendices
"BLUFF" YPRES	Sept 17th (cont.)		Other ranks (H&Signal Subsection) and 1 other rank II Battery evacuated wounded (gas).	
	18th		Three practice barrages carried out today by Batteries.	
	19th		2Lt H.V.RAMSEY admitted to Field Ambulance (accidental injury to wrist)	
	20th		The II Corps in conjunction with the X Corps on the left resumed the offensive at 5.40 pm. This morning advancing to depth of 800 yards on the left, the rest of 19th Divisional Front on the YPRES-COMINES Canal being right flank of attack. All Batteries fired on the 19.D.A. Barrage D/Battery being counter Battery work. All objectives gained. 1 Serg. of A Battery and 1 Sgt of B Battery wounded. 9 other ranks B Bty wounded (gas) and 13 wounded (gas) remained at duty. 1 other rank of Signal Subsection wounded.	
			BGRA. 47th Division inspected vapour lines.	
	21st		19 D.A. Artillery Groups reorganised — B and D now in No 3 Sub-Group commanded by Lt Col A.C. GORDON DSO. and A and C in No 7 Sub-Group commanded by Major P.H. BUSBY.	

T2134. Wt. W708—776. 500000. 4/15. Sir J. C. & S.

WAR DIARY
or
INTELLIGENCE SUMMARY.
(Erase heading not required.)

Army Form C. 2118.

Instructions regarding War Diaries and Intelligence Summaries are contained in F. S. Regs., Part II. and the Staff Manual respectively. Title pages will be prepared in manuscript.

Place	Date	Hour	Summary of Events and Information	Remarks and references to Appendices
"BLUFF" YPRES	Sept 21st	(am?)	One officer & 1 N.C.O. of A wounded and one of B gassed. 3 guns of A Battery damaged by shell fire. Console catwalks broken up.	
	22nd		One more gun of A Bty damaged by shellfire — this Battery now with two guns in action.	
	23rd		Major Cooper returned from liaison duties with 57th Infantry Brigade. One NCO of both B and C Batteries wounded, also one of D Battery. A preliminary Barrage fired on by Batteries at 5 p.m. SubGroups in which Batteries are arms under command of Lieut Coxyde of 19. D.R. Batteries fired on preliminary Barrage at 9 p.m. Two gunners of E Bty wounded.	
	24th			
	25th		Dawn. B Batteries heavily shelled at intervals. 2nd Lieut G. JAQUES & B Bty killed on the Battery position at 5.15 am. In B Bty this afternoon 1 N.C.O. killed, 1 NCO wounded and 2 gunners and a driver also wounded. In shelling of D Battery Lieut T.W. CUTHBERT wounded, two gunners killed and two NCOs and a gunner wounded.	

Army Form C. 2118.

WAR DIARY
or
INTELLIGENCE SUMMARY.
(Erase heading not required.)

Instructions regarding War Diaries and Intelligence Summaries are contained in F. S. Regs., Part II. and the Staff Manual respectively. Title pages will be prepared in manuscript.

Place	Date	Hour	Summary of Events and Information	Remarks and references to Appendices
"BLUFF"	Sept 25th (cont.)		B Bty's remaining three guns 12 hrs between A and B/235. Relieved and supercedes personnel advised to Wagon Lines. Cpl RUMBLE 9236 awarded Military Medal	
YPRES	26th		V Battery took part in barrage to cover the attack by X Corps on and Corps on left on POLYGON WOOD. Much work with ZONNEBEKE was restored. Zero hour 5:50 am. C Battery holding gun stood out of action during the day	
CROIX DE POPERINGHE (BAILLEUL)	27		Batteries all withdrew from action commencing at 6 p.m. to the wagon lines at CROIX DE POPERINGHE	
	28		Capt. N. ANDERSON awarded BAR to MILITARY CROSS	
STRAZEELE	30th	10.30 a.m	Brigade marched via STUBA'S CAMP and METEREN to billets in STRAZEELE area which were reached by 1 p.m. Inspection on the strength of Brigade	
			2/Lt H.Y. RAMSEY (Sick) struck off the strength on evacuation to England.	

A H Bayning
Lt Col RFA
Commanding

T2134. Wt. W708—776. 500000. 4/15. Sir J. C. & S.

WAR DIARY
or
INTELLIGENCE SUMMARY.

(Erase heading not required.)

Army Form C. 2118.

36th Bde RFA

WO 3 2

Place	Date	Hour	Summary of Events and Information	Remarks and references to Appendices
	Oct.			
TANNAY	1st	10 a.m	Brigade marched from billets at STRAZEELE via HAZEBROUCK to billets at TANNAY (on Mway to ARRAS, not Jnny 4/1925) arriving here at 3 p.m. after inspection en route by B.C.R.A.	
LAPUGNOY	2nd	7 a.m	Brigade continued march of 6 hours through MOLINGHEM, LILLERS and MARIES-LES-MINES to billets at LAPUGNOY arriving at 1 p.m.	
ACQ	3rd	9.30 a.m	Brigade marched Foley through CALONNE - RICOUART, RUITZ and REBREUVE at which three Batteries had midday halt. HQ and D Batty halting at CHOCOURT. Brigade reached billets at ACQ near AUBIGNY at 5.30 p.m.	
	4th		Advance section and C.O. to new front at OPPY to take over Arras battery positions and reconnoitre for relief of 63rd D.I.	
BAILLEUL (ARRAS)	5th		236 Brigade relieved 317th Brigade R.F.A. 63rd Divisional Artillery covering front held by 142 Inf Bde. 47th Division from North of OPPY Wood back OPPY to windmill North of GAVRELLE A/236 relieved A/317, B/236 relieved B/317, C/236 relieved C/317 and D/236 - D/317. (Half the Battery occupying a forward position NEST of ARLEUX the 3 Batteries in and around BAILLEUL village and	

Army Form C. 2118.

WAR DIARY
or
INTELLIGENCE SUMMARY.
(Erase heading not required.)

Place	Date	Hour	Summary of Events and Information	Remarks and references to Appendices
BAILLEUL (ARRAS)	Oct 5th (cont)		a front of 2000 yards (2 Battalions). B Bty at Roporliere but Brok on forward position	
	6th		The Greys (236 Bde) firing Cutmet 300 rounds per day in harassing fire. Visits by BGRA and Divisional Commander	
	7th		C Battery took part at 2.30 am in a barrage covering a raid by the 3rd Division on the left. B Battery working on Proulin West of APLEX.	
	8th		The BGRA visited all Battery positions	
	9th		Firing allotment per 24 hours now 400 rounds 18 pdr and 150 4.5 Hows.	
	10th		Capt T.H. FLYNN posted to command C/235; Lt. PFRD.RYDER posted from 235th Brigade to the staff of 9/236 vice Capt FLYNN (actual change temporarily suspended) 2Lt J. GLOVER posted from DAC to 9/236 and 2Lt N.E. LAWSON from DAC posted to B/236. All take effect from yesterdays date.	
	11th		A discharge of poison gas made on the enemy lines by OPPY at 3 am accompanied by bursts of fire from the Group (A, C and D Bty) many retaliation on Division on left on whose front Bellevue front assortype barrage. A/236 heavily shelled from 1 am to 2 pm — 110	

Army Form C. 2118.

WAR DIARY
or
INTELLIGENCE SUMMARY.
(Erase heading not required.)

Instructions regarding War Diaries and Intelligence Summaries are contained in F. S. Regs., Part II. and the Staff Manual respectively. Title pages will be prepared in manuscript.

Place	Date	Hour	Summary of Events and Information	Remarks and references to Appendices
BAILLEUL (ARRAS)	Oct 14th (Plan P9)		Casualties	
	15		Inspection of Brittany positions by GOC XIII Corps and CRA	
	18th	3.30	Zero line in a road on the enemys trenches immediately North of GAVRELLE by 141st (Rifle) Infantry Brigade — coming barrage fired on by A.C. and D.B. Batteries (the latter with only 2 guns) for half-an-hour. Enemy retaliation practically nil.	
	19th		2nd Bar to Military Cross awarded to Capt N. ANDERSON B/236 Battery.	
	20th		B/236 Battery came into action in forward position close to forward line.	
			D/236 with 2 guns in a rear position North of GAVRELLE. Lt. Ducky MILLWARD	
	21st		C/236 Bty registered and took over zone of D/236 Battery which went out of action to wagon lines	
	22nd		Latest honours :— Lieut H.L. BURGIS A Bty awarded MILITARY CROSS and Sergt STEVENS. H. A Bty and Bomb? CROSS A. A Bty and Gnr NIKINSON D Bty awarded Military Medal	
	24th		C/236 Battery pulled out to rest at FREVENT CHAPELLE	
			In addition to usual daily harassing fire and registration by aeroplane	

Army Form C. 2118.

WAR DIARY
or
INTELLIGENCE SUMMARY.
(Erase heading not required.)

Instructions regarding War Diaries and Intelligence Summaries are contained in F. S. Regs., Part II. and the Staff Manual respectively. Title pages will be prepared in manuscript.

Place	Date	Hour	Summary of Events and Information	Remarks and references to Appendices
BAILLEUL (ARRAS)	Oct 24th (contd)		Observation D/236 fired on a number of N.Z. Bns. in Billets Building firing during a raid by the Division on the right.	
	25th		Usual hostile and sniping fire carried out. A small raid carried out by the 8th Bn. 140 Bde. was covered by a barrage of all guns of the Brigade at 1.40 am. About 500 rounds fired. No retaliation.	
			A gas projection on Craylus immediately north of OPP4 and under 7/W. Batteries firing tin bottles.	
	27th		Much retaliation. Carried out measures to counter this fire.	
	28th		CO visited C Battery in rest. A/236 in BAILLEUL shelled all day — no damage done. Harassing by B/236 commenced.	
	29th		Received reports incendiary shells being used out by B/236.	
	30th		Much sniping and harassing of the enemy carried out. Position being disposed for OBty had inspected raid.	

A H Seaward
Commanding

WAR DIARY
or
INTELLIGENCE SUMMARY

Army Form C. 2118.

236th Brigade R.F.A.
November 1917

VII 33

Place	Date	Hour	Summary of Events and Information	Remarks and references to Appendices
BAILLEUL (ARRAS)	Nov 1st		The Brigade still in action in and near BAILLEUL on the OPPY front	
	2nd		C/236 brought into this renewing fire into action at the original position from out at FRESNOY–CAPELLE for the redoubt in 4" sector. Registration carried out today. Two guns of C/165 Battery 31st Division placed under orders of OC B/236 for operation. A feint barrage immediately North of OPPY Wood fired on by batteries on 4.15 pm in conjunction with the close of gas and smoke. No retaliation.	
	3rd		Harassing and registration carried on as well as bad weather permits	
	4th		A large daylight raid carried out by 142 Inf Brigade on enemy's trenches opposite GAVRELLE at 4.30 pm covered by artillery barrage (by Right Group (35th Inf Brigade) assisted by Left Group (V/236 Brigade) and the 31st and 61st Div Arty. All Batteries fired for 75 minutes and raid was successful (14 prisoners, 3 machine guns and 2 Trench Mortars) Enemy retaliated on Right Brigade front.	
	5th		Lieut HELLIOTT posted from C.By to HQrs as Orderly Officer	
	6th		Two howitzers of D/236 Battery lent to 31st D.A. and owned to D/170 position	

WAR DIARY or INTELLIGENCE SUMMARY

Army Form C. 2118.

Place	Date	Hour	Summary of Events and Information	Remarks and references to Appendices
BAILLEUL (ARRAS)	Nov 6.		In BAILLEUL. Section of B/236 Battery lent to C/165 Brigade. 31st Div. Both for raid by 31st Div.	
	7.		Registration for raid at TRESCAULT continued. B/236 and B/235 continued registration for raid at TRESCAULT. General MARKER M.G.R.A. 5 Army inspected Reports.	
	8.		Wagon lines shelled — one other rank A/236 Battery wounded. Zero hour for raid by 31st Div at TRESCAULT — one C/236 Battery OR (missing) killed by A/235 (not ?)	
			Brigade and B/235 Battery in position of opposition nearly 35 prisoners (above) had drawn. Barrage for 15 minutes. Raid very successful. A/236 Battery wounded of civilian. C/236 took over the Nieuport Sec.	
			in BAILLEUL. A/236 Battery Mess Room. Gunner posted from A/236. Lieut O.H. LLOYD posted to A/235. 2 Lieut TH. HUNTER to C/236. 2 Lieut TH. HUNTER posted to 71/236. 2 Lieut BROTHERS LIMERICK and MILTON attached to the Brigade.	
	9.		A/236 sent 4 guns and B/236 one to the 1st Corps. A/236 has moved up B.C. A/236 marched at 10am to rest billets of C/236 at PREBAYT CAPELLE C/B Battery wagon lines marching up to Brigade wagon lines.	

Army Form C. 2118.

WAR DIARY
or
INTELLIGENCE SUMMARY.
(Erase heading not required.)

Instructions regarding War Diaries and Intelligence Summaries are contained in F. S. Regs., Part II. and the Staff Manual respectively. Title pages will be prepared in manuscript.

Place	Date	Hour	Summary of Events and Information	Remarks and references to Appendices
BALLEUL (PRESS)	Nov 11th		A section of C Battery in BALLEUL shelled all day by 250 rounds — one gun put out of action, but no other damage. - B and The front buildings of D Battery also shelled this evening and one howitzer hit, but no serious	
	12th		General work on roads etc at the Waggon lines placing under RE supervision	
	14th		Successful registration by aeroplane observation of enemy Trench Mortars near BATTY village by D Battery and subsequent bombardment	
	16th		Heavy shelling of SUGAR FACTORY and near musketeen of 18/236 by the enemy Artillery barrages by 16 pdrs on enemy resrve defences carried out twice during the evening in addition to usual 250 rounds night firing	
	17		Very successful registration with aeroplane carried out by D/236 Battery. Maintenance of positions by CRA 31st DA and Battery commanders pending relief	
	20th		Advance parties from Batteries of 21st DA arrived to take over Group exchange of gun positions, and addresses party to take over Group at Exchange of Work as test station for the Group at Right Group H.Q.	

A6945 Wt. W17412/M1160 350,000 12/16 D. D. & L. Forms/C/2118/14.

WAR DIARY or INTELLIGENCE SUMMARY

Army Form C. 2118.

Place	Date	Hour	Summary of Events and Information	Remarks and references to Appendices
BAILLEUL	Nov 21st		Arrangements changed — The Group to be taken over by 170 Bde HQrs with Battery. The 212 Div Artillery D/236 withdrew all their howitzers to the wagon line during the night today and replaced them by 4 howitzers of D/94 Battery.	
ARRAS				
ESTRÉE-CAUCHIE	22nd		Group HQrs relieved by 170 Bde HQrs and Batteries relieved B/236 by B/94 Battery, C/236 by B/95 Battery and D/236 by D/94 Battery in the case of B/94 Battery using GPs in position. Brigade marched at 11.30 am from Mt Hyron Lines to ESTRÉE-CAUCHIE arriving at billets at 3.30 pm. Drew 17 spare guns of 21st DAC from I.O.M. Workshops.	
WAILRUS	23rd		Brigade marched at 9 am from ESTRÉE-CAUCHIE via CAMBLAIN L'ABBÉ ACQ and AGNEZ-LES-DUISANS to billets at WAILRUS arriving midday. Now complete with guns and almost with supplies after recent relief. Brigade M.O. — Capt W.R. Sadler R.A.M.C. left for home absent-Beauf.	
BEHAGNIES	24th		Marched at 10.30 am to WAILLY, BOISLEUX-AU-MONT and HAMELINCOURT (HQrs A and C Btys) and SAPIGNIES (B & D Btys) to billets at BÉHAGNIES.	

Army Form C. 2118.

WAR DIARY
or
INTELLIGENCE SUMMARY.
(Erase heading not required.)

Instructions regarding War Diaries and Intelligence Summaries are contained in F. S. Regs., Part II. and the Staff Manual respectively. Title pages will be prepared in manuscript.

Place	Date	Hour	Summary of Events and Information	Remarks and references to Appendices
BUS (BAPAUME)	Nov 25th		Marched at 10 a.m. at half an hours notice via BAPAUME and LE TRANSLOY to crowded billets at BUS reaching there at 2 p.m.	
	26th		Brigade still at BUS under 4 Corps orders	
	28th		Staff note and practice tactical operations carried out this morning. News received that Brig-General A.C. Lowe D.S.O. m. 266th D.A. and C.O. of 236 Brigade for 2¼ months from Sep 1915 to Sep 1917 has been killed in action at YPRES (8th Guns south FRICOURT) in celebration	
	29th		Reconnaissance of ground of GRANDCOURT and PLEUQUIÈRES carried out for the purpose of selecting positions for every guns.	
	30th		Orders received for Brigade to march to HAPINCOURT. Billeting parties dispatched but orders countermanded as result of enemy attack via GRANDCOURT and GUEUDECOURT — and Brigade shortly to all enemy at GONNELIEU and GUEUDECOURT. Guns arrived back from FRICOURT after celebrating today.	

CMSommerville
Brig General Comdg 236 Bde

WAR DIARY or INTELLIGENCE SUMMARY

Army Form C. 2118.

23oth Brigade R.A.   December 1917   Vol 34

Place	Date	Hour	Summary of Events and Information	Remarks and references to Appendices
GOUZEAUCOURT	Dec 1st	4.30am	The Brigade at 4 hours notice marched from billets at BUS and APPOLINE at 4.30am up into action following heavy enemy counterattack and advance yesterday. METZ-EN-COUTURE reached at 6am and under orders of 20 Div. Arty. Brigade got into action in the area just North of GOUZEAUCOURT during the counterattack on GONNELIEU in the afternoon. Much Battery backtrack. Batty area shelled and 2nd Lt McLAWSON B/236 wounded and two wires killed and 5 wounded on D/236. O.C. Brigade placed in tactical command of Group of 9 batteries including 91st Brigade RFA and 463 Battery RHA	
	2nd		Batteries continually firing. Barrages & Support Shoots at dawn of enemy onto WELSH RIDGE (North of LA VACQUERIE) when menacing. No serious attacks during the day	
	3rd		Very heavy enemy shelling of GOUZEAUCOURT and environs generally and in neighbourhood of Batteries and HQrs all night.	
	4th		Owing to advance of the enemy and capture of LA VACQUERIE A/236 and	

Army Form C. 2118.

WAR DIARY
or
INTELLIGENCE SUMMARY.
(Erase heading not required.)

Instructions regarding War Diaries and Intelligence Summaries are contained in F. S. Regs., Part II. and the Staff Manual respectively. Title pages will be prepared in manuscript.

Place	Date	Hour	Summary of Events and Information	Remarks and references to Appendices
GOUZEAUCOURT	Dec 4th		D/236 Battery shelled enemy back onto enemy in our outpost road. Much shelling by the enemy all day. Tramping intensely heavy all night particularly on GOUZEAUCOURT district. Barrage came down about a number of times today on everyone into festival situation.	
	5th		The Group moved to at 6 am soon after a very heavy barrage opened — the enemy attacking without success N.E. & S. of the neighbourhood of HARINCOURT. HQ moved back into the neighbourhood of HARINCOURT northern area, moved advanced and shelled position. Regrouping of Brigades countermanded — The Corps still being attacked.	
	6th		On the wings of WEST & EAST of the front. A number of barrages and SOS calls fired for during the day and evening and Harassing fire given to enemy attacks by the 182nd and 187th Brigades. 613th Div. Group now becomes Subsidiary 20th Div. Arty and awaits by 236 Buoy orders as the German form of the Corps enemy massing preparatory to a counter attack later opp by the German front of the Corps at 10.30 am.	

WAR DIARY or INTELLIGENCE SUMMARY

Army Form C. 2118.

Place	Date	Hour	Summary of Events and Information	Remarks and references to Appendices
GOUZEAUCOURT	Dec 7th (cont)		Brigade HQ shelled at 4.30pm and the MO was killed. Gun positions also shelled - one other rank (C Battery lightly wounded) and one slightly wounded. Brigade now covers LA VACQUERIE village on its SDS lines.	
	8th		New positions back in the TRESCAULT SPUR reconnoitred for B/236 and C/236 Batteries and a new Brigade HQ found. B/236 covered all guns onto TonyA Worl area shelling by the enemy. Near Kers covered base to FINS. Brigade now covering 184th Infantry Brigade.	
	9th		Brigade HQ moved a short distance back into HAVRINCOURT WOOD. C/236 Battery moved back into TRESCAULT SPUR this morning. Gunners brought guns back with old GOUZEAUCOURT position.	
	11th		First parties of relieving 173rd Brigade RFA arrived and first parties of 236 Brigade went across to HAVRINCOURT and new HQrs reconnoitred on new front.	
	12th		Triangular relief accomplished today. 173rd Brigade took over LA VACQUERIE front positions and guns and 236 Brigade took over positions and forms of 310 Brigade RFA at HAVRINCOURT covering GRAINCOURT front	

WAR DIARY
or
INTELLIGENCE SUMMARY.
(Erase heading not required.)

Army Form C. 2118.

Place	Date	Hour	Summary of Events and Information	Remarks and references to Appendices
HAVRINCOURT	Dec 12th	(cont)	Relief complete by 4 pm. OC 236 Brigade and commanding Group of all Artillery under 47th Division consisting of 236 Brigade, 235 Brigade and 77 Brigade Army F.A. covering whole 47th Divl Front (now held by 141st Brigade). Much rapid firing carried out by all Batteries consisting of barrages and bombardment by GRANDCOURT	
	13th		Bombardment by all guns of GRANDCOURT to 5 minutes at 8.30 am.	
	14th		A/236 Battery moved early this morning to position on edge of HAVRINCOURT village.	
	15th		5 ORs Rank of B/236 Battery wounded by bomb from aeroplane. B/236 Battery completed its own truce position 500 yards east of former position	
	16th		D/236 Battery moved to position with South section outskirts of HAVRINCOURT	
	17th		Lieut. P.S. AYRES reported from DAC to C/236 Battery	
	18th		77th Army Bde RFA went out of action and thus only the LEFT GROUP which consists of 235 and 236 Bdes only under command of OC 236 Bde	

WAR DIARY
or
INTELLIGENCE SUMMARY.

(Erase heading not required.)

Army Form C. 2118.

Place	Date	Hour	Summary of Events and Information	Remarks and references to Appendices
HAIRINCOURT	Dec 19th		Firing allotment increased. Two Howitzer rounds per Battery during first each night. Now covering 51st Inf Bde, 17th Div with one Colonel 140 Bde	
	20th		Positions to cover new line of defence reconnoitred	
	22nd		Firing of Howitzer decreased to 150 rounds per Battery. Usual harassing fire still being carried out.	
	23rd		At noon 48 17th DA relieved 48 59th DA.	
	24th		G.O.C. R.A. V Corps visited Battery Positions with a representative from GHQ. BGRA 17th Division visited Group HQrs and under this command. S.O.S. alarm at 9 pm.	
	25th		Positions for silent batteries reconnoitred. CO now acting as CRA during absence of B. General Whitty.	
	27th		The Left Group consisting of 47th Div Arty now covering whole 17th Divisional front as 59th Divisional Artillery in process of withdrawing. Allotment for firing doubled.	
	28th		Left Group now consists of 236 Brigade only - 235 Brigade RFA having relieve Right Group. Left Group still covering two (2) Battalions of 51st Bde	

Army Form C. 2118.

WAR DIARY
or
INTELLIGENCE SUMMARY.
(Erase heading not required.)

Place	Date	Hour	Summary of Events and Information	Remarks and references to Appendices
HAVRINCOURT	Dec 29th		Heavy enemy shelling during the night.	
	30th	6.30 am	Heavy bombardment by the enemy and the Bosche fired an SOS Lights and half an hour on 65th Divns wire front to the west. But main attack materialized	
	31st		Barrage over covering 52nd Inf Bde 17th Division attack relieved 51st Inf Bde	

31-12-16   236 BRIGADE R.F.A.

[signed] Lt. Col
Comm'd 236 Bde R.F.A.

Army Form C. 2118.

236 Bde RFA

Vol 33

WAR DIARY
or
INTELLIGENCE SUMMARY.

(Erase heading not required.)

Instructions regarding War Diaries and Intelligence Summaries are contained in F. S. Regs., Part II. and the Staff Manual respectively. Title pages will be prepared in manuscript.

Place	Date	Hour	Summary of Events and Information	Remarks and references to Appendices
HAVRINCOURT	Jan. 1918 1st		Brigade staff arriving. 52 Bde 17th Division in GRAINCOURT sector and we under 17th DA for tactical orders	
	2nd		BGRA 17th DIV held conference at HQrs 236 Bde on defensive measures	
	3rd		Defensive positions for four new cuns reconnoitred. SOS on left formerly of Brigade at 4pm. Defensive barrage also rate firstly. Batteries to help our group. Party of Bayoath on left on CANAL were sniped	
	4th		Our Batteries bombarded enemy approaches from 6.55 am to 7.30 at normal rate to prevent concentration. Capt H.E. YEATMAN VC. on months course to England.	
	5th		Majors W. COOPER and H.S. DUNCAN awarded Military Cross in New Years Honour List Firing allotment decreased to 100 rounds per Battery per day.	
	7th		A and D Batteries fired in a Slow Barrage from 7am to 8am covering a local attack by 52nd Brigade	
	8th		New LEFT GROUP drawn with Mr Boyrath and Hand D Batteries Mr Boyrath covering a CANAL frontage 235 Bayoath as well covering a CANAL frontage	

WAR DIARY
or
INTELLIGENCE SUMMARY

Army Form C. 2118.

Place	Date	Hour	Summary of Events and Information	Remarks and references to Appendices
HAVRINCOURT	Jan'y 10th		Headquarters moved forward East to dugouts named U.48. 235. Brigade R.F.A. Now covering 41st Infantry Bde. Sector. Preserves front nets 4 Batteries 23.6.6.18	
		11th	New O.Ps reconnoitred. Our Batteries fired 40 rounds. Three heavy Trench Mortars 15.15 in	
		12th	2/A? W? Trench Mortar Battery with 4 6"inch Newtons now C.T.S in position at FLESQUIERES is under command. 2x 234 Brigade	
		13th	Very heavy barrage on Bayard front, by enemy from 4.30 am until 3 am. Batteries fired on a protective barrage at the request of infantry, have been in action followed by counter gun by 2nd Army.	No casualty
		16th	New position on our of retirement near Ruyaulcourt reconnoitred	
		17th	Lt Col H.B. Huet arrived at Hqrs. over command of 187 Group in absence of Lt Col J.H. Adams D.S.O. on leave. Major H. Cooper R.C. attached Hqrs. 47th D.A. temporarily commanding Brigade. A bombing raid took place by Ryr. Battalion of 17 Division on the Left. 2nd and 19 Mortar assisted with a barrage and enemy saps caught on way back to their Trenches. Fire discontinued after 10 minutes	

WAR DIARY or INTELLIGENCE SUMMARY

Army Form C. 2118.

Place	Date	Hour	Summary of Events and Information	Remarks and references to Appendices
HAMINCOURT	Jan 19th		A, B and D Battery positions shelled by an 8 inch howitzer at intervals all day. Some little damage to pits. No casualties.	
	20th		Construction of tunnelled dug outs in progress on all Battery positions.	
	21st		Ten SOS calls from 1st Battalion 8 answered by batteries, several two each day.	
			Much movement enemy today.	
	24th		Reconnaissance for possible forward O.P. in a line of FLESQUIERES carried out. Group arm arranges 142 Inf Brigade.	
	25th		G.O.C 47 Division inspected thoroughly information from 1am to 7pm today, accompanied by C.R.A. Stating Battery positions very satisfactory.	
	26th		G.O.C 47 Division visits and inspected Brigade Headquarters at BUS.	
	27th		Gas shelling of Battery areas — no damage or casualties at RANSDEY catchments Vacloze temporarily.	
	28th		Continuous shelling of enemy strong points in & gun pits south of GRAINCOURT By Groups with 6 pdrs. A. Shows 8 and 6 inch Newton mortars.	

Army Form C. 2118.

WAR DIARY
or
INTELLIGENCE SUMMARY.

(Erase heading not required.)

Place	Date	Hour	Summary of Events and Information	Remarks and references to Appendices
HARINCOURT	Jan 29th		New gun position for B/236 Battery reconnoitred. Battery fired firing 10 rounds SOS for 24 hours mainly on harassing fire. Bomb instructions at Major Lew's command post. 3 Other ranks B/236 slightly gassed_orderly. 1 Other rank	
	30"		gassed — to Field Ambulance	

Feb 1" 1918

B. O. J. Major
commanding
236 Brigade R.F.A

236 B/c R4
JM 36

Army Form C. 2118.

WAR DIARY
or
INTELLIGENCE SUMMARY.
(Erase heading not required.)

Place	Date	Hour	Summary of Events and Information	Remarks and references to Appendices
	1918			
HAURINCOURT	Feb. 1st		The 236 Brigade as LEFT GROUP still covering 14th Bn on FLESQUIERES front. Bombardment by 2.A.17th TM Bty (March Left Group) with 6" mortars onto fitful bursts on enemy outpost line & O.Ps.	
	2nd		and 9.5 How's harassed their dumps night and 0.5 How's harassed their dumps night	
	3rd		After shells in C13b at 4.30 owing to many fortifications in MHH9 of 17th D.A. on the opposite bank of CANAL DU NORD	
	4th		Barrage and covers 170 Inf Bgde who attack & relieved 14th Bn. New position for B/236 Battery in south side of GRAIN DOWN selected by Major and country Reps and informal future battle	
	5th		A number of rocket and other S.O.S. attack tests carried out by batteries	
	6th		Lt-Col BORING relieved from leave and was attached to 47th Div. Actg HQ. as A/CRA	
	9th		C/236 Battery burnt out a single sniping gun near FLESQUIERES. Lieut AYERS attached HQrs in absence of the Adjutant on leave until	
	10th		Return antitank gun positions reconnoitred	
	11th		Shelling of A/236, B/236 and D/236 Battery position areas — 3	

WAR DIARY
INTELLIGENCE SUMMARY.
(Erase heading not required.)

Army Form C. 2118.

Place	Date	Hour	Summary of Events and Information	Remarks and references to Appendices
HAVRINCOURT	Feb. 11th (cont)		Other ranks of B/236 killed on this position.	
	13th		Visit by Col's RA 3rd Army and V th Corps. Work commenced upon reserve artillery positions to cover intermediate line.	
	16th		Lt Col H.B. ALLEN handed over command of LEFT GROUP to Lt Col BONRING on latter's return from duties of CRA. Hostile artillery very active.	
	17th		Single forward 4.5 howitzer placed forward in HAVRINCOURT village for night firing and sniping purposes.	
	22nd		LEFT GROUP now covering 188th Inf Bde 63rd Division on scene front.	
	24th		Brigade at 10 am came under orders of 63rd (R.N) Divisional Artillery. Ammunition allotment outdrawn to 150 rounds per day per Brigade.	
	25th		Two guns B/236 now in new Battery position. Work now erected round all Battery positions.	
	26th		Forward guns of B/236 in position.	

Army Form C. 2118.

WAR DIARY
or
INTELLIGENCE SUMMARY.
(Erase heading not required.)

Place	Date	Hour	Summary of Events and Information	Remarks and references to Appendices
HARINCOURT	Feb 28"		New O.P. which was captured enemy concrete structure in PLESQUIERE taken over.	
	1-3-18			

Act Osborn Lt Col
commanding 256 Brigade R.F.A.

47th Divisional Artillery.

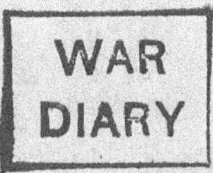

236th BRIGADE

ROYAL FIELD ARTILLERY

MARCH 1 9 1 8

236th Brigade R.F.A. March 1918
Vol 37

Army Form C. 2118.

WAR DIARY
or
INTELLIGENCE SUMMARY.
(Erase heading not required.)

Place	Date	Hour	Summary of Events and Information	Remarks and references to Appendices
HAVRINCOURT	Mar 1st		Brigade still in action at HAVRINCOURT and now covering 188th Inf Brigade 63rd (RN) Division on FLESQUIERE front with four Batteries and one Newton Mortar Battery in the LEFT GROUP	
	3rd		O.C. 88th F.A. Bde and first sections of Batteries arrived to relieve 236 Bde and reconnoitre positions and work on haul. Positions for forward sections chosen.	
BUS	4th		HQ and Batteries of 236 Bde relieved by 21mo and withdraw into V Corps Mobile Reserve at Inyou Lino at BUS under orders of HQ 47th Div. Arty.	
	5th		O.C Brigade and Battery commanders reconnoitred reinforcing positions between VELU and HERMIES and also North of main CAMBRAI road through BEUGNY and its necessary OPs. Vigorous training in open field, during signalling and laying now in progress. Further counter-attack reinforcing positions East of METZ reconnoitred.	
	6th		Lecture on CAMBRAI offensive given by ORA 47 Div to Battery	

A6945. Wt. W14427/M1160 35,000 12/16 D. D. & L. Forms/C./2118/14.

WAR DIARY
or
INTELLIGENCE SUMMARY.

(Erase heading not required.)

Army Form C. 2118.

Place	Date	Hour	Summary of Events and Information	Remarks and references to Appendices
BUS	7th		Commanders Reconnoitring and reserve positions for utmost defence line chosen and marked in neighbourhood of BARASTRE	
	8th		Positions to open counter-attacks on DOIGNIES or HERMIES in VELU and RUYAULCOURT districts reconnoitred by Brigade Commander and Battery representatives under supervision of HQ 19th Divisional Artillery. 2 Lieuts R. TALMAN and G.D. DAY attached Brigade.	
	9th		47 Divisional Artillery Gymkhana held on RUM LANE, near BUS, a number of entries by this Brigade. D/236 won great knockout competition.	
	10th		47th Div. Artillery Church Parade at BUS. CRA present.	
	11th		All Batteries practised coming into action in reinforcing positions near VELU. Major W.J. BUCHARD M.C. reported back from two months absence in England on course and leave.	
	12th		Had an alarm "Stand To" at 7.30 am. Brigade ready to move off by 8.30 and O.P.s and positions for counter attack in region of BEAUMETZ reconnoitred.	

WAR DIARY
or
INTELLIGENCE SUMMARY.
(Erase heading not required.)

Army Form C. 2118.

Place	Date	Hour	Summary of Events and Information	Remarks and references to Appendices
BUS	March 13.		Brigade and Battery Staffs out until 3pm practising taking up positions in action and reconnoitring observation stations in and around MESNIL-EN-ARROUAISE district	
	14th		47th Division practise counter-attack. MANANCOURT district. Wounded GOUZEAUCOURT RIDGE. Batteries of 236 Brigade covering 141st Infantry Bde, which was attacking as the Left Brigade in position between LECHELLE and MESNIL-EN-ARROUAISE. Very successful field day.	
	15		Counter attack positions around METZ visited and reconnoitred.	
	16		The Brigade practised by taking up positions west of BERTINCOURT where during private inspection was made by G.O.C. Division	
	17th		Several Gymkhana at BUS racecourse. Afternoons flat race won by Capt EDWARDS A.V.C. (attached to Brigade) on charger of Lieut DE WHEZ who was second in hurdles also. Inspection of Wagon Line Billets by C.R.A.	

Army Form C. 2118.

WAR DIARY
or
INTELLIGENCE SUMMARY.

(Erase heading not required.)

Place	Date	Hour	Summary of Events and Information	Remarks and references to Appendices
BUS	MARCH 19th		Orders received for relieving Artillery of 2nd Division in the line on WELSH RIDGE	
	20th		Whole Brigade out most of the day carrying out a practice counter-attack in the neighbourhood of BAPAUME Reconnaissance in conjunction with tanks and with infantry of the 19th Division	
BERTINCOURT	21st	4.95 AM	Commencement of GREAT GERMAN OFFENSIVE found by very heavy bombardment along the whole front. Brigade ordered to stand to at about 9.30 AM and at 10.0 am moved off complete to report to 19th Div Arty HQ at HAPLINCOURT	
		4.30 PM	17th Div Arty HQ at BERTINCOURT Batteries came into action at 4.30 PM from North East of the village and at 6.30 PM fired a barrage to cover a counter attack on DOIGNIES 2 Ohr ranks attd HQs killed.	
		11.0 PM	Brigade ordered to report complete north of BAPAUME at FAVREUIL north of BAPAUME	
FREMICOURT	22nd	6 am	Batteries arrived at BAPAUME - A and B/236 sent to form LEFT GROUP	
SAPIGNIES			6th DA at SAPIGNIES whilst HQs C and D/236 went into action	

WAR DIARY or **INTELLIGENCE SUMMARY.**
(Erase heading not required.)

Army Form C. 2118.

Place	Date	Hour	Summary of Events and Information	Remarks and references to Appendices
FREMICOURT & SAPIGNIES	MARCH 22nd		East of FREMICOURT covering the advancing German line East of BEUGNY	
		3.30pm	Barrage fired at 3.30pm against renewed enemy attacks	
		10.30pm	Orders from Group (2nd Bde RFA) to withdraw batteries to positions West of FREMICOURT and North of main BAPAUME - CAMBRAI road	
FAVREUIL	23rd	1am	HQrs withdrew to FAVREUIL and there covered 123rd Infy Bde on front between BEUGNY and VAUX now both in German occupation	
			Spr Signaller D/236 wounded	
			Major W.J. BARNARD OC B/236 Battery wounded at SAPIGNIES and evacuated	
			Continuous strong enemy attacks from VAUX & ables off during the day	
			All Wagon Lines retired to neighbourhood of POMMIER - LE - GRAND	
	24th		OC 187th Bde RFA took over command of RIGHT GROUP of which 236 Bde RFA is still B Sub Group.	
			Batteries now in rear of the enemy Objects withdraw a short distance continuous strong enemy attacks and frequent barrages fired.	

WAR DIARY
or
INTELLIGENCE SUMMARY.
(Erase heading not required.)

Army Form C. 2118.

Place	Date	Hour	Summary of Events and Information	Remarks and references to Appendices
	MARCH			
FONCREVIL	24th contd	2.30 P.M.	One section foes Battery withdrawn and sent to rear positions near BÉHUCOURT B/236 lost one gun thrown up - 5 men wounded.	
BÉHUCOURT		4.30 p.m.	HQrs and remainder of Batteries ordered by RIGHT GROUP to withdraw to positions near BÉHUCOURT - operation safely conducted under heavy fire.	
ACHIET-LE-PETIT		8.30 p.m.	Consequent on retirement of infantry to SAPIGNIES - BIEFVILLERS line Brigade ordered to withdraw further and take up positions East of ACHIET-LE-PETIT. HQrs C and D/236 in positions by midnight. Lieut CH de NATZ (attd D/236) wounded and missing by A/236 and B/236 Batteries joined the Brigade from LEFT GROUP and came into position.	
		11.0 am	Observing stations reported our infantry retiring from SAPIGNIES - BIEFVILLERS line.	
BUCQUOY		noon	Brigade ordered out of action and withdrew through ACHIET-LE-PETIT to positions in valley immediately East of BUCQUOY village and moved under orders of 41st Division.	

Army Form C. 2118.

WAR DIARY
or
INTELLIGENCE SUMMARY.
(Erase heading not required.)

Place	Date	Hour	Summary of Events and Information	Remarks and references to Appendices
BUCQUOY	March 25th		Batteries in action against enemy out-flanking Division in direction of IRLES	
	26th		Now under orders of 62nd DA which relieved 41st DA	
			Great difficulties as regards ammunition, forage and supplies	
		1.30pm	Brigade orders to retire on conformity with General withdrawal West of BUCQUOY and North East of TORQUENNES and on arrival in new positions on original No 1 Army Line, HQrs established on old German front line	
		11.30am	CO and Adjutant to 186 Inf Bde HQr BUCQUOY as liaison for 6 hours	
		5.0pm	Enemy attack on BUCQUOY first repulsed with loss OC J236 Bryntts new RIGHT GROUP commander with 187 Inf Bde RHA and 310 Bde RFA in the Group	
			Lieut CE. WILES (attd A236) wounded and evacuated	
	27th		Continuous attack and counter-attack in and around ROSSIGNOL WOOD. North of PUISIEUX. German Guards Division seen marching through PUISIEUX to SERRE. Australian division moved on our right	

WAR DIARY
or
INTELLIGENCE SUMMARY.

(Erase heading not required.)

Army Form C. 2118.

Instructions regarding War Diaries and Intelligence Summaries are contained in F. S. Regs., Part II. and the Staff Manual respectively. Title pages will be prepared in manuscript.

Place	Date	Hour	Summary of Events and Information	Remarks and references to Appendices
HANNESCAMPS	MARCH 28th		136 Brigade (RIGHT GROUP) HQrs moved back to HANNESCAMPS. Further enemy attacks beaten off. Brigade now covers fronts of	
	29th		187th Inf Bde and 186th Inf Bde. A/236 Batteries took strong point. Barrage line constantly changing. Much harassing fire carried out on masses of enemy transport and constituting Troops.	
	30th		New Observing Station on GOMMECOURT established. Heavy bombardment and attack on Division on the right during the afternoon. Brigade helped lines now at BIENVILLERS.	
	31st		Infantry of 62nd Division relieved by 37th Division. RIGHT GROUP now covering 112nd Inf Bde and partly 63rd Inf Bde on the right. Large harassing fire programme carried out during the night.	

Clements Touhy Capt RFA
for Lieut Col
Commanding 236 Bde RFA

1-4-18

47th Div.

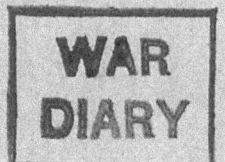

Headquarters,

236th BRIGADE, R.F.A.

A P R I L

1 9 1 8

236th Brigade R.F.A.   April 1918

WAR DIARY
INTELLIGENCE SUMMARY
(Erase heading not required.)

Army Form C. 2118.

47 Div   No 38

Place	Date	Hour	Summary of Events and Information	Remarks and references to Appendices
ESSARTS	April 1st		Heavy shelling of whole area at times during the day. Batteries shelled equally. 2/Lieut GRAND Headquarters in HANNESCAMPS shelled intermittently during the afternoon and evening. Lieut CER LLOYD wounded. Sick.	
	2nd		Group HQrs (236 Bde RFA) moved forward to Divisional Headquarters North of GOMMECOURT in old German front line. New Battery positions taken up same ROSSIGNOL WOOD front, connected immediately West of FONQUEVILLERS. 236 Brigade now covers 63rd Infantry Brigade of 37th Division.	
	3rd		The Right Group (on down to 1/236 Brigade and 187 Brigade RFA, 310 Brigade RFA) being transferred to the Left Group. A/236 and D/236 Batteries moved into new positions West of FONQUEVILLERS. Since 20th of March casualties have been 2 other ranks killed 15 wounded and three officers wounded.	
	5th		In accordance with orders received on 4th April the 63rd Infantry Brigade was to attack today and capture ROSSIGNOL WOOD. The	

WAR DIARY
or
INTELLIGENCE SUMMARY.
(Erase heading not required.)

Army Form C. 2118.

Place	Date	Hour	Summary of Events and Information	Remarks and references to Appendices
ESSARTS	April 5th (cont.)		Enemy had also arranged to attack on the whole front from BUQUOY round the Salient to South of LA SIGNY FARM and he opened a counter-battery bombardment of high explosive and yellow cross gas shell at 4.30 am. At 5 am all batteries of the Group of 236 and 187 Brigades formed a barrage at a slow rate across the advance of the Tanks on ROSSIGNOL WOOD. ZERO HOUR for the attack by the infantry was 5.30 am and the barrage at high rate of fire was placed at that hour and lifted afterwards decreasing in rate of fire until 7.10 am. At 6.30 am the 63rd Inf. Brigade reported that forward troops had been found but owing to strong enemy resistance ROSSIGNOL WOOD could not be attained and from 8.30 to 10 am a barrage was placed on by batteries of 236 Brigade and also by 16th Brigade on the South East edge of the wood. The bombardment by the enemy of all Batteries of Brigades and ridges increased in severity until reached its maximum at 8.30 am	

WAR DIARY or INTELLIGENCE SUMMARY

Army Form C. 2118.

Place	Date	Hour	Summary of Events and Information	Remarks and references to Appendices
ESSARTS	April 5th	(cont'd)	An attack by a number of Divisions took place both at BUCQUOY and LA SIGNY FARM where some only very slight advances were made, but no advance was made in front of 63rd Bn Bde. Enemy to attack at 5.30 am by the British. Batteries shelled with heavy bursts of fire, obviously enemy seen approaching our lines North of VENSIEUX several times during the morning so HQ 236 Bgde above had communication still standing with both forward infantry and batteries. Up to noon 7 officers and 200 men had been captured. Howitzers remained firing from 2 o'pm until 4 o'pm covering communication trenches and continual bursts of fire were placed on SOS lines by orders. Enemy however succeeded in working most of ROSSIGNOL WOOD during the afternoon by which time the enemy barrage had concluded. Three officers of the Brigade had been wounded by shellfire Lieut R.B. ULLMAN M.C. (C/236) and 2 Lieuts G.D. DAY (attached C/236)	

Army Form C. 2118.

WAR DIARY
or
INTELLIGENCE SUMMARY.
(Erase heading not required.)

Instructions regarding War Diaries and Intelligence Summaries are contained in F. S. Regs., Part II. and the Staff Manual respectively. Title pages will be prepared in manuscript.

Place	Date	Hour	Summary of Events and Information	Remarks and references to Appendices
ESSARTS	April 5th (contd)		and H.C.F. MILTON (attached B/236) evacuated gassed. One sergeant C/236 and one sergeant D/236 mortally wounded; 5 other ranks C/236, 3 other ranks B/236, 3 other ranks D/236 and one other rank A/236 wounded or gassed and evacuated during the day. Captain W. ANDERSON M.C. (B/236) and 5 other ranks of B/236 evacuated gassed from effects of yesterday's bombardment.	
		6pm	O.C. 236 Brigade took over command of new R.A. Group covering the line South East of the village of HEBUTERNE and consisting of 235 and 236 Brigades R.F.A. O.C. 235 Brigade remaining in action to command his Brigade as a subgroup. B/236 and C/236 Batteries moved to new positions west of FONQUEVILLERS from which new front to the South can more easily be fired upon.	

WAR DIARY
or
INTELLIGENCE SUMMARY.
(Erase heading not required.)

Army Form C. 2118.

Place	Date	Hour	Summary of Events and Information	Remarks and references to Appendices
FONQUEVILLERS	April 7th		RIGHT GROUP now covers 4th Australian Infantry Brigade. 236 Brigade Headquarters moved to dugouts Fonquevillers Vicarage intended for use in the Divisional area.	
	8th		Shelling of communications by the enemy.	
	10th		Came under orders CRA 37th D.A. who relieved CRA 62nd D.A.	
	11th		Information received that Lieut Ch. de WAEL wounded on 1st September on 25-3-16 has died in hospital. One Sept. C/236 who died in hospital.	
	12th	3pm	Hqrs 236 Brigade moved to CHATEAU-DE-LA-HAIE and relieved Hqrs 235th Brigade which noted moved to support Corps New Groups Hqrs established.	
	13th		Visit by Brig-General WHITLEY CRA 47th D.A. and in the morning by CRA 37th Div. Much harassing fire with 30 rounds per gun and 20 rounds per Howitzer was carried out each night.	
	14th		Counterpreparation barrage fired early morning B/236 and A/235 now made silent batteries.	

Army Form C. 2118.

WAR DIARY
or
INTELLIGENCE SUMMARY.
(Erase heading not required.)

Place	Date	Hour	Summary of Events and Information	Remarks and references to Appendices
FONQUEVILLERS	April 15th	From 4.45 am to 5.15 am a annihilation barrage was fired on enemy areas of 2nd Divn.	
	16th	5 pm	925.78 Battery ordered to infiltrate through New Zealand Division the immediate South and fired at L.J. My Gr Commd with W. 188th Battery and one troop of Battery M. Group. Liaison SOS barrage much praised the next evening.	
			CAPT S.E. PIXLEY posted from B/235 to command B/236 vice MAJOR W.J. BARNARD M.C. wounded vice/left from 25-3-18	
			Lieut H. DAWES posted a/Capt in B/236 Battery vice CAPT N. ANDERSON M.C. wounded (gas) with effect from 7-4-18	
			Lieut J.C. CORSON transferred from B/236 to HQrs	
			Lieut H.J. GLOVER from B/236 A/c Capt and Commd SAA Column D/C	
			2nd Lieut P.A. BATTY posted to B/236 and 2nd Lieut S.H. RANDALL? to C/236	
	17th		New Battery position to B/235 and new Group HQ. reconnoitred. Three enemy batteries in new forward positions located by air co-op observers and shelled.	

Army Form C. 2118.

WAR DIARY
or
INTELLIGENCE SUMMARY.
(Erase heading not required.)

Instructions regarding War Diaries and Intelligence Summaries are contained in F. S. Regs., Part II. and the Staff Manual respectively. Title pages will be prepared in manuscript.

Place	Date	Hour	Summary of Events and Information	Remarks and references to Appendices
FONQUEVILLERS	April 19th		Brigade (RIGHT GROUP) Headquarters moved to billets close to 118 4th Australian Brigade in SAILLY-AU-BOIS and communications to Batteries now nearly 3 miles further North arranged. Heavy bursts of harassing fire by enemy in neighbourhood of SAILLY during the day. Alternative positions in and around SAILLY for Batteries of 236 Bgde reconnoitred. Much enemy movement harassed.	
	20th		Our Battery wagons sent back at rear Wagon lines of C5WN and Limbers only kept forward.	
	21st		A reinforcement and several hostile field-gun batteries observed firing and heavily bombarded and silenced by A and D Batteries. One gunner of 236 badly wounded on battery position during the night.	
	22nd		Enemy batteries near STAR WOOD observed and Heavy Artillery ranged onto them in crashes of two hundred rounds three times during the day notably at 11.30 am and 5pm.	
	23rd		Positions for Batteries troops further in advance lines in the	

WAR DIARY
or
INTELLIGENCE SUMMARY.
(Erase heading not required.)

Army Form C. 2118.

Place	Date	Hour	Summary of Events and Information	Remarks and references to Appendices
FONQUEVILLERS	April 23rd		neighbourhood of HENU and ST LEGER reconnoitered. Bde HQrs at SAILLY-AU-BOIS shelled between 4.30 pm and 5.0 pm and one orderly wounded and 1 wounded.	
	24th		Enemy scouting airplane flying over Battery positions at FONQUEVILLERS at 2.30 pm shot down by Lewis guns of A/236 and C/236 Batteries and the pilot & Corporal wounded and officers passenger missed. The machine, a Fokker, crashed near B/236 Battery. C/236 and D/236 fired counter-ion enemy batteries seen firing at 12.30 pm in PUISIEUX-SERRE road	
		7pm	Front of Right Group held by 4.K Australian Brigade taken over by 1st NZ. Brigade and 236 and 235 Brigades R.F.A. came under orders (RANWZ Zealand) D.A. as LEFT GROUP. A/236 moved 3 guns to SAILLY. Bureau of firing ammunition 18pdr Battery 6700 rounds per gun per 24 hours, harassing fire increased. During the gas shell increase to 2400 rounds per 4.5 Howitzer Battery	
	25.		A/236 Battery moved two more guns to make five in there	

WAR DIARY or INTELLIGENCE SUMMARY

Army Form C. 2118.

Place	Date	Hour	Summary of Events and Information	Remarks and references to Appendices
SALLY-AU-BOIS	April 25 (cont'd)		position and D/236 moved all guns to SALLY-AU-BOIS and took up 236 posts position. Forward Infantry Lines moved to location North West of BAYENCOURT. Gas concentrations carried out by 4.5 Howitzers	and took 3 pns
	26th		C/236 moved took 3 guns forward position. Guns B/236 moved from to subset position in rear of A/236 and C/236 West of SALLY. Brigade O.P. now established at HEBUTERNE CEMETERY.	
	27th		Remaining two guns of B/236 moved South of forward position South East of SALLY.	
	28th		Registrations from new positions carried out. Enemy shelled Battery and SALLY-AU-BOIS area in trusts in retaliation for trusts of fire and crashes carried out continuously by Field and Heavy Artillery. Two signallers B/236 wounded.	
	29th 3pm		Command of Batteries of 235 Brigade for tactical purposes returned to OC. 235 (Bde R.F.A.) 236 Brigade now acting as "E" or Flank Brigade of NZ.D.A.	

Army Form C. 2118.

WAR DIARY
or
INTELLIGENCE SUMMARY.
(Erase heading not required.)

Place	Date	Hour	Summary of Events and Information	Remarks and references to Appendices
SAILLY-AU-BOIS	April 29 (con/d)		Enemy again shelled SAILLY-AU-BOIS in bursts of heavy howitzer and shrapnel shell. One gun A/236 Battery had primative whin bore - one man wounded.	
	30th		Captain N. ANDERSON M.C. (2 bars) late B/236 Battery awarded LEGION D'HONNEUR (CHEVALIER)	

R.H.Broring
Lt Col
Commanding 236 Brigade RFA

236th BRIGADE.
R.F.A.

236 Bde R.F.A.

WAR DIARY
or
INTELLIGENCE SUMMARY.
(Erase heading not required.)

Army Form C. 2118.

Vol 39

Place	Date	Hour	Summary of Events and Information	Remarks and references to Appendices
SAILLY-AU -BOIS	MAY 1st		Second new Battle OP adjacent to existing forward section B/236 constructed. Batteries now have practically completed new positions. Lieut M.G. BLACK attached from 47.D.A.C. to A/236	
	4th	8.50pm	An eighteen minutes barrage fired to cover a small attack on enemy salient in lines of 1st N.Z. Infantry Brigade immediately East of HEBUTERNE. Rapid relief fire carried out but no enemy barrage (retaliation) by the enemy. Ten prisoners were captured. Original SOS barrage lines taken over as final objective was not completely gained. Lieut H.C.T. MILTON reported for attachment to B/236 from OC 104th Army Brigade R.F.A. Evacuation due to gassing.	
	5th		OC 104th Army Brigade R.F.A. reconnoitred 236 Brigade Battery positions and Post sections of Batteries were relieved, guns being taken out.	
	6th		Completion of relief of Batteries completed by Trench and command handed over to OC 104 Army Brigade R.F.A.	

WAR DIARY
or
INTELLIGENCE SUMMARY.
(Erase heading not required.)

Army Form C. 2118.

Place	Date	Hour	Summary of Events and Information	Remarks and references to Appendices
BOVIN	May 6th	5pm	236 Brigade RFA returned to Wagon Lines at BOVIN	
GEZAINCOURT	7th		Orders for move out of III Corps area issued to the whole of the 47th Divisional Artillery and the No 1 Coy 47th Divisional Train and all moved to GEZAINCOURT and BUTSBERGUES near DOULLENS. 236 Brigade marched at 10am by route AUTHIE – SARTON to GEZAINCOURT.	
		10pm	Orders for move of 47th D.A. and Train again issued.	
STOUEN	8th		236 Brigade arty am marched via MONTRELET to STOUEN arriving 2 pm. O.C. Brigade now acting as V.C.R.A. in absence of Brig. Genl WHITLEY in action, and under orders of III Corps in 4th Army area. Staff Captain 47th D.A. attached to assist Staff of 236 Brigade in administration of Divisional Artillery.	
LIERCOURT	9th	9am	Marched via FUIXECOURT (where inspection by MGRA 4th Army took place) and LA CONDÉ to LIERCOURT arriving 3pm as last unit on road, 47th DAC having gone to BERNAY-LES-MAREUIL and 235 Brigade to ERONDELLE. Now under orders of O.C. 4th Army Artillery Rest Area and.	

WAR DIARY
INTELLIGENCE SUMMARY

Army Form C. 2118.

Place	Date	Hour	Summary of Events and Information	Remarks and references to Appendices
LIERCOURT	May 9th (cont)		completed refitting of Brigade ectn. horses. Lieut D.G. THOMAS formerly of D/236 reported and was posted to 151st withdrawn BASE	
	10th		Batman's horse Lewis changed and extensive stores received and further indented for. Charge course for specialists to be attended at HALLENCOURT	
	11th		Visit by O.C. 4th Army Rest Area - Major O'NEIL Y. KEYES formerly Adjutant of the Brigade - and O.C. 4th Army Artillery School - Lt Col. DICKSON. Gunnery Instructors attached	
	12th		Church Parade held in grounds of CHATEAU. Entertainments committee for sports and concert formed. Lieut Col A. BAILEY commanding 303 Brigade RFA 60th Division attached from PALESTINE front.	
	13th		Gunnery instructors (both Staff and A.S. Course) attached from 4th Army Artillery School and lectures commenced. Training area reconnoitred. Parties of men were being sent into RESOUILLE daily	

WAR DIARY
or
INTELLIGENCE SUMMARY.
(Erase heading not required.)

Army Form C. 2118.

Instructions regarding War Diaries and Intelligence Summaries are contained in F. S. Regs., Part II. and the Staff Manual respectively. Title pages will be prepared in manuscript.

Place	Date	Hour	Summary of Events and Information	Remarks and references to Appendices
LIERCOURT	MAY 15th		Physical training instructor attached for training of Junior N.C.O.s.	
	16th		Brigade Athletic Sports held from 2pm to 7pm in grounds of CHATEAU at LIERCOURT. Sgt LUPTON, Dvr HOLDWAY and Gnr STEVENS D/236 awarded M.M.	
	17	2.30pm	Inspection of Brigade in marching order on and near road D/Batteries fireworks by BGRA 47th Division.	
	18		Visit by MGRA IV Army and BGRA 47th Division. Brigade concert held in large marquee supplied by ETC and Army consisting of half of programme contributed by "LENA ASHWELL" Dramatic and Concert Company. Many visitors from other units of the Divisional Artillery.	
	19th		Church parade held in grounds of LIERCOURT CHATEAU.	

Army Form C. 2118.

WAR DIARY
or
INTELLIGENCE SUMMARY.
(Erase heading not required.)

Place	Date	Hour	Summary of Events and Information	Remarks and references to Appendices
LIERCOURT	MAY 20th		M.G.R.A. II Army inspected ramparts and roadways. Practically all deficiencies in stores and personnel now made up and all guns returned from Ordnance workshops. All rifles and sights returned from ordnance at HALLENCOURT. A Play given by "LENA ASHWELL" Dramatic Company performed before Brigade at 6pm very successfully. Gunr PATTERSON A/236 awarded M.M.	
BOURDON	22nd 8am		Brigade marched from IV Corps Artillery Res Area Billets LIERCOURT to billets at BOURDON via LONG and FLIXECOURT watering between LONG and LETOILE.	
CONTAY	23rd		Lt. J.H.O. PROTHERO attached A/236 Battery evacuated sick.	
		9am	236 Brigade marched from BOURDON who remainder of 47th Divisional Artillery via 47th Divn Train (mobile) under orders of OC 236. Brigade via VIGNACOURT - FLESSELLES - VILLERS - BOCAGE (Snow waiting late place) - MOLLIENS-AU-BOIS and BEAUCOURT-SUR-L'HALLUE to NAOURS-HOUS of 5th Army RHA Reserve at CONTAY and VADENCOURT ack came into III Corps Reserve. Batteries in billets and horse-lines bivouacs.	

WAR DIARY
or
INTELLIGENCE SUMMARY.
(Erase heading not required.)

Army Form C. 2118.

Place	Date	Hour	Summary of Events and Information	Remarks and references to Appendices
CONTAY	23rd		Rose of Billing of 5th Army Brigade which they were relieved in night. A/236 Battery which is in Wagon lines at BEAUCOURT next to those of 407 Battery 96 Army Bde RFA	
	24		A/236 Battery relieved 407 Battery in action at MILLENCOURT. B/236 Battery relieved an antitank gun detachment and Officer of 5th RHA Brigade and O/236 Battery relieved an antitank detachment and Officer of 408 Battery. O/Battery exchanges B/236 96 Army Brigade RHA in action. "O" Battery for the antitank gun manned handed over two guns to 58th Divisional Artillery. C/236 and 1.1 by 58th Divisional Artillery. Battery also handed over two guns to "Z" Battery RHA in exchange for one manned by C/236 and one manned by B/236 (83 Bde RFA) by 18th Divisional Artillery	
	25		Experiments with message-carrying rockets carried out. The Brigade Signal Officer Lieut L.T SIMEONS awarded M.C. as immediate award while under orders of 41st Divisional Artillery	

Army Form C. 2118.

WAR DIARY
or
INTELLIGENCE SUMMARY.
(Erase heading not required.)

Place	Date	Hour	Summary of Events and Information	Remarks and references to Appendices
	MAY			
CONTAY	25		Gnrs ANDRÉ and CLIFFORD, Signallers of A/236 awarded M.M.	
	26		HQrs and Battery positions of 83rd Brigade RFA near LAVIÉVILLE and BRESLE reconnoitred. Napoobines of 5th Army Bde RHA taken over by B, C and D Btys. Lieut Col HOBBS attached B/236 Battery.	
	27th		CONTAY and Major Innes men's Shelter at 6.30 pm, one horse killed	
	28th		One section of each Battery relieved one section of corresponding Battery of 83rd Brigade RFA in the ALBERT-AMIENS road Sector in their positions immediately South of HENENCOURT. The section of A/236 exchanged positions with section of A/83. Guns exchanged	
HENENCOURT	29th	5pm	Relief of 83rd Brigade RFA completed. A/236 has four horse guns in their Battery position and a forward section a mile East of LAVIÉVILLE. B/236 has four guns in main position and a forward section North of MILLENCOURT. C/236 has four guns in main position and forward section on Northern outskirts of LAVIÉVILLE. D/236 has four guns in main position and two manning A/82 Battery old position North of BRESLE. HQrs with 141 Inf Bde.	
			HQrs with 141 Inf Bde in the LEFT GROUP.	

WAR DIARY
INTELLIGENCE SUMMARY.
(Erase heading not required.)

Army Form C. 2118.

Place	Date	Hour	Summary of Events and Information	Remarks and references to Appendices
HÉNENCOURT	MAY. 29th		Brigade which it covers in Chalkpit immediately in front of Bellow positions. Forward wagon lines North of BRESLE WOOD civil at BAYSIEUX.	
	30th		The Group covers a front of 1500 yards. 1 Australian p.m. attached. Three bursts of harassing fire carried out during the night.	
	31st		New forward O.P. reconnoitred. Communication with forward anti-tank gun manned by C/83 established.	

A.M. Scott
Lieut. Col.
Commanding 236 Bde. R.F.A.

WAR DIARY
or
INTELLIGENCE SUMMARY
(Erase heading not required.)

Army Form C. 2118.

236 Bde R.F.A. Vol 40

Place	Date	Hour	Summary of Events and Information	Remarks and references to Appendices
HENENCOURT	JUNE 1st		All Batteries of 236 Brigade in main HENENCOURT position gas shelled from 4am to 5am	
	2nd		Battery positions again gas shelled at 4am - one gunner C/236 Battery wounded. Reserve and rear position manned by Tunnel dugouts between main Battery positions commenced by B/236 and D/236	
	3rd		Allotment for night harassing fire increased to 300 rounds of 18pdrs and 100 rounds 4.5 How on special targets	
	4th		Lieut Col H. BAILEY RFA attached 236 Bde HQrs took over temporary command of LEFT GROUP for 4 days from 5pm	
			A/236 Battery took a roving gun out in road due East of MILLENCOURT and 1500 yards from the front line and carried out harassing fire being withdrawn before morning	
	6th		a/Capt L. B. TANSLEY R.F.A. Adjutant of 236 Brigade awarded MILITARY CROSS in LONDON GAZETTE of 3rd inst (Kings Birthday Honours) Lieut H. HINDLEY attached to D/236 and Lieut L. EDGE to C/236 from	

Army Form C. 2118.

WAR DIARY
or
INTELLIGENCE SUMMARY.
(Erase heading not required.)

Place	Date	Hour	Summary of Events and Information	Remarks and references to Appendices
HENENCOURT	JUNE 6th		47th D.A.C.	
	7		A small raid was carried out at 11.15 p.m. by 19th Bn London Regt. opposite enemy trench immediately South of ALBERT-AMIENS road. Covering barrage found by the Brigade and the A/82 Battery in the Group for 30 minutes. Report by G.O.C. 141st Infy Bde pronounced artillery barrage excellent and prevented enemy machine guns and trench mortars from coming into action against the raiding party which killed some of the enemy. 2nd Lt H.B. DOUGLAS B/236 Battery acted as Liaison officer with O.C. Raid.	
			B/236 Battery carried out harassing fire with a roving gun placed about one mile from the front line	
	8th		At 2.30 am a gas projection opened by a burst of fire from B/236 and C/236 was carried out against the enemy trench which had been raided on the night of the 7th June G.O.C. 47th Division inspected Batteries of the Brigade this morning. C/236 officer and detachment received praise of C/R3 in charge of antitank gun.	

WAR DIARY
INTELLIGENCE SUMMARY

Army Form C. 2118.

Place	Date	Hour	Summary of Events and Information	Remarks and references to Appendices
HENENCOURT	JUNE 8th		Second line of enemy positions are 1 mile West of SAISIEUX reconnoitred. Lieut Col. A.H. BONRING assumed command of the Left Group at 5 p.m.	
	9th		Lieut Col. A.H. BONRING assumed temporary command of 47th Divisional Artillery in absence of BGRA on leave. Lieut Col H. BAYLEY D.S.O. resumed command of LEFT GROUP and Major W. COOPER M.C. became acting Brigade commander. Brigade now covering 142nd Inf Bde which today relieved 141st Inf Bde.	
	10th		At 9.45 p.m. Australian Corps on the right carried out an attack South of MORLANCOURT in conjunction with the 6th Australian Infantry Brigade carried out was runs at junction of 47th Division front and front immediately South of the 236 Brigade front to cover trenches on Northern slope of said spur. N.O.6.a.6.b. 11.45 p.m. General ROSENTHAL GOC 2nd Lieut Div reported that barrage was excellent and thanked on behalf of 6th Brigade to	

WAR DIARY or INTELLIGENCE SUMMARY

Army Form C. 2118.

Place	Date	Hour	Summary of Events and Information	Remarks and references to Appendices
HENENCOURT	JUNE		Valuable support	
	11th		D/236 Battery put outs forward harassing barrages up to dark. 80 officers and men of the Brigade have had or are now having short attacks of fever of unknown origin accompanied by high temperature lasting three or four days. Registration by A/236 and D/236 for small raid by Royal Bypach.	
	12th		8" The raid operation cancelled. A/236 Battery with heavy explosion own acting as Counter Battery. Liaison officers were supplied to the infantry Battalions in the line.	
	13th		New signs on double-entrance mined dugout for A/236 and CP236 between the two Battery positions. Eight to Eighteen enemy relief harassing fire allotment received to 450 18pdrs rds. 208 4.5How. Ammunition to the night.	
	14th			
	15th		Usual harassing fire kept up. No enemy comparatively quiet.	

act/CRA UCol A H DOWRING, visited all wagon lines the experience

Army Form C. 2118.

WAR DIARY
or
INTELLIGENCE SUMMARY.
(Erase heading not required.)

Place	Date 1918	Hour	Summary of Events and Information	Remarks and references to Appendices
HENEN-COURT	JUNE 15		from which the Brigade & other units of the Division have been suffering is abating.	
	16		The adjutant Capt. L.B. TANSLEY M.C. from L Dublin Ambulance with [?] Dengue Epidemic – not diagnosed as influenza. A/108 relieves A/82.	
	17	22.29	[An Enemy Aeroplane] (142 aprox) received many bombs from forward [?] areas at E.8.c.50.04 & E.14.a.2.5. Our Artillery replied.	
		11.30pm	4 Light Groups (236 Bde B.72 & A/108) & the 4th & 2 1/6 batteries & the [?] Ridge Groups. Seven minutes after our shelling Enemy barraged our front lines. Reply successful - 2 generous [?] in LT R. TALMAN acting as Liaison Officer to the Grid.	
	18		Lt Col. JONES at the Artillery commander (290 the Otago batts) returned with a [?] to [?] the brigade chief early start. Night 5/P changed to new location at D.4 + 6.2 followed [?] evening received from G.O.C 142 inf. Bde (Maj Gen. McDOUAL): - Please accept my thanks for 142 inf. Bde. for your cooperation in [?] and [?] [?] Plan & Counter attacks especially to [?] [?] our offices of [?] [?] [?] comrades [?].	

WAR DIARY
INTELLIGENCE SUMMARY

Army Form C. 2118.

Place	Date	Hour	Summary of Events and Information	Remarks and references to Appendices
HENENCOURT	JUNE 20th		236 B&RFA relieved in action by 290 Brigade RFA 58th Division and guns were exchanged. Relief complete by 5pm and detachments and HQrs withdrew to wagon lines at CONTAY. B/108 Battery in the Army had been relieved by 377th Battery.	
			Major W. J. BARNARD M.C. rejoined B/236 Battery and attached in absence of Major S.E. PIXLEY. Capt L.B. TANSLEY M.C. rejoined after three days at 6th F.A.	
	21st		Brigade marched at 6.15 am from wagon lines at CONTAY via BERNCOURT – POULAINVILLE and LONGPRÉ to billets at ARGOEUVRES and came into reserve in III Corps area.	
	23rd		Lieut J. RADFORD-NORCOP Staff Yeomanry attached to Brigade as Horsemaster. ADVS III Corps visited all horse lines of the Brigade and was pleased particularly with B Bty.	
	24th		Batteries commenced carrying out a programme of drill & training, first day was spent in Horsing drill & gun drill conducted by section.	
	25		Continuation of programme same as previous day. Colonel A.H. BOYRING resumed command of Brigade	

WAR DIARY
or
INTELLIGENCE SUMMARY.
(Erase heading not required.)

Army Form C. 2118.

Place	Date	Hour	Summary of Events and Information	Remarks and references to Appendices
	26		B.G.R.A 47 D.A. having returned from leave, LT. J.C. CORSAN M.C. acts as Adjutant 236 Brigade in place of Capt. L.B. TANSLEY M.C. transferred to B236 Battery & returned permanent rank of Lieutenant	
	26		Battery Commanders & Battery Staffs carried out a small scheme for practice in communications in action with units supervision of Brigade Commander on training area allotted to Bn Arty about 2 miles S.W.	
PICQUINY	27		LT. J. RADFORD-NORCOP Staffs Yeomanry attached to 236 R.F.A Brigade N.Q. These Batteries (A & B) carried out training in driving with gun drill in Supervision of Brigade Commander at PICQUINY. 236 Brigade orders to be prepared to move following night to a new location 12 miles distant.	
	28		Brigade Commander inspected Battalion marching order Parade	
		9.P.M.	Brigade moved from St Saveur Rest Area to DOUARS via LONGPRE AMIENS SWITCH ROAD & RIVERY arriving there in the following morning. 2nd Lt. H.B. DOUGLAS attacked were left behind to rejoin following day.	

Army Form C. 2118.

WAR DIARY
OF
INTELLIGENCE SUMMARY.
(Erase heading not required.)

Instructions regarding War Diaries and Intelligence Summaries are contained in F. S. Regs., Part II. and the Staff Manual respectively. Title pages will be prepared in manuscript.

Place	Date	Hour	Summary of Events and Information	Remarks and references to Appendices
	28		to 236 Bde HQ as Orderly Officer to replace LtJC Corson who has been killed	
DADURS	29		Brigade arrived DADURS 1 pm when billets had been arranged by BM	
			Australian D.A. Brigade HQ moved to BUSSY-LES-DAOURS	
		2pm	O.C. Brigade & Battery Commanders reported to 13th AH-GROUP H.Q	
			4th Australian D.A. for instructions & reconnoitred prospective battery positions	
			about 1000 yds south of CORBIE	
		9.30 pm	Batteries took up previously reconnoitred positions in action	
			& were ordered to have 600rds pr 18pr & 400 pr howitzers by 4AM July 1st 1918	
			Colonel H BAYLY DSO was attached to 21st Brigade Australian A.F.A.	
			for instruction. Brigade now covering 4th Australian Divisional Infantry	
FOUILLY	30		Batteries reported in the early morning but were ordered to remain silent	
			with the exception of B236 Battery even in event of S.O.S.	
			2nd Lt S.H RENVOIZE slightly wounded on Battery Positn C236 but	
			remained at duty	
	1 July 1918			

AWScann Major
Comd. 236 Bde RFA

236 "B" Bde R.F.A.

WAR DIARY
or
INTELLIGENCE SUMMARY.
(Erase heading not required.)

Army Form C. 2118.

Place	Date	Hour	Summary of Events and Information	Remarks and references to Appendices
July	1		Batteries with assistance of 4th Australian D.A.C. completed arrival & establishment of ammunition dumps in positions & spent day at work under cover, tasks for Battery Battans. 236 Brigade ammunition as "B" Sub Group	
	3		Preparations for projected attack continued. Z day agreed as 4th July.	
	4		Attack by 2nd & 4th Australian Divisions on villages of HAMEL, HAMEL WOOD, VAIRE WOOD, and spur running N.E. from main VILLERS-BRETONNEUX ridge. Attack was delivered at 3:10AM by 6th, 11th, 11th AUSTRALIAN INFANTRY BRIGADES plus four companies UNITED STATES INFANTRY, assisted by Tanks. Fifteen Brigades of Field Artillery and one RESERVE R.H.A. Battery put down a thick barrage in front of INFANTRY START LINE. 236 Brigade covered a front of 600 yds and moved forward the barrage in 100 yd jumps from lines including the Southern half of VAIRE WOOD to a final protective barrage about 200 yds north of CORBIE-WARFUSEE-ABANCOURT Road East to the outer of ACCROCHE WOOD. The programme was maintained very successfully & enemy defensive barrage was fifteen minutes late and weak and our troops were well inside it before it ought have become effective. Total prisoners 350 of whom	

WAR DIARY
or
INTELLIGENCE SUMMARY.
(Erase heading not required.)

Army Form C. 2118.

Instructions regarding War Diaries and Intelligence Summaries are contained in F. S. Regs., Part II. and the Staff Manual respectively. Title pages will be prepared in manuscript.

Place	Date	Hour	Summary of Events and Information	Remarks and references to Appendices
	July 4		and 1300 other ranks. Final objective taken and maintained	
			At 10.24 PM the enemy attempted a counter attack on the villages of HAMEL	
			but was repulsed with a loss of 50 prisoners	
	5		Expected counter attack in the early morning did not materialise.	
			Batteries harassed the enemy forward & intermediate trips by night	
			S.O.S lines moved slightly north being across ACCROCHE WOOD	
	6		Batteries took on charge ammunition of two 79th Brigade Artillery being	
			reduced now after the attack. Batteries fired on special counter preparation	
			Scheme at 3.5PM for twenty minutes. Major A.J YENCKEN promoted 2/Major	
			Lt Col B.H. WEST transferred No 2 Section 27th D.A.C. Lt HOBBS, C.R. from HQ	
			to B236 Battery.	
	8		At 12.15 Am a minor operation was carried out by 12th Australian Infantry	
			Brigade on a front on both sides of the River SOMME in order to	
			straighten out our existing front. 2.36 Brigade fired in continuation of	
			barrage reaching back 600 yds behind SOS lines. 1. 30 PM Operation	
			reported quite successful & all objectives taken. 1800 other ranks relieved	

WAR DIARY or INTELLIGENCE SUMMARY.

Army Form C. 2118.

(Erase heading not required.)

Place	Date	Hour	Summary of Events and Information	Remarks and references to Appendices
	July 8		For 236 Brigade to withdraw to wagon lines during the night 8/9 July and to march following night. Battery handed over ammunition both on positions and from echelon to 4th Australian Div Arty and withdrew from positions at 9 p.m. to wagon lines	
	July 9		On application to Australian Corps the Brigade received permission to march at 7.30 p.m. instead of after nightfall as previously ordered. Brigade marched at 7.30 p.m. to ARGOEUVRES via RIVERY, AMIENS SWITCH ROAD, LONGPRÉ arriving at ARGOEUVRES at 11.30 p.m.	
	July 10		Brigade spent day in cleaning up. 2nd Lt MILLER attached to D/236 Battery from 47th D.A.C.	
	July 12		2nd Lt DAY attached to C/236 Battery from 47th D.A.C. D.G.R.A. visited Battery Wagon & Horse lines. A and C/236 Batteries calibrated their guns on the Fourth Army Calibration Range near VAUX EN AMIENOIS	
	July 13		B/236 Battery calibrated two guns on Fourth Army Calibration Range at 10.30 a.m. 1 p.m. Battery commanders 2 officers and one gun detachment via Battery Staff proceeded on lorries to CONTAY to relieve 83rd Brigade R.F.A. 18th Divisional Artillery. The Brigade marched at 8 p.m. to CONTAY via LONGPRÉ = FOULAINVILLE	

WAR DIARY
INTELLIGENCE SUMMARY

Army Form C. 2118.

Place	Date	Hour	Summary of Events and Information	Remarks and references to Appendices
	July 13		CARDONETTE - BEAUCOURT arriving at CONTAY at about 12.30 pm the following morning	
	14		236 BRIGADE relieved 83rd BRIGADE RFA 18th DIVISIONAL ARTY in the LEFT GROUP, LEFT DIVISIONAL SECTOR. Third CORP. Battery positions located between SENLIS (inclusive) and HENENCOURT. S.O.S lines on a 9 gun 900 yards length fronting onto ALBERT BRICKWORKS. Brigade now covering 142 INFANTRY BRIGADE 47 DIVISION. Relief complete by midnight. Senior Liaison with Infantry Brigade established.	
	15		One gun of C236 Battery especially detailed in day light on enemy in forward areas. This gun to be built by all others. Its hostile fire practise in quickly replying from unexpected position.	
	16		A236 Battery registered by means of B Battery Observatia at N.11 Balloon Section. HARLEY MAJOR W COOPER M.C. D236 Battery occupied premoting Day harassing fire carried out aforwards by one Battery of the Brigade firing 36 rounds during the day. Night harassing fire carried out by one section of each battery in the Brigade firing a total of 450 rounds per night	

Army Form C. 2118.

WAR DIARY
or
INTELLIGENCE SUMMARY.
(Erase heading not required.)

Instructions regarding War Diaries and Intelligence Summaries are contained in F. S. Regs., Part II. and the Staff Manual respectively. Title pages will be prepared in manuscript.

Place	Date	Hour	Summary of Events and Information	Remarks and references to Appendices
July	16		B236 Battery working as a Counter battery with subsidiary and maximum range of 9000 yds in conjunction with Heavy Artillery	
	17		In order that all guns in the Corps on the line should be calibrated A236 Battery exchanged uncalibrated guns with calibrated guns of A169 BATTERY Army Field Artillery however owing to 169 ARMY BRIGADE being ordered South III app onwards the calibration between	
	18		B.G.R.A. noted battery positions 142 Infantry Brigade relieved the 143rd by	
	19		140 Infantry Brigade Brigade commander reconnoitred 6 observation positions 10 days of Rest camp near E.U. allowed for Brigade in the Brigade by 4th Army	
	21		MAJOR C.V.M TOWNSEND attached to A236 Battery for 3 pos.	
	22		Continued movement in enemy forward sectors throughout the day pointed to the early being observed B236 Battery had heavy to harass and enemy later proved reported to Relief by this Battalion	
	24		A small raid was carried out by the 2nd Battalion 7th LONDON REGT 142 INFY BDE at 3.45AM in a front of 300 yds about 1000 yds north of A. BENT RAILWAY STATION. 100 oil projectors were fired into the area to be raided before gas. Prisoners and an	

WAR DIARY
or
INTELLIGENCE SUMMARY.
(Erase heading not required.)

Army Form C. 2118.

Place	Date	Hour	Summary of Events and Information	Remarks and references to Appendices
July	24		Machine gun captured, raiding party sustained twelve casualties all slightly wounded. Only two hostile batteries responded to enemy's S.O.S. signal Lieut T. Proudfoot proceeded on 14 days leave to England. One battalion 131st AMERICAN REGT relieved	MORCOURT
	25		15th BATTALION THE LONDON REGT 140 BRIGADE in the line in the night 24/25 July. Brigade fired in support of raid carried out by 58th DIVISION on enemy front and support lines 1000 yds south of ALBERT-AMIENS ROAD at 10am. Raid reported successful. 20 prisoners taken. 2nd Lt R.H. SMITH proceeded on 14 days leave to England.	
	26		9am Projection of gas on enemy's front and support trenches 1000yds N.W. of ALBERT Brigade fired on its trackways roads to serve enemy batteries and field	
	27		during 16 the 47 DIVISION being ordered to take over more positions to the South, the Brigade front was increased by 500 yds and A103 BATTERY 107 (HANTS) BRIGADE was added to LEFT GROUP position on the outskirts of HERFORCOURT S.O.S. fired in front J and due east of ALBERT	
	29		236 Brigade inspected by Majn Cmer and Batteries in Munching order	
	30		Bombardment by 6" Guns in IIIrd Corps in 147 DIVISION of LEFT GROUP 47 DIVISION on enemy trenches in front of BOUZINCOURT and south of AVELUY. Bombardment lasted 25 minutes.	
	31		Activity from enemy trench mortars on LEFT GROUP front.	

A.T. Sowerby
Lieut Col
Commdg 236 Brigade R.F.A.

47th Divl. Artillery

236th BRIGADE

ROYAL FIELD ARTILLERY

AUGUST 1918.

WAR DIARY or INTELLIGENCE SUMMARY

Army Form C. 2118.

Place	Date	Hour	Summary of Events and Information	Remarks and references to Appendices
August 1918	1		B36 Brigade R.F.A. assisted in bgd barrage in a recent raid by 10th WEST YORKSHIRE REGT. 17th DIVISION on the trenches in front of AVELUY at 9.10 pm. Raid successful. 16 prisoners taken. A number of whom were found to be Polish, engaged in blowing up dugouts. Several explosions heard in ALBERT and prisoners report Division that enemy was preparing to retire on the RIVER ANCRE front.	
	2		Patrols reported enemy front line evacuated all along Divisional front. 58th Division entered DERNANCOURT. Reconnaissance patrols pushed forward during the day and reported the front line of RIVER ANCRE was clear of enemy troops. Posts were established on the east bank during the night. Posts in question pushed to the RIVER ANCRE where advanced posts joined the right Australian Troops S of HW 13.37 Sheet 57d. Occasional enemy encountered in ALBERT pair of whom witnessed to have been seen a patrol. SOS lines were east of RIVER ANCRE at maximum range.	
	3			
	4		Infantry posts withdrawn about 500 yds from banks of RIVER ANCRE. SOS lines readjusted B236 Battery exchanged two calibrated guns and C236 Battery exchanged one uncalibrated gun with the 108 ARMY BRIGADE R.F.A.	

Army Form C. 2118.

WAR DIARY
or
INTELLIGENCE SUMMARY.
(Erase heading not required.)

Instructions regarding War Diaries and Intelligence Summaries are contained in F. S. Regs., Part II. and the Staff Manual respectively. Title pages will be prepared in manuscript.

Place	Date	Hour	Summary of Events and Information	Remarks and references to Appendices
1918 August	6		Owing to withdrawal of enemy, rov'g forward sections established its hostile lines	
	7		by day & night. Sections to remain in same position for three or four days only	
	9		B/236 Battery put into forward section. Harassing fire on	
			Col. Bowring proceeded on senior Artillery Officers Course at Shoeburyness. Major	
			W. COOPER M.C. assumed command of 236 Brigade.	
	10		D/236 Battery put into section forward in the valley north of MILLENCOURT	
			HQ Divnl. Arty. relieved by the 18th Division Div. Artillery	
			2nd Lt. SMITH returned from leave	
	11		C/236 Battery withdrew their forward section. 17 Div Arty H.Q. relieved by 18 Div Arty	
			H.Q.	
	12		His Majesty the King inspected certain officers and men of the 47 Divisional Artillery	
			at QUERRIEU. CAPT. W. ANDERSON M.C. and CAPTAIN RYDER M.C. and 5 O.Rs	
			inspected & Brought 236 Brigade	
	13		A/236 Battery put into a forward section in valley north of MILLENCOURT to Harassing	
			fire on

Army Form C. 2118.

WAR DIARY
or
INTELLIGENCE SUMMARY.
(Erase heading not required.)

Instructions regarding War Diaries and Intelligence Summaries are contained in F. S. Regs., Part II. and the Staff Manual respectively. Title pages will be prepared in manuscript.

Place	Date	Hour	Summary of Events and Information	Remarks and references to Appendices
August 1918	14		O.C. Brigade reconnoitred forward area for battery positions also roving to enemy withdrawal beyond the ANCRE only the longer range was effective D236 Battery in Lettres Hararing action	
	15		Owing to signs that enemy intended withdrawing further an reconnaissance for advancing battery positions was abandoned C236 Battery however was ordered to move forward in case of need	
	16		Orders received for batteries to take up forward positions as enemy's resistance enemy still in force in and about ALBERT	
	17		Much movement having been observed LEFT GROUP fired on eastern side of MIRE as far South Reposition C came out 5am and 9pm All Batteries moved forward into valley between MILLENCOURT and SENLIS	
	18		Head Quarters 236 Brigade march forward to D236 Battery's vacated position near HENENCOURT MILL	
	20		Harassing fire by day and night Adjutant Headquarters 236 Brigade moved to HAM COPSE	

WAR DIARY
or
INTELLIGENCE SUMMARY.
(Erase heading not required.)

Army Form C. 2118.

Place	Date	Hour	Summary of Events and Information	Remarks and references to Appendices
August	21		18th Division attacked at 4.45 AM South of ALBERT and during RIVER ANCRE captured BELLEVUE FARM with some 236 Brigade given a barrage supporting 55 Infantry Brigade to three hours all objectives gained including ALBERT. During the afternoon Infantry reported in potations on machine guns on TARA & USNA hills.	
	22		During the Brigade Brooms reported tractates Inf.= nearly all positions guns had been destroyed, and had had to be replaced the two nights Battins fired on a small "snack" straightening out enemy mobility early. ALBERT	
	23		4.43 AM 18th Division attacked TARA & USNA Hills. 236 Brigade awarded in barrage immediately south of Bapaume—ALBERT Road During the afternoon batteries moved forward to positions north of the ALBERT QUARRY	
	24		Attack by 18th Division on OVILLERS & LA BOISELLE. 236 Brigade assisted with barrage at 1 AM in attack and capture of CHAPES SPUR, all objectives taken	

WAR DIARY
or
INTELLIGENCE SUMMARY.

Army Form C. 2118.

Place	Date	Hour	Summary of Events and Information	Remarks and references to Appendices
August	24		contd S.O.S thro' N.R.S through BECOURT WOOD. 2nd Lt ELLOWITZ returned from 4th Army Course. LT AYERS wounded. MAJOR DUNCAN & 2nd LT CULLERNE woke 27 other ranks went into hospital as a result of gas shelling on the previous day. 2nd Lt FRASER rejoined	
	25		Battery fired at an extreme range on FRICOURT VILLAGE & WOOD took up which were captured at 6 P.M. at 8 P.M. O.C. Bryatt accompanied by Battery Commanders reconnoitred battery position south of LABOISSELLE.	
	26		Batteries moved forward at 10 A.M. and during the day fired on Machine gun posts in the neighbourhood of MAMETZ WOOD that were still holding out. Lt LIELL reported from D.A.C. and was attached to D.236 Battery. Batteries remained in position as position as LA BOISSELLE to cultivate was observed and during day fired on MONTAUBAN RIDGE where certain element of the enemy were still holding out. 2nd Lt INGHAM reported for attachment to Brigade & joined D.236 Battery	

WAR DIARY
or
INTELLIGENCE SUMMARY.
(Erase heading not required.)

Army Form C. 2118.

Place	Date	Hour	Summary of Events and Information	Remarks and references to Appendices
August	26		Batteries fired on MONTAUBAN RIDGE and 18th Division Infantry advanced and captured village and ridge during the morning. The enemy retired to line TRONES WOOD and SE of (full) LONGUEVAL. 2.35 Brigade who had most severe fighting north of FRICOURT lost four officers from severe shell. MAJOR R.J. CLIFTON and RAT BATTERY Commander of 117th London Battery 6th London Bgde R.F.A. died late from wounds received. 7.30 P.M. Orders issued for next movement. O.C. Brigade reconnoitred Battery Position in CATERPILLAR VALLEY on this eastern edge of MAMETZ WOOD at 6 A.M. all Batteries were in 8 A.M. and fired on TRONES WOOD. 53rd INFANTRY BRIGADE (18th Division) were ordered to advance from 4.21 to 6.30 P.M. Batteries fired a barrage for	
	27		this. TRONES WOOD at 7 P.M. Infantry attacked and captured event to 50 Prisoners and large Toll on a grand succession of 2nd GRENADIER GUARDS DIVISION extreme heavy casualties. General retired opposite the night	

WAR DIARY or INTELLIGENCE SUMMARY

Army Form C. 2118.

Place	Date	Hour	Summary of Events and Information	Remarks and references to Appendices
August	27		LEUZE & BOULEAUX WOODS and left machine guns & guns on plateau east of TRONES WOOD. At 7.10 p.m. Battery fired counter-preparation back to GUILLEMONT. LAYER S.P.S. around MILTON CROSS.	
	28		Counter-preparation fired at midnight and 4.30 a.m. next day.	
	29		54 rounds GF fired in reply to LEUZE WOOD & trench & battery N.E. of LEUZE WOOD protecting right of Enemy Battery Reporting heavy fire East of LEUZE WOOD.	
			At 2 p.m. 236 Brigade moved up to positions ouest GINCHY — COMBLES.	
			GUILLEMONT ROAD, west of heavily shelled the new position. 6 casualties.	
	30		Enemy artillery very active.	
			British patrols east on road north-east coming near COMBLES — FREGICOURT & PRIEZ FARM. Enemy holding line 2.35 m.m. ?? ?? ??. Accurate ?? shooting on LEUZE WOOD and C.6 morning & afternoon & night.	
	31		Casualties by sniping	
			Position unchanged. Enemy artillery comparatively quiet.	

Signed
Comm. 236 Bde R.F.A.

Army Form C. 2118.

WAR DIARY
or
INTELLIGENCE SUMMARY.
(Erase heading not required.)

Place	Date	Hour	Summary of Events and Information	Remarks and references to Appendices
	1918 Sep 1		At 5.30am the Barrage fell on a line 25yds in rear of the BAPAUME-PERONNE road when the attack was effected. Quite a barrage arranged to commence with troops on our 1st objective proceeding in a northerly direction thus ensuring the village of MORVAL which was strongly held by the enemy. The attack was entirely successful and at 9am PRINCES TRENCH was captured and posts of the 18 Division were reported as exerting pressure left of ST PIERRE VAAST WOOD (?) at about 10.30am MORVAL was reported captured by the 38th Division. Enemy in large numbers were holding a line where SAILLY-SAILLISEL, a large number of the enemy retiring from MORVAL were captured. At 11.am Battalion fell down a slope & houses to the enemy & were seen retiring to a ridge east of the town. During the day hostile artillery was much scarcer & small &

Place	Date	Hour	Summary of Events and Information	Remarks and references to Appendices
	Sep 2		of the enemy were fired on with success. At 4 pm the Brigade fired our barrage for our attack on SAILLY-SAILLISEL which was captured. The Brigade moved to positions in the neighbourhood of COMBLES at 5 pm with Head Quarters about a mile from COMBLES on the road to PRIEZ FARM. Batteries fired on hostile aeroplanes & hostile guns which had been left to cover their retirement. While the 236 Brigade were engaging forward 18th Division attack Government Farm & ST PIERRE VAAST WOOD Such a tilt although the firm had to terminate owing to enemy in line.	
		4.30 pm	Batteries fired on enemy Machine guns in support of an attack by the 47th Division on left	
	3		Enemy having retired to the East of CANAL DU NORD. 236 Brigade pushed forward to positions on the north outskirts of ST PIERRE VAAST WOOD. Guns registered fire by Moon 10 cm & 150m guns & howitzers	

Army Form C. 2118.

WAR DIARY
or
INTELLIGENCE SUMMARY.
(Erase heading not required.)

Place	Date	Hour	Summary of Events and Information	Remarks and references to Appendices
Sept	4		During the morning the Battery fired on enemy movement with good effect. Infantry patrols pushed forward to the eastern edge of RIVERSIDE WOOD and cleared MOISLAINS & MANANCOURT.	
		5 P.M.	B/236 Brigade was ordered to withdraw to wagon lines and to come under orders of the 47 Divisional Arty in the divisional sector immediately south of the 18 Division. 12th Division relieved 18th Division. MAJOR W.J. BARNARD M.C. & LT. HALL B/236 Battery mounted geo.	
	5	10.30 P.M.	B/236 Battery was ordered to take up a position about one mile north east of BOUCHAVESNES to await in bivouac for attack to capture NURLU-PERONNE Road the following morning. 236 Brigade now working in liaison with 140 Infantry Brigade. Battery moved wagon lines from FREGICOURT to MARIEUX WOOD during the morning. Head Quarters established in BOUCHAVESNES close to 140 Infantry Brigade H.Q. During the afternoon battery commanders reconnoitred positions east of MOISLAINS.	
	6	1.30 A.M.	Batteries took up already reconnoitred position near & TORTILLE RIVER & MOISLAINS and had communication in AYESCOURT & LIERAMONT while 140 Infantry Brigade pushed forward from NURLU-ETANG DE RONNE roads. A/ & C/ 236 Brigade were ordered	

WAR DIARY
or
INTELLIGENCE SUMMARY

Army Form C. 2118.

Place	Date	Hour	Summary of Events and Information	Remarks and references to Appendices
	1918 Sep 6		to a heavy fire of 5.9's + 4.2" shells and sustained 17 casualties (2 killed) During the afternoon CAPTAIN A F R RYDER. M.C. pushed forward a section to the outskirts of LIERAMONT. C236 Battery have moved forward and took up position at FACTORY on NURLU-PERONNE Road and LT. ULMAN and C235 moved forward with a section to LIERAMONT at 4.30 pm both brought section forward with effort on enemy movement 9 pm. 47th Division relieved by 58th Division 236 Brigade not seen to troops to-day	A236 Battery
	7		236 Brigade marched to VILLE-SUR-ANCRE via MADREPAS - MARICOURT. FRICOURT & MEAULTE. Am heavy mustard gas bombard 6 pm. Batteries rested during the day. At 11.30 pm 236 Bde + 4 p5 marched to HENIN and entrained	
	9		for CHOCQUES, train left 8.30 pm. A236 Battery entrained at MERICOURT at 1.38 AM for LILLERS - B236 Battery entrained at CORBIE at 2.51 AM for CALONNE RICQUART - C236 Battery entrained at MERICOURT at 4.35 AM for LILLERS - D236 entrained at CORBIE at 5.51 AM for CALONNE-RICQUART. Batteries arrived at destinations between 3 pm - 12 midnight and marched from detraining stations to MEDONCHELLE	
	10		47th Division resting in ADCHEL area. 2nd 4.5 or any shoots the first week to determine SOS	

Army Form C. 2118.

WAR DIARY
or
INTELLIGENCE SUMMARY.
(Erase heading not required.)

Place	Date	Hour	Summary of Events and Information	Remarks and references to Appendices
Sept	10		horses and repair and overhaul of guns. Brigade now interview VIII Corps 5th Army	
	12		MAJOR H. BAILEY was attached to D/236 Battery from VIII Corps	
			CAPTAIN N. CHRISTOPHERSON M.C. promoted acting major and posted to command B/236 Battery. LT. C.E. WILLS posted to B/296 Battery and from HQ D.A.C.	
	15		A special Thanksgiving Service conducted by Divisional Chaplain was held at NEDONCHELLE. 2nd LT. J. MILLER returned from leave	
	16		Col A.M. BOWRING returned from leave and Senior Course Shoeburyness and resumed command of the Brigade	
	17		Battery training commenced. Two batteries carried out Battery drill on manoeuvre at BAILLEUL-LEZ-PERNES and two batteries carried out gun drill & laying in wagon parks	
	18		C.R.A. XIII Corps visited and inspected the Brigade during the afternoon	
	19		MAJOR A.F. YENCKEN, M.C. was attached to HQ Divisional Artillery H.Q. to carry out the duties of Brigade Major during the absence on leave of MAJOR H. BRIDGEHAMMER.	
			MAJOR H BAILEY received orders to report to XIII Corps R.A. Rest Camp and carry out Chief duties	

Army Form C. 2118.

WAR DIARY
or
INTELLIGENCE SUMMARY.
(Erase heading not required.)

Instructions regarding War Diaries and Intelligence Summaries are contained in F. S. Regs., Part II. and the Staff Manual respectively. Title pages will be prepared in manuscript.

Place	Date	Hour	Summary of Events and Information	Remarks and references to Appendices
Sept	19		of Commandant	
	20		236 Brigade marched to BOURS via AUMERVAL-PERNES road arriving at 11 AM. 2 Lorries carried baggage to BRYAS STATION but intended entrainment was postponed	
	21		CAPT. A.F.R.D. RYDER. M.C. A236 Battery proceeded to England on Battery Commanders course SHOEBURYNESS and fourteen day leave	
	26		2nd Q.R. DAY. C236 Battery proceeded on fourteen days leave to ENGLAND	
	27		47th Division moved to the ST POL area. 47 R Divisional Artillery is the ANVIN sub area. 236 Brigade marched out 12.30 P.M at midnight - CAYEUX via VALHUON-HUCLIER-CONTEVILLE-WAVRANS arriving at 3.30 P.M.	
	28		Capt R.K HASLAM. C.F. joined the Brigade	
	29		MAJOR A.E. Y. COCKRAN M.C. reassumed command of C236 Battery	

Army Form C. 2118.

WAR DIARY
or
INTELLIGENCE SUMMARY.
(Erase heading not required.)

Place	Date	Hour	Summary of Events and Information	Remarks and references to Appendices
Sept	29		MAJOR. H. BRIDGEMAN. M.C. having returned from leave.	
	30		Capt S. TAYLOR. promoted a/Major whilst in command of a sub section.	Not Promoted whilst comd 1 2 3 or 5 Br M G C

Army Form C. 2118.

WAR DIARY
or
INTELLIGENCE SUMMARY.

(Erase heading not required.)

Instructions regarding War Diaries and Intelligence Summaries are contained in F. S. Regs., Part II. and the Staff Manual respectively. Title pages will be prepared in manuscript.

Place	Date	Hour	Summary of Events and Information	Remarks and references to Appendices
Oct 1918	1		236 Brigade marched to NEDONCHELLE from MONCHY-CAYEUX via ANVIN and BERGENEUSE at 12.30 PM arriving at 4.30 PM. MAJOR A. FYENCKEN M.C. proceeded to England on fourteen day's leave	
	2		236 Brigade marched to ROBECQ at 11.15 AM arriving at 4.30 PM via HURIONVILLE - LILLERS - BUSNES	
	3		236 Brigade ordered to take over from 296 Brigade 59th Division in the neighbourhood of LAVENTIE owing to the enemy having withdrawn on its front considerable difficulty was experienced in the relief. O.C. Brigade went forward with Battery Commanders to reconnoitre at 9.30 AM. Batteries marched to their prospective wagon lines at 11.30 PM but found them to have been vacated by the 296 Brigade. B.G.R.A 47 Div Arty took over from 59th Div Arty at 9 AM and ordered 236 Brigade RFA to take up positions east of FROMELLES. Positions were taken up during the night. Much difficulty was experienced from the blowing up of roads by the enemy before retiring. The Brigade now covering the whole Divisional front with the 141 and 142 Infantry Brigades in the line	
	4		236 Brigade relieved 296 Brigade RFA at 5 AM. 47 Division attempted to advance by means of "peaceful penetration" but were held up on the railway embankment.	

Army Form C. 2118.

WAR DIARY
or
INTELLIGENCE SUMMARY.
(Erase heading not required.)

Instructions regarding War Diaries and Intelligence Summaries are contained in F. S. Regs., Part II. and the Staff Manual respectively. Title pages will be prepared in manuscript.

Place	Date	Hour	Summary of Events and Information	Remarks and references to Appendices
in the neighbourhood of ERQUINHEM & BEAUCAMP	4		A236 Battery RFA worked in cooperation with the 142 Infantry Brigade.	
	5		B236 Battery RFA worked in cooperation with the 141 Infantry Brigade pushing forward detours in close support of Infantry and fired with effect on machine guns etc. Infantry consolidated above line and battalion adjusted communications. Reason. 236 Brigade RFA now only covering 141 Infantry Brigade in the northern half of the Divisional sector.	
	6		140 Infantry Brigade relieved 141 Infantry Brigade	
	7			
	8		Capt. J.C. COWAN. M.C. proceeded to England on fourteen days leave. Lt. R.B. ULLMAN M.C. rejoined from 1st Army ARTILLERY Course.	
	9		2Lt. T. HUNTER. proceeded to England on fourteen days leave. Lt. L.B. TANSLEY. proceeded to England on fourteen days leave. 141 Infantry Brigade relieved 140 Infantry Brigade. Lt. Col. A.W. BOWRING wounded slightly in left forearm, remaining at duty.	
	10		B/236 Wagon Line shelled 3 Casualties & horses wounded	

Army Form C. 2118.

WAR DIARY
or
INTELLIGENCE SUMMARY.
(Erase heading not required.)

Place	Date	Hour	Summary of Events and Information	Remarks and references to Appendices
Oct.	11		D/236 Battery fired on BONTEMS in Conjunction with 235" in Support of Raid by 142 Infantry Brigade.	
	12		B.G.R.A. inspected B.C.D. 236 Battery Wagon Lines.	
	13		Capt. W.P.S. EDWARDS proceeded to England on fourteen days leave.	
	14		236, 13th R.F.A. fired barrage in support of 142 Infantry Brigades patrol to ascertain if enemy still holding line of railway. Enemy retired from Railway Central trench. 141 Infantry Brigade moving up posts to ENNETIERES. 142 Infantry Brigade on right moving on position to line of line east of ESCOBECQUES and FIN de la GUEIZE on the ROUBAIX 7th Div the right.	
	15		A/236 and B/236 Batteries fired a barrage in support of 142 Infantry Brigade who resumed the advance.	
	16		172 Infantry Brigade relieved 141 Infantry Brigade. C.O. 236 Bde R.F.A. and Battery Commanders reconnoitered new Battery positions East of Railway Embankment. 236 Brigade R.F.A. relieved by 286 Brigade R.F.A. at 1100 57th Div Art	
	17		236 Brigade marched to ESTAIRES from FROMELLES via LAVENTIE at 1200 arriving at 1500.	

Army Form C. 2118.

WAR DIARY
or
INTELLIGENCE SUMMARY.
(Erase heading not required.)

Instructions regarding War Diaries and Intelligence Summaries are contained in F. S. Regs., Part II. and the Staff Manual respectively. Title pages will be prepared in manuscript.

Place	Date	Hour	Summary of Events and Information	Remarks and references to Appendices
Oct 1918	18		236 Brigade marched to St VENANT via LA GORGUE, MERVILLE St VENANT at 0900 arriving at 1330.	
	19		2nd Lt J. ELLOWITZ proceeded to England on fourteen days leave.	
	20		MAJOR A.F. YENCKEN rejoined G 147th Div. for Staff course/duties. O.C. Brigade attended conference at Divisional Headquarters NOPPEN FERME at 3 P.M.	
	21			
	22			
	23		2nd Lt J. CHEYNE proceeded to England on fourteen days leave. Section of B/236 Battery carried out manoeuvres with 23rd Battn 142 Infantry Brigade at 1400.	
	24		Lt Col. A.H. BOWRING proceeded to England on Tour of Home Service. MAJOR W. COOPER assumed command of the Brigade.	
	25		Capt W. ANDERSON M.C. C/236 Battery admitted to 56th Ambulance P.U.O. 236 Brigade marched to RIEZ BAILLEUL via CALONNE MERVILLE - LA GORGUE leaving 0945 arriving 1300. Captain J.C. CORSON M.C. returned from fourteen days leave in England.	
	26		236 Brigade marched to HAVERDIN via FROMELLES - ESCOBECQUES leaving 0830 arriving 1400. Lt L.B. TANSLEY M.C. & Lt H. HUNTER returned from fourteen days leave in England.	

Army Form C. 2118.

WAR DIARY
or
INTELLIGENCE SUMMARY.
(Erase heading not required.)

Place	Date	Hour	Summary of Events and Information	Remarks and references to Appendices
October 1918	28		On the occasion of the official entry of the Fifth Army Commander into LILLE: The 47th Division marched through the city after the Fifth Army Commander had presented the standard to the Mayor. 236 Brigade RFA under the command of LIEUT COL THE HON. H.G.O. BRIDGEMAN DSO. MC. marched in rear of the 141 Infantry Brigade, entering the city by the CHATELEU GATE at 1100 hrs, proceeded to the GRANDE PLACE thence to LILLE or BROUCK near ROUBAIX arriving at 1300 hrs. 2nd LT H.B. DOUGLAS proceeded on 14 days leave to England.	
	29		LT H. RENWICK C/236 Battery RFA proceeded on 14 days leave to England. LIEUT COLONEL THE HON. H.G.C. BRIDGEMAN DSO. MC. resumed command of the Brigade MAJOR W. COOPER M.C. was attached to 47 D.A. HQ to do the duties of Brigade Major.	
	30		236 Brigade received orders to relieve part of the 256 Brigade RFA 51st Divisional Artillery in the Right sector of the 11th Army front. C.O. Brigade reconnoitred battery positions and made lines accompanied by Battery Commanders of B, C & D/236 Battery RFA. HQ 236 Brigade with three guns or howrs of B/236 Battery moved into action occupying the day H.Q. attached in TEMPLEUX. B/236 Battery RFA in position with 4 guns new RAMICOURT. C/H/ C/236 Battery RFA in position with 4 guns north of BLONDAIN D/236 Battery RFA is in position with three hours only, north of FOURCROIX, the remainder in reserve at ANNAPES. A/236 Battery RFA in reserve at ANNAPES, Batteries under command of 236 Brigade RFA until completion of relief	
	31			

H.B. Bridgeman Lt Col RFA 24/11

WAR DIARY
or
INTELLIGENCE SUMMARY.

(Erase heading not required.)

Army Form C. 2118.

236 Bde R.F.A.

Place	Date	Hour	Summary of Events and Information	Remarks and references to Appendices
Nov 1918	1		236 Brigade R.F.A. relieved part of 89th Brigade in action one mile north of TOURNAI and covering the 141 Infantry Brigade at 1000 hours.	
	2		B & C 236 moved their remaining guns into action.	
			A 236 & half of D 236 Batteries marched to ANNAPES & remainder billeted in village.	
			Lt H.L. BURGIS M.C. proceeded on fourteen days leave to England.	
	3		Capt W.R.S. EDWARDS A.V.C. and Lt A. MITCHELL A 236 Battery returned from fourteen days leave in England.	
	4		Batteries carried out a large number of counter battery shoots throughout the day.	
	6		Major W.J. BARNARD M.C. reported from Base and was attached B 236 Battery R.F.A.	
	7		Lt P. BATTY B 236 Battery admitted Field Ambulance wounded gas.	
			4.2 Howitzer shell struck signallers quarters on C 236 Battery position and wounded 6 men.	
	8		Found very active with machine guns and artillery a/a midday. Enemy reported to be withdrawing west of TOURNAI. Any advance on night enemy retired from the east bank of the River ESCAUT. 141 Infantry Brigade crossed	
	9		the river at about 0500 hours and found enemy line of the railway running from TOURNAI to HERINNES. During the afternoon 236 Brigade HQ and C 236 Battery R.F.A. crossed the river	

WAR DIARY
or
INTELLIGENCE SUMMARY.

Army Form C. 2118.

Place	Date	Hour	Summary of Events and Information	Remarks and references to Appendices
9100	9		and occupied billets at MAIN. A, B & D236 remaining at PONT-A-CHIN for the night. 2nd Lt. J. CHEYNE C236 Battery R.F.H. reported from sick leave and is on duty.	
	10		The remaining batteries joined the Bde. SCHELDT and the 236 Brigade R.F.A. marched in support of 141 Infantry Brigade to FRASNES-LEZ-BUISSENAL via BIZENCOURT Bridge & occupied billets near DIME	
	11		236th Brigade R.F.A. were ordered to return to MOURCOURT as the Division was being relieved by the 74th Division. The Brigade marched at 13.30 hours arriving at MOURCOURT at 15.30 hours. Orders for the Brigade's approaching move to MOORSEELE via LA PLAIZ	
	12		236 A. Brigade marched to ESTEMPLEUVE at 10.00 hours arriving 13.30 hours 117 Divisional Bounds was held. No experience in which the extreme anxiety for the education, employment and entertainment of troops during the coming struggle to be given passed before came obligation. MAJOR W. CHRISTOPHER A336 proceeded on one month's leave to England	
	13		LT. F. OXLEY md C236 Battery proceeded for 14 days leave to E. & land	
	14		236 Brigade R.F.A. marched to billets in BOURGHELLES via SIN and BAIZIEUX leaving at 0900 hours arriving at 1400 hours	

Army Form C. 2118.

WAR DIARY
or
INTELLIGENCE SUMMARY.
(Erase heading not required.)

Instructions regarding War Diaries and Intelligence Summaries are contained in F.S. Regs, Part II. and the Staff Manual respectively. Title pages will be prepared in manuscript.

Place	Date	Hour	Summary of Events and Information	Remarks and references to Appendices
Nov.	16		2nd Lt. H.O. DOUGLAS returned from 14 days leave in England	
	17		Lt. RENVOIZE C236 Battery returned from 14 days leave in England	
	18		Lt. THOMAS D236 Battery " "	
	19		Lt. BURRAIS M.C. A236 Battery " "	
			CAPT STAYLOR & CAPTAIN H. DAVIES proceeded on fourteen days leave to England	
	25		236 Brigade R.F.A. marched from BOURGHELLES to FOURNES leaving at 0715 hours and proceeding via BOUVINES - SAINGHIN - LESQUIN - ENNEQUIN - LOOS - HAUBOURDIN arriving at 1530 hours	
	26		236 Brigade R.F.A. marched from FOURNES to LABEUVRIERE leaving at 0900 hours and proceeding via LA BASSEE and BETHUNE arriving at 1500 hours. A.B. & C 236 Batteries marched to HESDIGNEUL arriving at 1530 hours. D236 Battery marched to LA BEUVRIERE at 1530 hours	
	27		A.B. & C 236 Batteries marched from HESDIGNEUL to FOQUIERES leaving at 0930 hours arriving 1000 hours	
	30		Lt. R.F. OXLEY M.C. returned from fourteen days leave from ENGLAND	
			CAPT A.F.R.D. RYDER M.C. rejoined Brigade. MAJOR A.F. YENCKEN M.C. rejoined the Brigade from Junior Staff Course.	

M. Morison
Lt. Col. Comdg. 236 Brigade R.F.A.

236 Bde R.F.A
WB 176

WAR DIARY
INTELLIGENCE SUMMARY

Place	Date	Hour	Summary of Events and Information	Remarks and references to Appendices
1918 December	6		Lieut Col. Hon. H.G.O. BRIDGEMAN, D.S.O, M.C. proceeded to England on Senior Artillery Officers Overseas Course at SHOEBURYNESS & SALISBURY. MAJOR H.S. DUNCAN M.C. D236 Batty assumed command during his absence.	
	11		Capt H. DAVIES, B236 Battery returned from fourteen days leave in England. First dispatch of Coalminers under Provisional Demobilization Scheme. 2nd Lt. G THOMPSON A236 Battery returned from fourteen days leave in England. Lecture to 236 Brigade R.F.A at LA BEUVRIERE on "Industrial Leeds" by H DUDBURY ESQ	
	12		MAJOR N. CHRISTOPHERSON. M.C. A236 Battery returned from one month leave in England	
	13		CAPTAIN S. TAYLOR, D236 Battery returned from fourteen days leave in England	
	17		CAPTAIN S. TAYLOR D236 Battery Lt A. MITCHELL A236 Battery one sergeant one corporal and one Bombardier detailed to proceed to La Havre on Temporary duty	
	24		Lieut Col. HON. H.G.O. BRIDGEMAN, D.S.O, M.C returned from England from Senior Artillery Officers Overseas Course and reassumed command of Brigade	

R.R... [signature]
Lieut Col
Commdg 236 Brigade RFA

236 Bde RFA
1919

Index..........................

SUBJECT.

No.	Contents.	Date.
	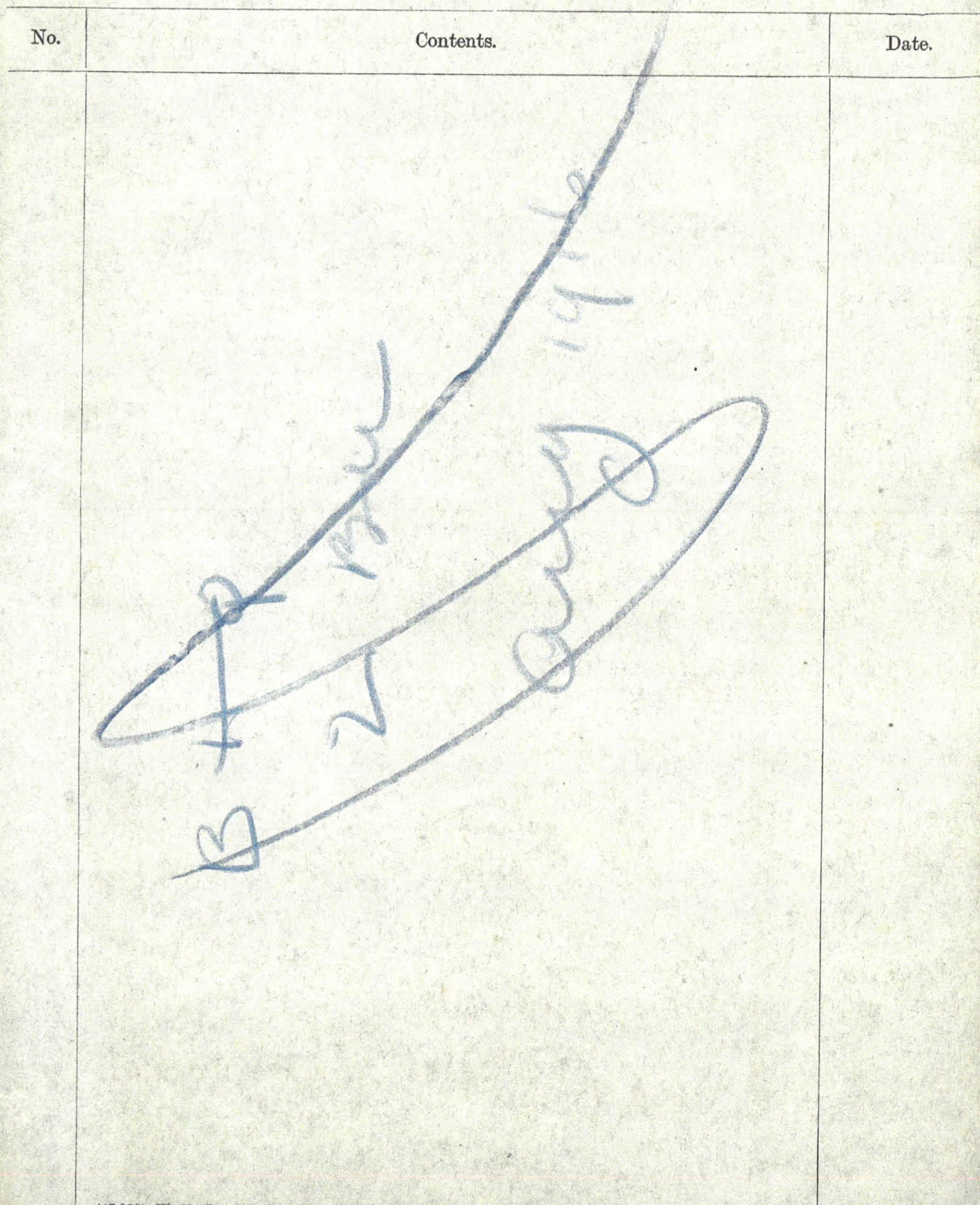	

(47,308). Wt.33,632—122. 500. 1/20. **Gp.164.** A.&E.W.

D236 Bty R.F.A
47

WAR DIARY
or
INTELLIGENCE SUMMARY.
(Erase heading not required.)

Army Form C. 2118.

Place	Date	Hour	Summary of Events and Information	Remarks and references to Appendices
1919 January	2		3 men despatched for demobilization to Scottish Area	
	10		18 men despatched for demobilization to London Midland & Scottish Area	
	11		19 men and 1 Officer (Capt T.H. Hunter. D236 Battery R.F.A.) despatched for demobilization. London Midland & Scottish Area	
	12		10 men despatched for demobilization. Midland Area & M.G. Buck proceeded on 14 days leave on expiration of which he will proceed to demob. area 9/1/19	
	13		11 men despatched for demobilization Lancashire & West Counties Area	
	14		9 men " " " West Country Area	
	17		11 " " " "	
	18		25 " " " London & Scottish Area	
	20		17 " sent to England	
	21		13 " " "	
			Major W.T. Barker M.D. & 2nd Lt. F. Smith 6th K of B236 Battery R.F.A. returned from leave in England	
	24		30 men despatched for demobilization London Area	
	25		17 " " " London & West Country Area	
	26		Medical Officer R.G. Thompson. A236 Battery R.F.A.	
	27		10 men & one Officer despatched for demobilization London Lancashire Area, including Captain H. Davies B236 Battery R.F.A.	

WAR DIARY
or
INTELLIGENCE SUMMARY.
(Erase heading not required.)

Army Form C. 2118.

WD 48

Place	Date	Hour	Summary of Events and Information	Remarks and references to Appendices
1919	1		Lt. P.F. OXLEY & 2nd Lt P. BATTY proceeded to Dispersal Concentration Camp for demobilisation to Horsham Northumbrian Area September.	
	2		8 other ranks proceeded to England for dem: posting to Northumberland County Area	
	3		3 men proceed for demob'g via No. 2 Dispersal Middle Area	
	4		1 man " " " " "	
	6		2nd Lt R. TALMAY proceeded on 14 days leave to England	
	7		1 man proceeded for demobilization via Scotland	
	8		5 men " " " " Midlands & Eastern Area	
	15		8 " " " " London Area	
	20		5 Horses despatched to No 4 Base Remount Depot for disposal. 5 Brigade	
	22		1 mail proceeded for demobilisation to London Area	
			Lt Col A.H.G.O BRIDGEMAN. D.S.O. M.C proceeded on 6 months special leave to England Major H.S. DUTTON. M.C. assumed command of the Brigade having 2nd in command	
	24		1 Horse despatched to No 4 Base Remount Depot	
	25		24 animals proceeded to No.915 for Silver Construction	
			Lt D.C THOMAS proceeded on 14 days special leave to England	
	27		5 men dispatched for demob'g via Dispersal Area	
			236 Brigade R.F.A. now reduced to Cadre B. Establishment in men	

M.S. Dutton Major
Commanding 236 Brigade R.F.A.

Army Form C. 2118.

WAR DIARY
or
INTELLIGENCE SUMMARY.
(Erase heading not required.)

Instructions regarding War Diaries and Intelligence Summaries are contained in F. S. Regs., Part II. and the Staff Manual respectively. Title pages will be prepared in manuscript.

Place	Date	Hour	Summary of Events and Information	Remarks and references to Appendices
	1919			
	January 31		13 men inspected for tomorrows London Leave.	

W. Lindsey
Lieut Col.
Comdg 236 Brigade R.F.A.

WAR DIARY
or
INTELLIGENCE SUMMARY.

(Erase heading not required.)

Army Form C. 2118.

236 Bde RFA
J S 49

Place	Date	Hour	Summary of Events and Information	Remarks and references to Appendices
1919 March	1st		82 Animals despatched to Base Depot CALAIS for sale on Continent	
	2		2nd Lt. J. MILLER D.236 Battery RFA returned from 14 days leave in England	
	8		23 Animals despatched to Base Depot CALAIS for sale on Continent	
	10		Lt. A.J. MITCHELL A.236 Battery proceeded on 14 days leave to Egypt	
	12		Lt. D.G. THOMAS D.236 Battery returned from 14 days leave in England	
	.		45 Animals despatched to LILLERS for public sale	
	20		3 men despatched for demobilization to Midland Area	
	21		29 Animals despatched to LILLERS for public sale	
	23		Lt. Col. Hon. H.G.O. Bridgeman D.S.O. M.C. returned from six months special leave in England	
	25		53 Animals despatched to LILLERS for public sale	
	27		Lt. A.J. MITCHELL A.236 Battery returned from 14 days leave in England	
			The following officers despatched for demobilization B.H.L. BURGISS 08 Lt. R. TALMAN A.236 Battery RFA 2nd Lt R.H. SMITH D.236 Battery RFA 2nd Lt J. MILLER D.236 Battery RFA also 9 ORs for London Area	
	28		20 Other Ranks despatched for demobilization to Midland & London Areas	
	31		Animals despatched to LILLERS for public sale	

J Rod Swain
Lt. Col.
Commanding 236 Brigade RFA

WAR DIARY
or
INTELLIGENCE SUMMARY

Army Form C. 2118.

236 B↑ R.F.A.

Place	Date	Hour	Summary of Events and Information	Remarks and references to Appendices
1919 April	3rd		Lieut C.S. JACQUES B/236 Battery promoted a/Captain & to command B/236 Battery London	
	6		12 Other ranks despatched for demobilization	
	7		Major J.C. CORSAN M.C. proceeded on 14 days leave to England 4 Other ranks proceeded to Divisional reception camp for demobilization	
	14		Major H.S. DUNCAN M.C. D/236 Battery & Lt M.G. BLACK A/236 Battery proceeded to Divisional Reception Camp for demobilization	
	22		236 Brigade moved two D/236 Battery RFA moved from FOUQUIERES to CHOCQUES at 11:00 hours. Lt D.G. THOMAS D/236 Battery R.F.A. transferred to 2nd Army, also Lt C.J.K. HILL B/236 Battery. Lt C.E. WILES transferred to 47th Divisional Company. All remaining personnel wanted for Army of Occupation transferred to 47th Divisional Company. All remaining released personnel for demobilization supplied to Base Reinforcement Battalion to Divisional reception camp.	
	23		Capt J.C. CORSAN M.C. returned from 14 days leave in England	
	26		HQ 236, A/236 Battery, B/236 Battery, 10 Ammunition wagons & 2 G.S. wagons & D/236 & B/235 Battery entrained at CHOCQUES STATION at 18.53 hours 26-4-1919	
	27		for HAVRE arriving at 14.30 hours 27-4-1919 & proceeded to HARFLEUR forming up guns & vehicles later at this station	Cancel

WAR DIARY
or
INTELLIGENCE SUMMARY.

Army Form C. 2118.

Place	Date	Hour	Summary of Events and Information	Remarks and references to Appendices
April	27		C236 Battery RFA and D236 Battery RFA entrained at CHOCQUES STATION at 2000 hours	
	28		LT. S.H. RENVOIZE proceeded to Dunnairal Reception Camp for demobilization	
	29		C236 Battery RFA and D236 Battery RFA arrived at HAVRE at 1500 hours and proceeded to HARFLEUR CAMP leaving guns & vehicles at the station. H.Q. 236 Bde, A236 Battery and B236 Battery RFA loaded guns & vehicles on S.S. IONNIA and sailed per U.S.S. CHARLES at 1730 hours	
May	1		C236 Battery & D236 Battery RFA loaded guns & vehicles on S.S. ORION and sailed per S.S. ST GEORGE	

for O.C. 236 Brigade RFA

J. Roberts Capt. RFA